In the Name of Allah, the Gracious, the Merciful

****

Study the Qur'aan in Qur'aanic light to understand Islam in its pristine simplicity, clarity, beauty and purity

****

QUR'AANIC STUDIES – A Modern Tafsir

Manzil III

by
Mohammad Shafi

<u>PREFACE</u>

Below the Arabic text of every Verse of the Qur'aan in this book, its transliteration, followed by translation and Chapter Notes, if any, essentially based on the Qur'aan itself, is given. Please remember that the Arabic text is divine and, therefore, sacrosanct, but the transliteration, translation and the Notes are human and, therefore, subject to correction. Please also remember that the human-made Notes cannot, and do not, explain the divine Verses. They seek to explain the human translation only and/or to relate the Verse to present circumstances or to divine explanations given in other Verses of the Qur'aan.

I have adopted the transliteration method employed by the Muslim Students' Association (MSA) of the University of Southern California. And, in this regard, I may usefully quote from their site:

> "MSA-USC would like to thank muslimnet.net for making their transliteration of the Qur'an publicly available.

> 'We would like to emphasize that this [transliteration] text is not a substitute for the original Arabic Qur'an. It is only an attempt to help those who are trying to learn to read the Arabic text, since it is as close to the written text as possible.

> It is important to practice pronouncing the letters as directed in the transliteration table, especially the underlined letters, before starting to read. It will be helpful if an Arabic speaker can help you.

> This work is free for use to everyone as long as no changes that might distort it are done to it. We request from those who benefit from it to pray for us. We pray to Almighty Allah to help you learn to read the Holy Qur'an, and to do every good thing.'"

I present this humble work in the earnest hope that it will prompt my Readers to try and understand the divine Message in its original Arabic text. They should remember that no translation however meticulously done can ever equal the original Arabic text in its divine grandeur and pristine clarity.

One may wonder why this yet another addition to the existing plethora of Translations and Commentaries! The answer to this question lies in the beauty of the fact that the divine Message of the Qur'aan remains valid for all times and ages since its revelation until the Last Day. The Message therefore needs to be studied from time to time in the changing perspectives of the changing times. It would be wrong to confine this universal Message for mankind to the circumstances and situations of a period in the past. Unfortunately, however, most of the commentators so far have based their understanding of the Qur'aan in the strict perspective of the circumstances and situations prevailing at the time of its revelation way back in 7th century A.D. The Muslim mindset generally has thus got stagnated and therefore unable to cope with the changing situations of the changing times. This humble attempt of mine is to help Muslims generally to come out, Allah willing, of that crippling stagnation.

This Part (Manzil) of my Qur'aanic Studies is on Chapters 10 to 16 of the Qur'aan. It may please be noted that hyperlinks to Verses/notes would be active only to places within the Part.

Mohammad Shafi
Mumbai, INDIA,
20th Decembaer 2018.

Arabic		Example	Arabic		Example
فتحة+آ	a	about	ن	n	nurse
آ	a	cat	و	oo	pool
ع	AA	say "a" twice distinctly with an open mouth	أ	o	on
ب	b	box	ق	q	queen ("k" sound made in back of throat)
د	d	door	ر	r	rabbit (Rolled "r" sound, similar to Spanish "r")
ض	d	heavy "d" sound (Open jaw but keep lips slightly round i.e: duh)	ش	sh	ship
ي	ee	feet	س	s	sea
ف	f	fish	ص	s	heavy "s" sound (Open jaw but keep lips slightly round)
غ	gh	the sound you make when gurgling (Touch very back of tongue to very back of mouth)	ت	t	tan
ه	h	hat	ط	t	heavy "t" sound (Open jaw but keep lips slightly round)
ح	h	heavy "h" sound (Drop back of tongue to open back of throat, then force air out for "h")	ث	th	think
كسرة+ا	i	ink	ذ	th	the
ج	j	jar	ظ	th	"th" sound as in "the", but heavier (Open jaw but keep lips slightly round)
ك	k	kit	ضمة	u	put
خ	kh	gravely "h" sound (Touch back of tongue to roof of mouth and force air out)	و	w	water
ل	l	look	ء+ا	/	pronounce the letter before but cut it short by stopping suddenly
م	m	man	ي	y	yarn
Bold letters are silent i.e **w**: write			ز	z	zebra
			(-) is to make some words easier to read		

CONTENTS

[Against the Qur'aanic Chapter No. in every line below are: the Chapter name & no. of Verses in it in ()]

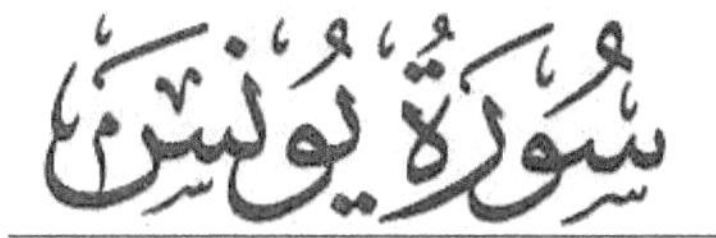

Chapter 10: Yunus (Jonah)

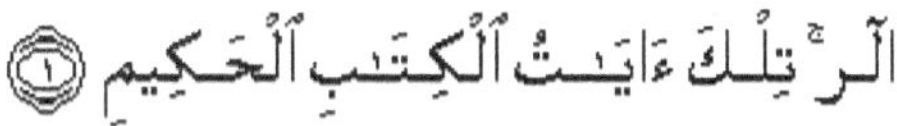

In the Name of Allah, the Gracious, the Merciful

1 Aliflamra tilka ayatu alkitabi alhakeemi

10:1. Alif Lam Ra.[1] Those are Verses of the Book of Wisdom.

---

1. Regarding letters like these at the beginning of some Chapters of the Qur'aan, please see study note 1 on Verse 2.1 of these Studies.

---

2 Akana lilnnasi AAajaban an awhayna ila rajulin minhum an anthiri alnnasa wabashshiri allatheena amanoo anna lahum qadama sidqin AAinda rabbihim qala alkafiroona inna hatha lasahirun mubee**nun**

5

Manzil II: 10: Yunus

10:2. Is it a matter to wonder at for the people that We revealed to a man from among themselves that he should warn the people and give good news to those who believe that there shall be a truly secure position for them with their Lord? The suppressors of the Truth say, "This man is clearly indeed a magician!"

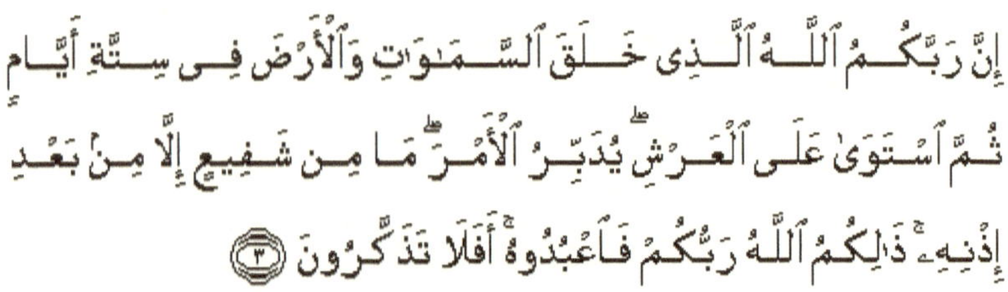

3 Inna rabbakumu Allahu allathee khalaqa alssamawati waalarda fee sittati ayyamin thumma istawa AAala alAAarshi yudabbiru alamra ma min shafeeAAin illa min baAAdi ithnihi thalikumu Allahu rabbukum faoAAbudoohu afala tathakkaroona

10:3. Indeed, Allah, your Lord, is He Who created the heavens and the earth in six periods in time[2], then ascended to the Throne[3], assuming absolute command. No intercessor can dare intercede except after His permission.[4] That is Allah, your Lord; so, worship Him! Would you not then take heed?

2. The Arabic word used here is *ayyaam*, plural of *yawm*. The English equivalent of *yawm* is 'day'. Normally, a 'day' means a 'perioid of time' during which the Sun shines on any part of the earth. In the Arabic language too, *yawm* has the same meaning normally. But just as the English day is also used to denote a 24-hour period which includes night, the Arabic *yawm* is used in the Qur'aan to denote other periods of time too extending to thousands of years. In Verses 22:47 and 32:5, *yawm* is taken to mean a thousand years, while in Verse 70:4, it is taken to mean fifty thousand years. So, the 'six *ayyaam*' mentioned in Verse 10.3 here is translated as 'six periods in time', every period of which may constitute an unspecified time of thousands and thousands of years or eons.

3. See study note 55 on Verse 9:129.

4. In the Hereafter, there is no question of any intercession – not even by any Prophet. This is clear from Verses 2:254 and 2:255 (also see study notes 482 and 483 on Verse2: 255). But here, in the context of this Verse 10:3, Allah Almighty may, if He wills, concede the prayer of a living person in this world for another living person in respect of any action in this world.

إِلَيْهِ مَرْجِعُكُمْ جَمِيعًا وَعْدَ ٱللَّهِ حَقًّا إِنَّهُ يَبْدَؤُاْ ٱلْخَلْقَ ثُمَّ يُعِيدُهُ لِيَجْزِىَ ٱلَّذِينَ ءَامَنُواْ وَعَمِلُواْ ٱلصَّٰلِحَٰتِ بِٱلْقِسْطِ وَٱلَّذِينَ كَفَرُواْ لَهُمْ شَرَابٌ مِّنْ حَمِيمٍ وَعَذَابٌ أَلِيمٌ بِمَا كَانُواْ يَكْفُرُونَ ۝

4 Ilayhi marjiAAukum jameeAAan waAAda Allahi *h*aqqan innahu yabdao alkhalqa thumma yuAAeeduhu liyajziya alla*th*eena amanoo waAAamiloo al*ss*ali*h*ati bialqis*t*i waalla*th*eena kafaroo lahum shar*a*bun min *h*ameemin waAAa*th*abun aleemun bima *k*anoo yakfuroon*a*

10:4. To Him is your return all together – a promise of Allah in truth. He originates creation, and then He recreates it so that He may justly recompense those who believe and do good deeds. And as for those who suppress the Truth, they shall have boiling water to drink and shall suffer a painful punishment for their suppression of the Truth.

هُوَ ٱلَّذِى جَعَلَ ٱلشَّمْسَ ضِيَآءً وَٱلْقَمَرَ نُورًا وَقَدَّرَهُ مَنَازِلَ لِتَعْلَمُواْ عَدَدَ ٱلسِّنِينَ وَٱلْحِسَابَ مَا خَلَقَ ٱللَّهُ ذَٰلِكَ إِلَّا بِٱلْحَقِّ يُفَصِّلُ ٱلْأَيَٰتِ لِقَوْمٍ يَعْلَمُونَ ۝

5 Huwa alla*th*ee jaAAala alshshamsa *d*iy*a*an waalqamara nooran waqaddarahu mana*z*ila litaAAlamoo AAadada alssineena waal*h*isaba m*a* khalaqa Alla*h*u *th*alika ill*a* bial*h*aqqi yufa*ss*ilu al*a*yati liqawmin yaAAlamoon*a*

10:5. He it is Who made the sun a source of light and the moon a light and ordained for it phases that you might count years and keep accounts. Allah did not create all that but on purpose. He explains the Verses/signs for people who know.[5]

---

5. People who do believe in the existence of Allah as the One Creator of all things, big or small, do know that all His creations serve some purpose. The things are not created in vain. Allah Almighty informs us here that the phases of the moon serve the purpose of enabling mankind to keep account of time. The phase of the new moon marks the end of one month and the start of the next. Elsewhere in the Qur'aan it is mentioned that 12 such months constitute a year. The divinely ordained measurement of time is therefore based on the lunar year. The lunar system, if implemented properly, ought to be more accurate than the solar system wherein adjustments must be made every now and then to keep the time accurate. No such adjustments need be made in the lunar system. Also, please note here that the sun has been described as a source of light, and the moon as just a light. This description is perfectly in tune with the scientifically verified fact that the moon just reflects the light of the sun on to the earth. It is by itself not the source of that light.

إِنَّ فِى ٱخْتِلَٰفِ ٱلَّيْلِ وَٱلنَّهَارِ وَمَا خَلَقَ ٱللَّهُ فِى ٱلسَّمَٰوَٰتِ وَٱلْأَرْضِ لَءَايَٰتٍ لِّقَوْمٍ يَتَّقُونَ ۝

6 Inna fee ikhtilafi allayli waalnnahari wama khalaqa Allahu fee alssamawati waalardi laayatin liqawmin yattaqoona

10:6. Indeed, in the variation of the night and the day, and in what Allah has created in the heavens and the earth, there are signs for people who fear Him.[6]

6. The variation of the night and the day suits mankind perfectly. Without this variation, human life – or, for that matter, any life as we know it on earth – would not be possible. Volumes can be written on the ingenuity and wonder of everything created in the heavens and the earth but suffice it to know for these Studies that the mathematical precision of the balance among the gravitational pulls of innumerable heavenly bodies so that they do not collide with one another, is simply mind-boggling. It is indeed a super-human feat. The Creator Who can demonstrate such a feat should no doubt be capable of adequately punishing all those who choose not to abide by His laws. To fear Allah is to realize this Reality.

إِنَّ ٱلَّذِينَ لَا يَرْجُونَ لِقَآءَنَا وَرَضُوا بِٱلْحَيَوٰةِ ٱلدُّنْيَا وَٱطْمَأَنُّوا بِهَا وَٱلَّذِينَ هُمْ عَنْ ءَايَٰتِنَا غَٰفِلُونَ ۝

Manzil II: 10: Yunus

7 Inna allatheena la yarjoona liqaana waradoo bialhayati alddunya waitmaannoo biha waallatheena hum AAan ayatina ghafiloona

---

10:7. Indeed, those who do not expect to meet Us and are pleased with this world's life and are content with it, and those who are heedless of Our Verses/signs,

---

أُوْلَـٰئِكَ مَأْوَىٰهُمُ ٱلنَّارُ بِمَا كَانُواْ يَكْسِبُونَ ۝

8 Olaika mawahumu alnnaru bima kanoo yaksiboona

10:8. Their abode is the Fire because of what they earned.[7]

---

7. Verses 7 and 8 constitute one sentence. Modern-day Muslims are heedless of the the divine commandments in the Qur'aan. This is a clear warning to them.

إِنَّ ٱلَّذِينَ ءَامَنُواْ وَعَمِلُواْ ٱلصَّـٰلِحَـٰتِ يَهْدِيهِمْ رَبُّهُم بِإِيمَـٰنِهِمْ تَجْرِى مِن تَحْتِهِمُ ٱلْأَنْهَـٰرُ فِى جَنَّـٰتِ ٱلنَّعِيمِ ۝

9 Inna allatheena amanoo waAAamiloo alssalihati yahdeehim rabbuhum bieemanihim tajree min tahtihimu alanharu fee jannati alnnaAAeemi

---

10:9. Indeed, those who believe and do good deeds, their Lord shall guide them by their faith. There shall flow from beneath them rivers in gardens of bliss.

دَعْوَىٰهُمْ فِيهَا سُبْحَٰنَكَ ٱللَّهُمَّ وَتَحِيَّتُهُمْ فِيهَا سَلَٰمٌ وَءَاخِرُ دَعْوَىٰهُمْ أَنِ ٱلْحَمْدُ لِلَّهِ رَبِّ ٱلْعَٰلَمِينَ ۝

10 DaAAwahum feeha subhanaka allahumma watahiyyatuhum feeha salamun waakhiru daAAwahum ani alhamdu lillahi rabbi alAAalameena

10:10. Their call in it shall be, 'Glory to You, O Allah!' and their greeting in it shall be, 'Peace.' And their call shall end with, 'Praise is to Allah, the Lord of the worlds.'

۞ وَلَوْ يُعَجِّلُ ٱللَّهُ لِلنَّاسِ ٱلشَّرَّ ٱسْتِعْجَالَهُم بِٱلْخَيْرِ لَقُضِىَ إِلَيْهِمْ أَجَلُهُمْ فَنَذَرُ ٱلَّذِينَ لَا يَرْجُونَ لِقَآءَنَا فِى طُغْيَٰنِهِمْ يَعْمَهُونَ ۝

11 Walaw yuAAajjilu Allahu lilnnasi alshsharra istiAAjalahum bialkhayri laqudiya ilayhim ajaluhum fanatharu allatheena la yarjoona liqaana fee tughyanihim yaAAmahoona

10:11. And if Allah should hasten bad things to happen to men as they desire the good things to hasten to them, their doom should certainly have been decreed for them. But We leave them to wander blindly in their inordinateness – those who expect not to meet Us.

وَإِذَا مَسَّ ٱلْإِنسَٰنَ ٱلضُّرُّ دَعَانَا لِجَنبِهِۦٓ أَوْ قَاعِدًا أَوْ قَآئِمًا فَلَمَّا كَشَفْنَا عَنْهُ ضُرَّهُۥ مَرَّ كَأَن لَّمْ يَدْعُنَآ إِلَىٰ ضُرٍّ مَّسَّهُۥ كَذَٰلِكَ زُيِّنَ لِلْمُسْرِفِينَ مَا كَانُوا۟ يَعْمَلُونَ ۝

12 Wai*tha* massa alins*a*na al*d*durru daAA*a*na lijanbihi aw q*a*AAidan aw q*a*iman falamm*a* kashaf*na* AAanhu *d*urrahu marra kaan lam yadAAun*a* il*a* *d*urrin massahu ka*tha*lika zuyyina lilmusrifeena m*a* k*a*noo yaAAmaloon**a**

10:12. And when any bad thing afflicts man, he calls Us, lying on his side, sitting or standing. But when We remove his affliction from him, he goes on as if he had never called to Us regarding the bad thing that afflicted him. Their deeds are thus made to look good to the transgressors.

وَلَقَدْ أَهْلَكْنَا ٱلْقُرُونَ مِن قَبْلِكُمْ لَمَّا ظَلَمُواْ وَجَآءَتْهُمْ رُسُلُهُم بِٱلْبَيِّنَـٰتِ وَمَا كَانُواْ لِيُؤْمِنُواْ كَذَٰلِكَ نَجْزِى ٱلْقَوْمَ ٱلْمُجْرِمِينَ ﴿١٣﴾

13 Walaqad ahlak*na* alquroona min qablikum lamm*a* *th*alamoo waj*a*athum rusuluhum bialbayyin*a*ti wam*a* k*a*noo liyuminoo ka*tha*lika najzee alqawma almujrimeen**a**

10:13. And certainly We did destroy generations before you when they became unjust. And their Messengers had come to them with clear signs, but they would not believe. We did thus give the sinning people their dues.

ثُمَّ جَعَلْنَـٰكُمْ خَلَـٰٓئِفَ فِى ٱلْأَرْضِ مِنۢ بَعْدِهِمْ لِنَنظُرَ كَيْفَ تَعْمَلُونَ ﴿١٤﴾

14 Thumma jaAAaln*a*kum khal*a*ifa fee alar*d*i min baAAdihim linan*th*ura kayfa taAAmaloon**a**

10:14. Then We made you vicegerents on the earth to see how you act.

وَإِذَا تُتْلَىٰ عَلَيْهِمْ ءَايَاتُنَا بَيِّنَـٰتٍ قَالَ ٱلَّذِينَ لَا يَرْجُونَ لِقَآءَنَا ٱئْتِ بِقُرْءَانٍ غَيْرِ هَـٰذَآ أَوْ بَدِّلْهُ قُلْ مَا يَكُونُ لِىٓ أَنْ أُبَدِّلَهُۥ مِن تِلْقَآيِٕ نَفْسِىٓ إِنْ أَتَّبِعُ إِلَّا مَا يُوحَىٰ إِلَىَّ إِنِّىٓ أَخَافُ إِنْ عَصَيْتُ رَبِّى عَذَابَ يَوْمٍ عَظِيمٍ ۝

15 Waitha tutla AAalayhim ayatuna bayyinatin qala allatheena la yarjoona liqaana iti biquranin ghayri hatha aw baddilhu qul ma yakoonu lee an obaddilahu min tilqai nafsee in attabiAAu illa ma yooha ilayya innee akhafu in AAasaytu rabbee AAathaba yawmin AAatheemin

---

10:15. And when Our clear Verses are recited to them, those who expect not to meet Us, say, "Bring a Qur'aan other than this, or change it." Say, "I cannot change it on my own initiative. I follow naught but what is revealed to me. I do indeed fear the punishment of a great Day, if I disobey my Lord."

قُل لَّوْ شَآءَ ٱللَّهُ مَا تَلَوْتُهُۥ عَلَيْكُمْ وَلَآ أَدْرَىٰكُم بِهِۦ فَقَدْ لَبِثْتُ فِيكُمْ عُمُرًا مِّن قَبْلِهِۦٓ أَفَلَا تَعْقِلُونَ ۝

16 Qul law shaa Allahu ma talawtuhu AAalaykum wala adrakum bihi faqad labithtu feekum AAumuran min qablihi afala taAAqiloona

---

10:16. Say, "If Allah had so willed, I would not have recited it to you, nor would you have known anything about it. I did live a lifetime among you before it.[8] Don't you then understand?"

---

8. The Prophet had lived for 40 long years among his people before Verses of the Qur'aan started being revealed to him.

فَمَنْ أَظْلَمُ مِمَّنِ افْتَرَىٰ عَلَى اللَّهِ كَذِبًا أَوْ كَذَّبَ بِآيَاتِهِ ۚ إِنَّهُ لَا يُفْلِحُ الْمُجْرِمُونَ ۝

17 Faman a_th_lamu mimmani iftar_a_ AAal_a_ All_a_hi ka_th_iban aw ka_thth_aba bi_a_y_a_tihi innahu l_a_ yufli_h_u almujrimoon**a**

10:17. Who is then more unjust than he who forges a lie against Allah or denies His Verses/signs? Never shall the sinners succeed.

وَيَعْبُدُونَ مِن دُونِ اللَّهِ مَا لَا يَضُرُّهُمْ وَلَا يَنفَعُهُمْ وَيَقُولُونَ هَٰؤُلَاءِ شُفَعَاؤُنَا عِندَ اللَّهِ ۚ قُلْ أَتُنَبِّئُونَ اللَّهَ بِمَا لَا يَعْلَمُ فِى السَّمَاوَاتِ وَلَا فِى الْأَرْضِ ۚ سُبْحَانَهُ وَتَعَالَىٰ عَمَّا يُشْرِكُونَ ۝

18 WayaAAbudoona min dooni All_a_hi m_a_ l_a_ ya_d_urruhum wal_a_ yanfaAAuhum wayaqooloona h_ao_l_ai_ shufaAA_ao_n_a_ AAinda All_a_hi qul atunabbioona All_a_ha bim_a_ l_a_ yaAAlamu fee alssam_a_w_a_ti wal_a_ fee alar_d_i sub_h_anahu wataAA_a_l_a_ AAamm_a_ yushrikoona

10:18. And they worship, besides Allah, what can neither harm them nor benefit them, and they say, "These are our intercessors with Allah." Say, "Do you inform Allah of what He knows not in the heavens and the earth!?" Glorified and supremely exalted is He above what they worship besides Him.

وَمَا كَانَ ٱلنَّاسُ إِلَّا أُمَّةً وَاحِدَةً فَٱخْتَلَفُواْ وَلَوْلَا كَلِمَةٌ سَبَقَتْ

مِن رَّبِّكَ لَقُضِىَ بَيْنَهُمْ فِيمَا فِيهِ يَخْتَلِفُونَ ۝

19 Wama kana alnnasu illa ommatan wahidatan faikhtalafoo walawla kalimatun sabaqat min rabbika laqudiya baynahum feema feehi yakhtalifoona

---

10:19. And mankind is naught but a single community, and yet they differ. Had it not been for a word already gone forth from your Lord, the issues, on which they differ, would have certainly been decided among them.[9]

---

9. Whether one is an Indian, African, American, Chinese or Japanese, the same basic rules of existence are applicable to all the human beings living or have been living on this planet. That single fact of life makes them a single community, irrespective of their colour, race or region. If they would all abide by the same divine laws enunciated in the Qur'aan, there could be no fundamental differences cropping up among them. But, barring the infinitesimal few, the overwhelming majority does not abide by the divine laws. That is why there is hostility and discord all around, fuelled by man's undue pride and prejudice. Allah Almighty could, if He would, give them instant punishment, but, in that case, all, except a few, on this earth would perish. HE has therefore reserved His final judgment for the Hereafter, giving mankind ample scope for reform or further slide into the pit of crime. HE does however intervene decisively whenever man oversteps his Allah-given bounds of freedom on this earth.

وَيَقُولُونَ لَوْلَا أُنزِلَ عَلَيْهِ ءَايَةٌ مِّن رَّبِّهِ فَقُلْ إِنَّمَا ٱلْغَيْبُ لِلَّهِ

فَٱنتَظِرُواْ إِنِّى مَعَكُم مِّنَ ٱلْمُنتَظِرِينَ ۝

20 Wayaqooloona lawla onzila AAalayhi ayatun min rabbihi faqul innama alghaybu lillahi faintathiroo innee maAAakum mina almuntathireena

---

10:20. And they say, "Why is no sign sent to him from his Lord?" Say, "The knowledge of the unseen is only with Allah. Well, wait! I am indeed with you among those who wait."[10]

14

10. Refer study note 8 on <u>Verse 6:37</u> **in this context. When the polytheists of Makkah repeatedly insisted on a divne sign for them to recognize Muhammad as a duly accredited Messenger of Allah, the matter was thus made clear to them that it is for Allah alone to give or not to give them the sign they demanded. The Messenger cannot, of his own volition, produce it for them. Why Allah did or did not do a certain thing is entirely in the realm of the unseen, which Allah alone knows.**

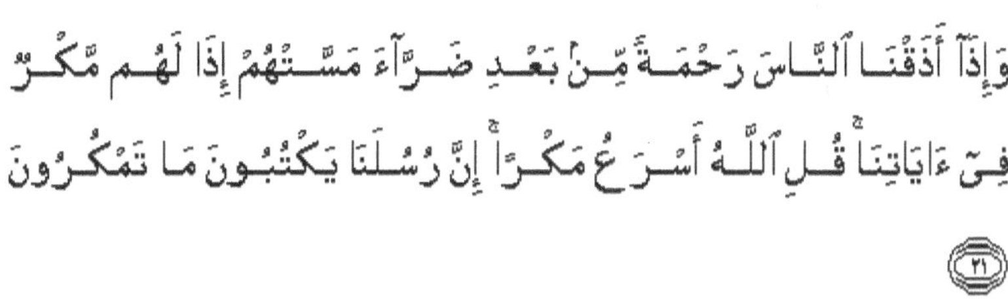

21 Waitha athaqna alnnasa rahmatan min baAAdi darraa massathum itha lahum makrun fee ayatina quli Allahu asraAAu makran inna rusulana yaktuboona ma tamkuroona

10:21. And when We make people taste mercy after a bad thing afflicts them, then it is that they plan to subvert Our Verses/signs.[11] Say, "Allah is quicker in planning. Our messengers[12] do indeed write down what you plan."

11. It is in times of well-being and prosperity that man tends to delude himself that he would continue to remain in that happy state for ever. He ignores the divine signs abounding around him. He sees death suddenly striking every now and then among his kith and kin and neighbourhood. But he brushes aside the disturbing thought that he himself could be its victim anytime. He often sees prosperity change to adversity but tends to forget that the same thing could happen to him himself. He may pay lip-service to Islam and say that it is the finest way of life, but when it comes to implementing the Qur'aanic code of life, he flinches and thinks that it is not practical to abide by everything that the Qur'aan says. When a Qur'aanic edict does not suit his lifestyle, he tries to undermine the divine meaning of the relevant Qur'aanic Verse with the help of man-made and error-prone *ahaadeeth* **and** *fatwas.*

12. Angels assigned to keep records of all things done and said.

هُوَ ٱلَّذِى يُسَيِّرُكُمْ فِى ٱلْبَرِّ وَٱلْبَحْرِ حَتَّىٰ إِذَا

كُنتُمْ فِى ٱلْفُلْكِ وَجَرَيْنَ بِهِم بِرِيحٍ طَيِّبَةٍ وَفَرِحُواْ بِهَا جَآءَتْهَا

رِيحٌ عَاصِفٌ وَجَآءَهُمُ ٱلْمَوْجُ مِن كُلِّ مَكَانٍ وَظَنُّوٓاْ أَنَّهُمْ أُحِيطَ بِهِمْ

دَعَوُاْ ٱللَّهَ مُخْلِصِينَ لَهُ ٱلدِّينَ لَئِنْ أَنجَيْتَنَا مِنْ هَٰذِهِۦ لَنَكُونَنَّ

مِنَ ٱلشَّٰكِرِينَ ﴿٢٢﴾

22 Huwa allathee yusayyirukum fee albarri waalbahri hatta itha kuntum fee alfulki wajarayna bihim bireehin tayyibatin wafarihoo biha jaatha reehun AAasifun wajaahumu almawju min kulli makanin wathannoo annahum oheeta bihim daAAawoo Allaha mukhliseena lahu alddeena lain anjaytana min hathihi lanakoonanna mina alshshakireena

---

10:22. He it is Who facilitates your movement by land and sea and you get into the ship. And the ship sails on with a pleasant breeze blowing and with people rejoicing the ride, until a violent wind overtakes them and the billows surge in on them from all sides, and they become certain that they are engulfed therein. They then pray to Allah in all sincerity and obedience to Him, "If You do deliver us from this, we will most certainly be grateful."

فَلَمَّآ أَنجَىٰهُمْ إِذَا هُمْ يَبْغُونَ فِى ٱلْأَرْضِ بِغَيْرِ ٱلْحَقِّ يَٰٓأَيُّهَا ٱلنَّاسُ إِنَّمَا

بَغْيُكُمْ عَلَىٰ أَنفُسِكُم مَّتَٰعَ ٱلْحَيَوٰةِ ٱلدُّنْيَا ثُمَّ إِلَيْنَا مَرْجِعُكُمْ فَنُنَبِّئُكُم

بِمَا كُنتُمْ تَعْمَلُونَ ﴿٢٣﴾

23 Falamma anjahum itha hum yabghoona fee alardi bighayri alhaqqi ya ayyuha alnnasu innama baghyukum AAala anfusikum mataAAa alhayati alddunya thumma ilayna marjiAAukum fanunabbiokum bima kuntum taAAmaloona

10:23. But when He delivers them, behold! They become unduly rebellious on earth. "O mankind! Your rebellion will affect you yourselves. These here are the provisions only of this temporal life. To Us is your return thereafter. Then We will relate to you what you did."

إِنَّمَا مَثَلُ ٱلْحَيَوٰةِ ٱلدُّنْيَا كَمَآءٍ أَنزَلْنَـٰهُ مِنَ ٱلسَّمَآءِ فَٱخْتَلَطَ بِهِۦ نَبَاتُ ٱلْأَرْضِ مِمَّا يَأْكُلُ ٱلنَّاسُ وَٱلْأَنْعَـٰمُ حَتَّىٰ إِذَآ أَخَذَتِ ٱلْأَرْضُ زُخْرُفَهَا وَٱزَّيَّنَتْ وَظَنَّ أَهْلُهَآ أَنَّهُمْ قَـٰدِرُونَ عَلَيْهَآ أَتَىٰهَآ أَمْرُنَا لَيْلًا أَوْ نَهَارًا فَجَعَلْنَـٰهَا حَصِيدًا كَأَن لَّمْ تَغْنَ بِٱلْأَمْسِ كَذَٰلِكَ نُفَصِّلُ ٱلْأَيَـٰتِ لِقَوْمٍ يَتَفَكَّرُونَ ﴿٢٤﴾

24 Innama mathalu alhayati alddunya kamain anzalnahu mina alssamai faikhtalata bihi nabatu alardi mimma yakulu alnnasu waalanAAamu hatta itha akhathati alardu zukhrufaha waizzayyanat wa*th*anna ahluha annahum qadiroona AAalayha ataha amruna laylan aw naharan fajaAAalnaha haseedan kaan lam taghna bialamsi kathalika nufassilu alayati liqawmin yatafakkaroona

---

10:24. This life is but like water which We send down from the sky. Spring forth therewith all kinds of vegetation on the earth, of which men and cattle eat. Until, when the earth puts on its golden raiment and it becomes adorned, and its people think that they have mastery over it, Our command comes to it, by night or by day, and We make it barren, as though it had not flourished anytime in the recent past. Thus, do We explain the Verses/signs for a people who reflect.

وَٱللَّهُ يَدْعُوٓاْ إِلَىٰ دَارِ ٱلسَّلَـٰمِ وَيَهْدِى مَن يَشَآءُ إِلَىٰ صِرَٰطٍ مُّسْتَقِيمٍ ﴿٢٥﴾

25 WaAllahu yadAAoo ila dari alssalami wayahdee man yashao ila siratin mustaqeemin

10:25. And Allah invites to the abode of peace and guides, whom He pleases, to the Straight Path.

﴿لِّلَّذِينَ أَحْسَنُوا الْحُسْنَىٰ وَزِيَادَةٌ وَلَا يَرْهَقُ وُجُوهَهُمْ قَتَرٌ وَلَا ذِلَّةٌ أُولَـٰئِكَ أَصْحَابُ الْجَنَّةِ هُمْ فِيهَا خَالِدُونَ ۝﴾

26 Lillatheena ahsanoo alhusna waziyadatun wala yarhaqu wujoohahum qatarun wala thillatun olaika ashabu aljannati hum feeha khalidoona

10:26. There is good – and more besides – for those who do good. And no gloom and no ignominy shall cover their faces. Those shall be the inmates of the Garden. Therein they shall abide.

﴿وَالَّذِينَ كَسَبُوا السَّيِّئَاتِ جَزَاءُ سَيِّئَةٍ بِمِثْلِهَا وَتَرْهَقُهُمْ ذِلَّةٌ مَّا لَهُم مِّنَ اللَّهِ مِنْ عَاصِمٍ كَأَنَّمَا أُغْشِيَتْ وُجُوهُهُمْ قِطَعًا مِّنَ اللَّيْلِ مُظْلِمًا أُولَـٰئِكَ أَصْحَابُ النَّارِ هُمْ فِيهَا خَالِدُونَ ۝﴾

27 Waallatheena kasaboo alssayyiati jazao sayyiatin bimithliha watarhaquhum thillatun ma lahum mina Allahi min AAasimin kaannama oghshiyat wujoohuhum qitaAAan mina allayli muthliman olaika ashabu alnnari hum feeha khalidoona

10:27. And as for those who have earned evil, the punishment for an evil is the like thereof, and ignominy shall cover them – they shall have none to protect them from

Allah – as if their faces were covered with slices of the dense darkness of night. Those shall be the inmates of the Fire. Therein they shall abide.

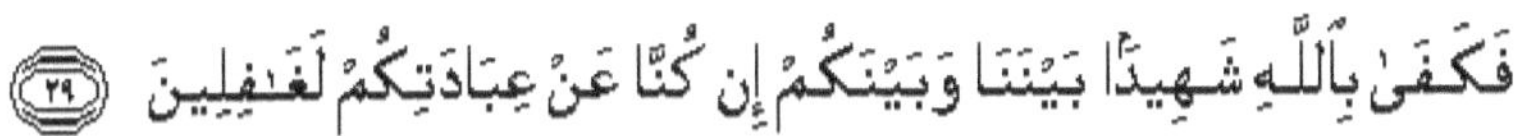

28 Wayawma na<u>h</u>shuruhum jameeAAan thumma naqoolu lilla<u>th</u>eena ashrakoo mak<u>a</u>nakum antum washurak<u>a</u>okum fazayyaln<u>a</u> baynahum waqa<u>l</u>a shurak<u>a</u>ohum m<u>a</u> kuntum iyy<u>a</u>n<u>a</u> taAAbudoon<u>a</u>

10:28. And on the day We gather them all together, We will say to those who worshipped others besides Allah, "Be there where you are – you and your gods other than Allah!" We shall then separate them, one from another. And their gods would say, "It was not us that you worshipped."

29 Fakaf<u>a</u> biAll<u>a</u>hi shaheedan baynan<u>a</u> wabaynakum in kunn<u>a</u> AAan AAib<u>a</u>datikum lagh<u>a</u>fileena

10:29. "And Allah is sufficient as a witness, between us and you, that we were quite unaware of your worship."

هُنَالِكَ تَبْلُواْ كُلُّ نَفْسٍ مَّآ أَسْلَفَتْ وَرُدُّواْ إِلَى ٱللَّهِ مَوْلَـٰهُمُ ٱلْحَقِّ وَضَلَّ

عَنْهُم مَّا كَانُواْ يَفْتَرُونَ ﴿٣٠﴾

30 Hunalika tabloo kullu nafsin ma aslafat waruddoo ila Allahi mawlahumu alhaqqi wadalla AAanhum ma kanoo yaftaroona

---

10:30. There, everyone will be tried for what it did before, and they shall be brought back to Allah, their true Patron. And what they concocted shall desert them.

قُلْ مَن يَرْزُقُكُم مِّنَ ٱلسَّمَآءِ وَٱلْأَرْضِ أَمَّن يَمْلِكُ ٱلسَّمْعَ وَٱلْأَبْصَـٰرَ وَمَن

يُخْرِجُ ٱلْحَىَّ مِنَ ٱلْمَيِّتِ وَيُخْرِجُ ٱلْمَيِّتَ مِنَ ٱلْحَىِّ وَمَن يُدَبِّرُ ٱلْأَمْرَ

فَسَيَقُولُونَ ٱللَّهُ فَقُلْ أَفَلَا تَتَّقُونَ ﴿٣١﴾

31 Qul man yarzuqukum mina alssamai waalardi amman yamliku alssamAAa waalabsara waman yukhriju alhayya mina almayyiti wayukhriju almayyita mina alhayyi waman yudabbiru alamra fasayaqooloona Allahu faqul afala tattaqoona

---

10:31. Ask them, "Who provides for you means of sustenance from the heavens and the earth? Or Who controls the hearing and the sights? And Who brings out the living from the dead, and the dead from the living? And Who plans the affairs prudently and executes them well?" They will reply, "Allah." Then ask, "Won't you then fear Him!?"

فَذَٰلِكُمُ ٱللَّهُ رَبُّكُمُ ٱلْحَقُّ ۖ فَمَاذَا بَعْدَ ٱلْحَقِّ إِلَّا ٱلضَّلَـٰلُ ۖ فَأَنَّىٰ تُصْرَفُونَ

32 Fathalikumu Allahu rabbukumu alhaqqu famatha baAAda alhaqqi illa alddalalu faanna tusrafoona

10:32. This then is Allah, your true Lord! And what remains there after the truth but error? How could you then be turned away from this Absolute Truth?

كَذَٰلِكَ حَقَّتْ كَلِمَتُ رَبِّكَ عَلَى ٱلَّذِينَ فَسَقُوٓاْ أَنَّهُمْ لَا يُؤْمِنُونَ ﴿٣٣﴾

33 Kathalika haqqat kalimatu rabbika AAala allatheena fasaqoo annahum la yuminoona

10:33. Thus[13] is your Lord's word, that they will not believe, proved true about such as defiantly disobey Allah.

13. I.e. the transgressors' being defiantly disobedient of Allah Almighty, despite the unreasonableness of the transgression, as shown in Verses 31 and 32 above.

قُلْ هَلْ مِن شُرَكَآئِكُم مَّن يَبْدَؤُاْ ٱلْخَلْقَ ثُمَّ يُعِيدُهُۥ ۚ قُلِ ٱللَّهُ يَبْدَؤُاْ ٱلْخَلْقَ

ثُمَّ يُعِيدُهُۥ ۖ فَأَنَّىٰ تُؤْفَكُونَ ﴿٣٤﴾

34 Qul hal min shurakaikum man yabdao alkhalqa thumma yuAAeeduhu quli Allahu yabdao alkhalqa thumma yuAAeeduhu faanna tufakoona

10:34. Say, "Is there any one among those whom you worship besides Allah, who can pioneer the creation and then reproduce it?" Say, "Allah pioneers the creation and then He reproduces it. How then are you fooled by falsehood?"

قُل هَل مِن شُرَكَآئِكُم مَّن يَهدِى إِلَى ٱلحَقِّ قُلِ ٱللَّهُ يَهدِى لِلحَقِّ أَفَمَن يَهدِى إِلَى ٱلحَقِّ أَحَقُّ أَن يُتَّبَعَ أَمَّن لَّا يَهِدِّى إِلَّا أَن يُهدَىٰ فَمَا لَكُم كَيفَ تَحكُمُونَ ۝

35 Qul hal min shurakaikum man yahdee il<u>a</u> al<u>h</u>aqqi quli All<u>a</u>hu yahdee lil<u>h</u>aqqi afaman yahdee il<u>a</u> al<u>h</u>aqqi a<u>h</u>aqqu an yuttabaAAa amman l<u>a</u> yahiddee ill<u>a</u> an yuhd<u>a</u> fam<u>a</u> lakum kayfa ta<u>h</u>kumoon<u>a</u>

10:35. Say, "Is there anyone, among those whom you worship besides Allah, who guides to the truth?" Say, "Allah it is Who guides to the truth. Is He then Who guides to the truth more worthy to be followed, or he who himself does not go aright unless he is guided? What's the matter with you? How wrongly do you make your decisions?"

وَمَا يَتَّبِعُ أَكثَرُهُم إِلَّا ظَنًّا إِنَّ ٱلظَّنَّ لَا يُغنِى مِنَ ٱلحَقِّ شَيئًا إِنَّ ٱللَّهَ عَلِيمٌ بِمَا يَفعَلُونَ ۝

36 Wam<u>a</u> yattabiAAu aktharuhum ill<u>a</u> *th*annan inna al*thth*anna l<u>a</u> yughnee mina al<u>h</u>aqqi shayan inna All<u>a</u>ha AAaleemun bim<u>a</u> yafAAaloon<u>a</u>

10:36. And most of them do not follow anything but conjecture. Conjecture will avail nothing indeed against the Truth. Allah is indeed aware of what they do.

وَمَا كَانَ هَـٰذَا ٱلْقُرْءَانُ أَن يُفْتَرَىٰ مِن دُونِ ٱللَّهِ وَلَـٰكِن تَصْدِيقَ ٱلَّذِى بَيْنَ يَدَيْهِ وَتَفْصِيلَ ٱلْكِتَـٰبِ لَا رَيْبَ فِيهِ مِن رَّبِّ ٱلْعَـٰلَمِينَ ﴿٣٧﴾

37 Wama kana hatha alquranu an yuftara min dooni Allahi walakin tasdeeqa allathee bayna yadayhi watafseela alkitabi la rayba feehi min rabbi alAAalameena

10:37. And this Qur'aan is not such as could be forged by those besides Allah. But it is a confirmation of what came before it. And it is, no doubt, the book, explained in detail, from the Lord of the worlds.[14]

14. When the Lord Himself confirms that the Qur'aan is a <u>detailed</u> instruction Book for mankind, it is nothing short of blasphemy to say – as do many of our religious leaders – that the Qur'aan is not detailed and needs the *ahaadeeth* for providing the details!

أَمْ يَقُولُونَ ٱفْتَرَىٰهُ قُلْ فَأْتُوا۟ بِسُورَةٍ مِّثْلِهِۦ وَٱدْعُوا۟ مَنِ ٱسْتَطَعْتُم مِّن دُونِ ٱللَّهِ إِن كُنتُمْ صَـٰدِقِينَ ﴿٣٨﴾

38 Am yaqooloona iftarahu qul fatoo bisooratin mithlihi waodAAoo mani istataAAtum min dooni Allahi in kuntum sadiqeena

10:38. Or do they say that he (the Prophet) has forged it? Say, "Then bring a chapter like this and invite whom you can, besides Allah, if you are truthful."[15]

15. Refer study note 16 on <u>Verse 2:23</u> in this context.

بَلْ كَذَّبُواْ بِمَا لَمْ يُحِيطُواْ بِعِلْمِهِۦ وَلَمَّا يَأْتِهِمْ تَأْوِيلُهُۥ ۚ كَذَٰلِكَ كَذَّبَ
ٱلَّذِينَ مِن قَبْلِهِمْ ۖ فَٱنظُرْ كَيْفَ كَانَ عَٰقِبَةُ ٱلظَّٰلِمِينَ ﴿٣٩﴾

39 Bal kaththaboo bima lam yuheetoo biAAilmihi walamma yatihim taweeluhu kathalika kaththaba allatheena min qablihim faonthur kayfa kana AAaqibatu alththalimeena

10:39. Nay, they reject all that is beyond their knowledge and comprehension, as false. So, did those before them. And see what happened to those wicked people[16]!

16. I.e., the people like those of Noah, Lot and the Pharaoh.

وَمِنْهُم مَّن يُؤْمِنُ بِهِۦ وَمِنْهُم مَّن لَّا يُؤْمِنُ بِهِۦ ۚ وَرَبُّكَ
أَعْلَمُ بِٱلْمُفْسِدِينَ ﴿٤٠﴾

40 Waminhum man yuminu bihi waminhum man la yuminu bihi warabbuka aAAlamu bialmufsideena

10:40. And among them is he who believes in it[17] and among them is he who does not believe in it, and your Lord knows the troublemakers.

17. The existence of things that are beyond human knowledge and comprehension.

وَإِن كَذَّبُوكَ فَقُل لِّى عَمَلِى وَلَكُمْ عَمَلُكُمْ أَنتُم بَرِيٓـُٔونَ مِمَّآ أَعْمَلُ وَأَنَا۟ بَرِىٓءٌ مِّمَّا تَعْمَلُونَ ۝

41 Wain ka_ththa_booka faqul lee AAamalee walakum AAamalukum antum bareeoona mimm_a aAAmalu waan_a bareeon mimm_a taAAmaloon**a**

10:41. And if they belie you, say, "I am responsible for what I do, and you, for what you do. You are free of any responsibility for what I do and I am free of any responsibility for what you do.

وَمِنْهُم مَّن يَسْتَمِعُونَ إِلَيْكَ أَفَأَنتَ تُسْمِعُ ٱلصُّمَّ وَلَوْ كَانُوا۟ لَا يَعْقِلُونَ

42 Waminhum man yastamiAAoona ilayka afaanta tusmiAAu al_s_summa walaw k_anoo l_a yaAAqiloon**a**

10:42. And there are those of them who appear to be listening to you. But can you make the deaf to listen even when they cannot understand?

وَمِنْهُم مَّن يَنظُرُ إِلَيْكَ أَفَأَنتَ تَهْدِى ٱلْعُمْىَ وَلَوْ كَانُوا۟ لَا يُبْصِرُونَ ۝

43 Waminhum man yan_th_uru ilayka afaanta tahdee alAAumya walaw k_anoo l_a yub_siroon**a**

10:43. And there are those of them who appear to be looking at you. But can you give guidance to the blind even when they cannot see?

إِنَّ ٱللَّهَ لَا يَظْلِمُ ٱلنَّاسَ شَيْـًٔا وَلَـٰكِنَّ ٱلنَّاسَ أَنفُسَهُمْ يَظْلِمُونَ ۝

44 Inna Allaha la yathlimu alnnasa shayan walakinna alnnasa anfusahum yathlimoona

10:44. Indeed, Allah does not wrong mankind in anything, but they wrong themselves.

وَيَوْمَ يَحْشُرُهُمْ كَأَن لَّمْ يَلْبَثُوٓا۟ إِلَّا سَاعَةً مِّنَ ٱلنَّهَارِ يَتَعَارَفُونَ بَيْنَهُمْ قَدْ خَسِرَ ٱلَّذِينَ كَذَّبُوا۟ بِلِقَآءِ ٱللَّهِ وَمَا كَانُوا۟ مُهْتَدِينَ ۝

45 Wayawma yahshuruhum kaan lam yalbathoo illa saAAatan mina alnnahari yataAAarafoona baynahum qad khasira allatheena kaththaboo biliqai Allahi wama kanoo muhtadeena

10:45. And the day He will resurrect them and gather them all together, they will introduce one another as if they had halted but for a little while of daytime. Those who belied their meeting with Allah are indeed doomed, and they were not on right guidance.

وَإِمَّا نُرِيَنَّكَ بَعْضَ ٱلَّذِى نَعِدُهُمْ أَوْ نَتَوَفَّيَنَّكَ فَإِلَيْنَا مَرْجِعُهُمْ ثُمَّ ٱللَّهُ شَهِيدٌ عَلَىٰ مَا يَفْعَلُونَ ۝

46 Waimma nuriyannaka baAAda allathee naAAiduhum aw natawaffayannaka failayna marjiAAuhum thumma Allahu shaheedun AAala ma yafAAaloona

10:46. And if We show you some of the things We promised to them, or if We cause you to die, yet to Us is their return, and Allah is witness to what they do.

$$\text{وَلِكُلِّ أُمَّةٍ رَّسُولٌ فَإِذَا جَاءَ رَسُولُهُمْ قُضِىَ بَيْنَهُم بِالْقِسْطِ وَهُمْ لَا يُظْلَمُونَ ﴿٤٧﴾}$$

47 Walikulli ommatin rasoolun fai_tha_ _jaa_ rasooluhum qu_d_iya baynahum bialqis_t_i wahum l_a_ yu_th_lamoona

10:47. And for every *Ummah*[18] a Messenger. And when their Messenger came, they were judged equitably, and they were not wronged.[19]

18. The Arabic word connotes the entire populace for whom any Messenger of Allah was sent. Muhammad (peace and Allah's blessings upon him) was sent for all mankind till the Last Day. So, his *Ummah* includes all mankind that inhabited this earth and would inhabit this earth from the day he was appointed as Messenger till the Last Day.

19. The Muslims, in today's world, are a disgraced community, even when they are the custodians of the last divine Message. Why? Aren't they thus wronged? Not al all! They deserve the disgrace. For, despite having the Maker's Own Manual in their hands, they refuse to conduct their lives as per instructions therein!

$$\text{وَيَقُولُونَ مَتَىٰ هَـٰذَا الْوَعْدُ إِن كُنتُمْ صَـٰدِقِينَ ﴿٤٨﴾}$$

48 Wayaqooloona mat_a_ ha_tha_ alwaAAdu in kuntum _s_adiqeena

10:48. And they ask, "When will this prophecy come about, if what you say is true?"

قُل لَّآ أَمۡلِكُ لِنَفۡسِى ضَرًّا وَلَا نَفۡعًا إِلَّا مَا شَآءَ ٱللَّهُ لِكُلِّ أُمَّةٍ أَجَلٌ إِذَا جَآءَ أَجَلُهُمۡ فَلَا يَسۡتَـٔۡخِرُونَ سَاعَةً وَلَا يَسۡتَقۡدِمُونَ ﴿٤٩﴾

49 Qul la amliku linafsee darran wala nafAAan illa ma shaa Allahu likulli ommatin ajalun itha jaa ajaluhum fala yastakhiroona saAAatan wala yastaqdimoona

10:49. Say, "I have no control over any harm, or any benefit, coming to me, except what Allah pleases. Every *Ummah* has its term. When their term comes, they shall not then remain here a moment more, nor can they go before their time."

قُلۡ أَرَءَيۡتُمۡ إِنۡ أَتَىٰكُمۡ عَذَابُهُۥ بَيَـٰتًا أَوۡ نَهَارًا مَّاذَا يَسۡتَعۡجِلُ مِنۡهُ ٱلۡمُجۡرِمُونَ ﴿٥٠﴾

50 Qul araaytum in atakum AAathabuhu bayatan aw naharan matha yastaAAjilu minhu almujrimoona

10:50. Say, "Have you ever considered that if His punishment overtakes you by night or by day, what then would there be for the sinners to ask for hastening of?"[20]

20. Verse 49 contains the answer to the query posed in Verse 48 above. Verses 50 and 51 (below) drive the point home by telling the non-believers that if Allah Almighty were to punish them the moment they committed any offence, they would not get the opportunity either to demand hastening of their punishment or for their own reform.

أَثُمَّ إِذَا مَا وَقَعَ ءَامَنتُم بِهِۦٓ ءَآلَْٔـٰنَ وَقَدْ كُنتُم بِهِۦ تَسْتَعْجِلُونَ ﴿٥١﴾

51 Athumma itha ma waqaAAa amantum bihi alana waqad kuntum bihi tastaAAjiloona

---

10:51. And will you believe in it only when it comes to pass? What then!? And you did want it hastened?

ثُمَّ قِيلَ لِلَّذِينَ ظَلَمُواْ ذُوقُواْ عَذَابَ ٱلْخُلْدِ هَلْ تُجْزَوْنَ إِلَّا بِمَا كُنتُمْ تَكْسِبُونَ ﴿٥٢﴾

52 Thumma qeela lillatheena thalamoo thooqoo AAathaba alkhuldi hal tujzawna illa bima kuntum taksiboona

---

10:52. Then those who did wrong shall be told, "Taste the everlasting punishment! Was it not but what you deserved?"

۞ وَيَسْتَنۢبِئُونَكَ أَحَقٌّ هُوَ قُلْ إِى وَرَبِّىٓ إِنَّهُۥ لَحَقٌّ وَمَآ أَنتُم بِمُعْجِزِينَ

﴿٥٣﴾

53 Wayastanbioonaka ahaqqun huwa qul ee warabbee innahu lahaqqun wama antum bimuAAjizeena

---

10:53. And they ask you, "Is that true?" Say, "Yes, by my Lord! It is indeed the truth. And you cannot elude it."

وَلَوْ أَنَّ لِكُلِّ نَفْسٍ ظَلَمَتْ مَا فِى ٱلْأَرْضِ لَٱفْتَدَتْ بِهِۦ وَأَسَرُّواْ ٱلنَّدَامَةَ لَمَّا رَأَوُاْ ٱلْعَذَابَ وَقُضِىَ بَيْنَهُم بِٱلْقِسْطِ وَهُمْ لَا يُظْلَمُونَ ۝

54 Walaw anna likulli nafsin *th*alamat m*a* fee alar*d*i laiftadat bihi waasarroo alnnad*a*mata lamm*a* raawoo alAAa*th*aba waqu*d*iya baynahum bialqis*t*i wahum l*a* yu*th*lamoona

10:54. And had every unjust Person all that is in the earth, he would certainly offer it to ransom himself. And they will feel regret in their hearts the moment they see the punishment they would be made to suffer. And they shall be judged equitably, and they shall not be wronged!

أَلَا إِنَّ لِلَّهِ مَا فِى ٱلسَّمَٰوَٰتِ وَٱلْأَرْضِ أَلَا إِنَّ وَعْدَ ٱللَّهِ حَقٌّ وَلَٰكِنَّ أَكْثَرَهُمْ لَا يَعْلَمُونَ ۝

55 Al*a* inna lill*a*hi m*a* fee alssam*a*w*a*ti waalar*d*i al*a* inna waAAda All*a*hi *h*aqqun wal*a*kinna aktharahum l*a* yaAAlamoona

10:55. Beware! To Allah does certainly belong all that is in the heavens and the earth. Beware! Allah's promise is indeed true, but most of them know not.

هُوَ يُحْىِۦ وَيُمِيتُ وَإِلَيْهِ تُرْجَعُونَ ۝

56 Huwa yu*h*yee wayumeetu wailayhi turjaAAoona

10:56. He it is Who gives life and causes death, and to Him you shall be returned!

بِتَأَيُّهَا ٱلنَّاسُ قَدْ جَآءَتْكُم مَّوْعِظَةٌ مِّن رَّبِّكُمْ وَشِفَآءٌ لِّمَا فِى ٱلصُّدُورِ وَهُدًى وَرَحْمَةٌ لِّلْمُؤْمِنِينَ ﴿٥٧﴾

57 Ya ayyuha alnnasu qad jaatkum mawAAithatun min rabbikum washifaon lima fee alssudoori wahudan warahmatun lilmumineena

10:57. O mankind! Admonition from your Lord and remedy for what the hearts harbour has surely come to you, and guidance and mercy for the believers.

قُل بِفَضْلِ ٱللَّهِ وَبِرَحْمَتِهِۦ فَبِذَٰلِكَ فَلْيَفْرَحُواْ هُوَ خَيْرٌ مِّمَّا يَجْمَعُونَ

﴿٥٨﴾

58 Qul bifadli Allahi wabirahmatihi fabithalika falyafrahoo huwa khayrun mimma yajmaAAoona

10:58. Say, "In the grace of Allah and in His mercy – in **that** they should rejoice. **That** is better than what they gather."

قُـلْ أَرَءَيْتُـم مَّـآ أَنـزَلَ ٱللَّـهُ لَكُـم مِّـن رِّزْقٍ فَجَـعَلْتُم مِّنْـهُ حَرَامًا وَحَلَـلًا قُلْ ءَآللَّـهُ أَذِنَ لَكُمْ أَمْ عَلَى ٱللَّهِ تَفْتَرُونَ ﴿٥٩﴾

59 Qul araaytum ma anzala Allahu lakum min rizqin fajaAAaltum minhu haraman wahalalan qul allahu athina lakum am AAala Allahi taftaroona

---

10:59. Say, "Do you see that you make a part of what Allah has sent down for you as sustenance unlawful, and a part, lawful." Say, "Has Allah commanded you to do so? Or do you forge a lie against Allah?"

وَمَا ظَنُّ ٱلَّذِينَ يَفْتَرُونَ عَلَى ٱللَّهِ ٱلْكَذِبَ يَوْمَ ٱلْقِيَـمَةِ إِنَّ ٱللَّهَ لَذُو فَضْلٍ عَلَى ٱلنَّاسِ وَلَـكِنَّ أَكْـثَرَهُمْ لَا يَشْكُرُونَ ﴿٦٠﴾

60 Wama thannu allatheena yaftaroona AAala Allahi alkathiba yawma alqiyamati inna Allaha lathoo fadlin AAala alnnasi walakinna aktharahum la yashkuroona

---

10:60. And what will be the thought of those who forge lies against Allah on the day of Resurrection? Allah is indeed full of grace for mankind, but most of them are ungrateful.

وَمَا تَكُونُ فِى شَأْنٍ وَمَا تَتْلُواْ مِنْهُ مِن قُرْءَانٍ وَلَا تَعْمَلُونَ مِنْ عَمَلٍ إِلَّا كُنَّا عَلَيْكُمْ شُهُودًا إِذْ تُفِيضُونَ فِيهِ وَمَا يَعْزُبُ عَن رَّبِّكَ مِن مِّثْقَالِ ذَرَّةٍ فِى الْأَرْضِ وَلَا فِى السَّمَاءِ وَلَآ أَصْغَرَ مِن ذَٰلِكَ وَلَآ أَكْبَرَ إِلَّا فِى كِتَـٰبٍ مُّبِينٍ

61 Wama takoonu fee shanin wama tatloo minhu min quranin wala taAAmaloona min AAamalin illa kunna AAalaykum shuhoodan ith tufeedoona feehi wama yaAAzubu AAan rabbika min mithqali tharratin fee alardi wala fee alssamai wala asghara min thalika wala akbara illa fee kitabin mubeenun

---

10:61. And you are engaged not in anything, and you read not concerning it in any portion of the Qur'aan, and you do not do any deed, but We are witnesses over you when you get involved therein. And not an atom-weight of anything, in the earth or in the heavens, lies concealed from your Lord. Nor is there anything, less than that or greater, but recorded in a book manifest.

أَلَآ إِنَّ أَوْلِيَآءَ اللَّهِ لَا خَوْفٌ عَلَيْهِمْ وَلَا هُمْ يَحْزَنُونَ

62 Ala inna awliyaa Allahi la khawfun AAalayhim wala hum yahzanoona

---

10:62. Verily, those that are close to Allah[21] shall indeed have no fear. Nor shall they grieve.

---

21. Refer study note 154 under <u>Verse 2:107</u>. **The next 2 Verses, 63 and 64, further describe those who are close to (*awliya* of) Allah.**

ٱلَّذِينَ ءَامَنُوا۟ وَكَانُوا۟ يَتَّقُونَ ۝

63 Alla_th_eena amanoo waka_n_oo yattaqoon**a**

10:63. Those that believe and fear Allah.

لَهُمُ ٱلْبُشْرَىٰ فِى ٱلْحَيَوٰةِ ٱلدُّنْيَا وَفِى ٱلْءَاخِرَةِ ۚ لَا تَبْدِيلَ لِكَلِمَٰتِ ٱللَّهِ ۚ ذَٰلِكَ هُوَ ٱلْفَوْزُ ٱلْعَظِيمُ ۝

64 Lahumu albushr_a_ fee al_h_ay_a_ti aldduny_a_ wafee ala_kh_irati l_a_ tabdeela likalim_a_ti All_a_hi _th_alika huwa alfawzu alAAa_th_eem**u**

10:64. For them there is good news in this world's life and in the Hereafter. - Allah's words never change! - **That** is the highest success.

وَلَا يَحْزُنكَ قَوْلُهُمْ ۘ إِنَّ ٱلْعِزَّةَ لِلَّهِ جَمِيعًا ۚ هُوَ ٱلسَّمِيعُ ٱلْعَلِيمُ ۝

65 Wal_a_ ya_h_zunka qawluhum inna alAAizzata lill_a_hi jameeAAan huwa alssameeAAu alAAaleem**u**

10:65. And let not what they say grieve you. To Allah indeed belongs all the honour[22]. He is the One Who hears and knows all things.

---

22. Man is wont to have a false sense of honour. He tends to forget that he is merely a creature. It was this false sense of honour (pride) that caused Satan's downfall. He disobeyed Allah's command to prostrate before Adam because the latter was created of matter while he himself was created of energy. This satanic trait is inherent in man also. It is this false sense of honour that generates violence among individuals and nations. It can prove to be his downfall like that of Satan. It can cause grief in him. A is grieved when B accuses him falsely. A wouldn't grieve if he strongly believes that Allah hears and knows everything.

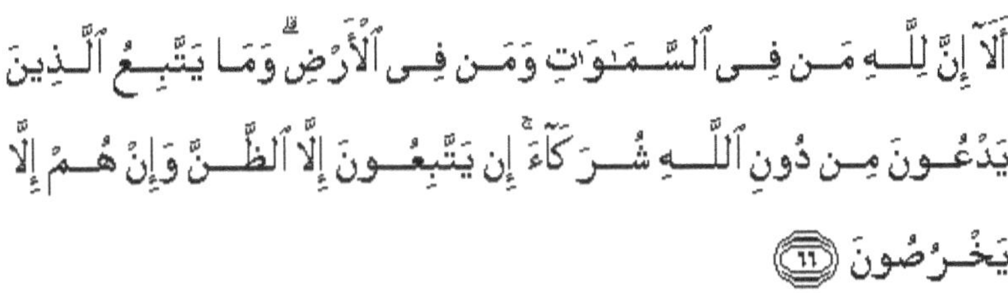

66 Ala inna lillahi man fee alssamawati waman fee alardi wama yattabiAAu allatheena yadAAoona min dooni Allahi shurakaa in yattabiAAoona illa alththanna wain hum illa yakhrusoona

10:66. Verily, indeed, to Allah belongs whatever there is in the heavens and whatever there is in the earth. And they, who call on others besides Allah, follow not any associates of His! They follow not but conjectures and they do not but guess.

67 Huwa allathee jaAAala lakumu allayla litaskunoo feehi waalnnahara mubsiran inna fee thalika laayatin liqawmin yasmaAAoona

10:67. He it is Who made for you the night that you might rest in it, and the day wherein one can see things clearly. Indeed, there are signs therein for people who would hear.[23]

23. The night and the day are not man-made. These are intentionally caused obviously by that Intelligent Being, Who has created the entire universe, for the convenience of man and other living creatures on the surface of this earth. These creatures cannot go on working indefinitely without a break. They need rest. This is one of the innumerable signs that the Creator has not neglected to provide any need of His creatures. But, alas, man, by and large, remains ungrateful! He won't listen to anyone pointing out such clear signs to him.

قَالُوا۟ ٱتَّخَذَ ٱللَّهُ وَلَدًا ۗ سُبْحَـٰنَهُۥ ۖ هُوَ ٱلْغَنِىُّ ۖ لَهُۥ مَا فِى ٱلسَّمَـٰوَٰتِ وَمَا فِى ٱلْأَرْضِ ۚ إِنْ عِندَكُم مِّن سُلْطَـٰنٍۭ بِهَـٰذَآ ۚ أَتَقُولُونَ عَلَى ٱللَّهِ مَا لَا تَعْلَمُونَ

۶۸

68 Qaloo ittakhatha Allahu waladan subhanahu huwa alghaniyyu lahu ma fee alssamawati wama fee alardi in AAindakum min sultanin bihatha ataqooloona AAala Allahi ma la taAAlamoona

---

10:68. They say, "Allah has got a son!" Glorified is He – the Self-sufficient. His is what is in the heavens and what is in the earth. You have no authority over any of this. How can you say about Allah what you do not know?

قُلْ إِنَّ ٱلَّذِينَ يَفْتَرُونَ عَلَى ٱللَّهِ ٱلْكَذِبَ لَا يُفْلِحُونَ

69 Qul inna allatheena yaftaroona AAala Allahi alkathiba la yuflihoona

---

10:69. Say, "They, who forge a lie about Allah, shall not succeed!"

مَتَـٰعٌ فِى ٱلدُّنْيَا ثُمَّ إِلَيْنَا مَرْجِعُهُمْ ثُمَّ نُذِيقُهُمُ ٱلْعَذَابَ ٱلشَّـدِيدَ بِمَا كَانُوا۟ يَكْفُرُونَ ۝

70 MataAAun fee alddunya thumma ilayna marjiAAuhum thumma nutheequhumu alAAathaba alshshadeeda bima kanoo yakfuroona

---

10:70. After this temporary provision in this world, to Us shall be their return. Then We shall make them taste severe punishment because they suppressed the Truth.

۞ وَٱتْلُ عَلَيْهِمْ نَبَأَ نُوحٍ إِذْ قَالَ لِقَوْمِهِۦ يَـٰقَوْمِ إِن كَانَ كَبُرَ عَلَيْكُم مَّقَامِى وَتَذْكِيرِى بِـَٔايَـٰتِ ٱللَّـهِ فَعَلَى ٱللَّـهِ تَوَكَّلْتُ فَأَجْمِعُوا۟ أَمْرَكُمْ وَشُرَكَآءَكُمْ ثُمَّ لَا يَكُنْ أَمْرُكُمْ عَلَيْكُمْ غُمَّةً ثُمَّ ٱقْضُوا۟ إِلَىَّ وَلَا تُنظِرُونِ ۝

71 Waotlu AAalayhim nabaa noohin ith qala liqawmihi ya qawmi in kana kabura AAalaykum maqamee watathkeeree biayati Allahi faAAala Allahi tawakkaltu faajmiAAoo amrakum washurakaakum thumma la yakun amrukum AAalaykum ghummatan thumma iqdoo ilayya wala tunthirooni

---

10:71. And recite to them the story of Noah when he said to his people, "O my people! If my stay and my reminding (you) of the signs/Verses of Allah is hard on you – and on Allah yet do I rely – then combine your efforts and of those whom you worship besides Allah, then let not your effort remain dubious to you, then have it executed against me and give me no respite."

$$\text{فَإِن تَوَلَّيْتُمْ فَمَا سَأَلْتُكُم مِّنْ أَجْرٍ ۖ إِنْ أَجْرِىَ إِلَّا عَلَى}$$

$$\text{ٱللَّهِ ۖ وَأُمِرْتُ أَنْ أَكُونَ مِنَ ٱلْمُسْلِمِينَ ﴿٧٢﴾}$$

72 Fain tawallaytum fama saaltukum min ajrin in ajriya illa AAala Allahi waomirtu an akoona mina almuslimeena

---

10:72. "And if you turn away, I did not ask for any reward from you; my reward is only with Allah. And I am commanded that I should be of those who submit."

$$\text{فَكَذَّبُوهُ فَنَجَّيْنَـٰهُ وَمَن مَّعَهُۥ فِى ٱلْفُلْكِ وَجَعَلْنَـٰهُمْ خَلَـٰئِفَ وَأَغْرَقْنَا}$$

$$\text{ٱلَّذِينَ كَذَّبُوا۟ بِـَٔايَـٰتِنَا ۖ فَٱنظُرْ كَيْفَ كَانَ عَـٰقِبَةُ ٱلْمُنذَرِينَ ﴿٧٣﴾}$$

73 Fakaththaboohu fanajjaynahu waman maAAahu fee alfulki wajaAAalnahum khalaifa waaghraqna allatheena kaththaboo biayatina faon*th*ur kayfa kana AAaqibatu almunthareena

---

10:73. Then they rejected him, so We saved him, and those with him, in the Ark, and We made them vicegerents[24] and drowned those who rejected Our Verses/signs. See then what happened in the end to those who were warned.

---

24. Refer study notes 22 to 25 on <u>Verse 2:30</u> **for the Qur'aanic meaning of** *khalaif* **(plural of** *khalifa*).

ثُمَّ بَعَثْنَا مِنْ بَعْدِهِۦ رُسُلًا إِلَىٰ قَوْمِهِمْ فَجَآءُوهُم بِالْبَيِّنَـٰتِ فَمَا كَانُوا۟ لِيُؤْمِنُوا۟ بِمَا كَذَّبُوا۟ بِهِۦ مِن قَبْلُ كَذَٰلِكَ نَطْبَعُ عَلَىٰ قُلُوبِ ٱلْمُعْتَدِينَ ﴿٧٤﴾

74 Thumma baAAathna min baAAdihi rusulan ila qawmihim fajaoohum bialbayyinati fama kanoo liyuminoo bima kaththaboo bihi min qablu kathalika natbaAAu AAala quloobi almuAAtadeena

---

10:74. Then did We raise up after him Messengers to their people, and they came to them with clear evidences. But they could not believe in what they had rejected before. Thus, it is that We set seals upon the hearts of those who exceed the limits.

ثُمَّ بَعَثْنَا مِنْ بَعْدِهِم مُّوسَىٰ وَهَـٰرُونَ إِلَىٰ فِرْعَوْنَ وَمَلَإِيْهِۦ بِـَٔايَـٰتِنَا فَٱسْتَكْبَرُوا۟ وَكَانُوا۟ قَوْمًا مُّجْرِمِينَ ﴿٧٥﴾

75 Thumma baAAathna min baAAdihim moosa waharoona ila firAAawna wamalaihi biayatina faistakbaroo wakanoo qawman mujrimeena

---

10:75. Then did We raise up after them Moses and Aaron and send them to Pharaoh and his nobles with Our signs. But they were too proud, and they were a sinning people.

فَلَمَّا جَآءَهُمُ ٱلْحَقُّ مِنْ عِندِنَا قَالُوٓا۟ إِنَّ هَـٰذَا لَسِحْرٌ مُّبِينٌ ﴿٧٦﴾

76 Falamma jaahumu alhaqqu min AAindina qaloo inna hatha lasihrun mubeenun

10:76. So when the truth came to them from Us they said, "This indeed is magic manifest!"

$$\text{قَالَ مُوسَىٰٓ أَتَقُولُونَ لِلْحَقِّ لَمَّا جَآءَكُمْ أَسِحْرٌ هَٰذَا وَلَا يُفْلِحُ ٱلسَّٰحِرُونَ ۝}$$

77 Qala moosa ataqooloona lilhaqqi lamma jaakum asihrun hatha wala yuflihu alssahiroona

10:77. Moses said, "Do you say this of the truth when it comes to you? Is this magic? And the magicians prevail not!"

$$\text{قَالُوٓا۟ أَجِئْتَنَا لِتَلْفِتَنَا عَمَّا وَجَدْنَا عَلَيْهِ ءَابَآءَنَا وَتَكُونَ لَكُمَا ٱلْكِبْرِيَآءُ فِى ٱلْأَرْضِ وَمَا نَحْنُ لَكُمَا بِمُؤْمِنِينَ ۝}$$

78 Qaloo ajitana litalfitana AAamma wajadna AAalayhi abaana watakoona lakuma alkibriyao fee alardi wama nahnu lakuma bimumineena

10:78. They said, "Have you come to us to turn us away from what we found our fathers upon, and is greatness bestowed just on you two on earth? And we are not going to believe in you."

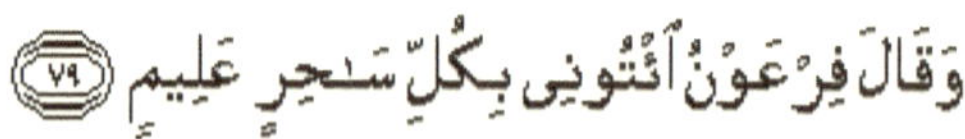

10:79. And Pharaoh ordered, "Bring to me every expert magician."

فَلَمَّا جَآءَ ٱلسَّحَرَةُ قَالَ لَهُم مُّوسَىٰٓ أَلْقُوا۟ مَآ أَنتُم مُّلْقُونَ ۝

80 Falamma jaa alssaharatu qala lahum moosa alqoo ma antum mulqoona

10:80. And when the magicians came, Moses said to them, "Cast down what you have to cast."

فَلَمَّآ أَلْقَوْا۟ قَالَ مُوسَىٰ مَا جِئْتُم بِهِ ٱلسِّحْرُ إِنَّ ٱللَّهَ سَيُبْطِلُهُۥٓ إِنَّ ٱللَّهَ لَا يُصْلِحُ عَمَلَ ٱلْمُفْسِدِينَ ۝

81 Falamma alqaw qala moosa ma jitum bihi alssihru inna Allaha sayubtiluhu inna Allaha la yuslihu AAamala almufsideena

10:81. So when they cast down their contraptions, Moses said to them, "What you have brought is deception. Allah will indeed bring it to naught. Allah does indeed not promote the work of those who spread discord."

وَيُحِقُّ ٱللَّهُ ٱلْحَقَّ بِكَلِمَٰتِهِۦ وَلَوْ كَرِهَ ٱلْمُجْرِمُونَ ۝

10:82. And Allah will show the truth to be the truth by His commands, even though the criminals may not like it.[25]

25. Criminals in human history – like Hitler – may for some time think that they are invincible, and that none can bring them to book for their injustices. But, like Hitler, they are bound to meet their doomsday.

فَمَآ ءَامَنَ لِمُوسَىٰ إِلَّا ذُرِّيَّةٌ مِّن قَوْمِهِۦ عَلَىٰ خَوْفٍ مِّن فِرْعَوْنَ وَمَلَإِيْهِمْ أَن يَفْتِنَهُمْ وَإِنَّ فِرْعَوْنَ لَعَالٍ فِى ٱلْأَرْضِ وَإِنَّهُۥ لَمِنَ ٱلْمُسْرِفِينَ ۝

83 Fama amana limoosa illa thurriyyatun min qawmihi AAala khawfin min firAAawna wamalaihim an yaftinahum wainna firAAawna laAAalin fee alardi wainnahu lamina almusrifeena

10:83. So then none believed in Moses – except for the progeny of his own people – out of fear of Pharaoh and their nobles, lest he should persecute them. And, indeed did Pharaoh have some power on the earth and indeed he was of those who committed excesses.

وَقَالَ مُوسَىٰ يَٰقَوْمِ إِن كُنتُمْ ءَامَنتُم بِٱللَّهِ فَعَلَيْهِ تَوَكَّلُوٓا۟ إِن كُنتُم مُّسْلِمِينَ ۝

84 Waqala moosa ya qawmi in kuntum amantum biAllahi faAAalayhi tawakkaloo in kuntum muslimeena

10:84. And Moses said, "O my people! If you do believe in Allah and if you are of those who do submit to Him, then do trust Him."[26]

---

26. It is as if, through this Verse, Allah Almighty is Himself addressing the Muslims of this age. They are, by and large, Muslims only in name. They have no real belief in Allah. They neither submit to Him completely, nor do they trust Him wholeheartedly.

فَقَالُواْ عَلَى ٱللَّهِ تَوَكَّلْنَا رَبَّنَا لَا تَجْعَلْنَا فِتْنَةً لِّلْقَوْمِ ٱلظَّـٰلِمِينَ ﴿٨٥﴾

85 Faqaloo AAala Allahi tawakkalna rabbana la tajAAalna fitnatan lilqawmi alththalimeena

---

10:85. So they said, "On Allah do we trust. O our Lord! Subject us not to the persecution of the unjust people."

وَنَجِّنَا بِرَحْمَتِكَ مِنَ ٱلْقَوْمِ ٱلْكَـٰفِرِينَ ﴿٨٦﴾

86 Wanajjina birahmatika mina alqawmi alkafireena

10:86. "And do deliver us, by Your mercy, from the people who suppress the Truth."

وَأَوْحَيْنَآ إِلَىٰ مُوسَىٰ وَأَخِيهِ أَن تَبَوَّءَا لِقَوْمِكُمَا بِمِصْرَ بُيُوتًا وَٱجْعَلُواْ بُيُوتَكُمْ قِبْلَةً وَأَقِيمُواْ ٱلصَّلَوٰةَ وَبَشِّرِ ٱلْمُؤْمِنِينَ ﴿٨٧﴾

43

87 Waaw<u>h</u>ayna il<u>a</u> moos<u>a</u> waakh<u>e</u>ehi an tabawwa<u>a</u> liqawmikum<u>a</u> bimi<u>s</u>ra buyootan wa<u>ij</u>AAaloo buyootakum qiblatan waaqeemoo al<u>ss</u>al<u>a</u>ta wabashshiri almumineena

---

10:87. And We told Moses and his brother, "Prepare some houses in Egypt as spiritual centres for your people and establish prayer. And give good tidings to the believers."[27]

---

27. This Verse is best understood in the context of Verses preceding and following it. One may not understand it fully, if it is read in isolation. And it has also to be read in the context of the historical situation the Children of Israel were in at that time. They had come to Egypt when Prophet Joseph had come to acquire a position of considerable authority with the then rulers of that country. As years passed, although the community increased in numbers, they lost their political clout after the passing away of Prophet Joseph. And at the time of Moses, they were reduced to the status of a persecuted minority – relentlessly persecuted by the ruling clan of the Pharaohs. Moses came to deliver the Children of Israel from the cruel clutches of the Pharaoh, but he wouldn't let them go. So they had to remain a persecuted minority in Egypt for some more time. It was during this continued period of persecution that Moses asked them to have trust in Allah (Verse 84 above). They reiterated their trust in Him and prayed for their delivery from Pharaoh's oppression (Verses 85 and 86). It was in this context that in this Verse 86, Allah Ta'ala asked them to earmark some houses as spiritual centres and establish prayers there. This, in fact, should serve as the divine mantra for any persecuted Muslim minority anywhere in the world today. If they just pray sincerely to Allah and have trust in Him, they are sure to be delivered from their ignominious position today, as the Children of Israel were from Pharaoh's persecution. But, alas, the Muslims today exhibit their lack of trust in Allah by resorting to dubious other means, which only help make their position worse.

وَقَالَ مُوسَىٰ رَبَّنَآ إِنَّكَ ءَاتَيْتَ فِرْعَوْنَ وَمَلَأَهُۥ زِينَةً وَأَمْوَٰلًا فِى ٱلْحَيَوٰةِ ٱلدُّنْيَا رَبَّنَا لِيُضِلُّوا۟ عَن سَبِيلِكَ رَبَّنَا ٱطْمِسْ عَلَىٰٓ أَمْوَٰلِهِمْ وَٱشْدُدْ عَلَىٰ قُلُوبِهِمْ فَلَا يُؤْمِنُوا۟ حَتَّىٰ يَرَوُا۟ ٱلْعَذَابَ ٱلْأَلِيمَ ۝

88 Waq<u>a</u>la moos<u>a</u> rabban<u>a</u> innaka <u>a</u>tayta firAAawna wamalaahu zeenatan waamw<u>a</u>lan fee al<u>h</u>ayati alddunya rabban<u>a</u> liyu<u>d</u>illoo AAan sabeelika rabban<u>a</u> i<u>t</u>mis AAal<u>a</u> amw<u>a</u>lihim waoshdud AAal<u>a</u> quloobihim fal<u>a</u> yuminoo <u>h</u>atta yarawoo alAAa<u>tha</u>ba aleema

---

10:88. And Moses said, "Our Lord! You have indeed given Pharaoh and his nobles glamour and riches in the life of this world. Our Lord! You have given them this so that they go astray from Your Path. Our Lord! Spread destruction over their riches and harden their hearts so that they believe not until they see the painful punishment."

قَالَ قَدْ أُجِيبَت دَّعْوَتُكُمَا فَاسْتَقِيمَا وَلَا تَتَّبِعَآنِّ سَبِيلَ ٱلَّذِينَ لَا يَعْلَمُونَ

89 Qala qad ojeebat daAAwatukuma faistaqeema wala tattabiAAanni sabeela allatheena la yaAAlamoona

10:89. Allah said, "The prayer of you two has indeed been accepted, be steadfast and follow not the path of those who do not know."

وَجَوَزْنَا بِبَنِىٓ إِسْرَٰٓءِيلَ ٱلْبَحْرَ فَأَتْبَعَهُمْ فِرْعَوْنُ وَجُنُودُهُۥ بَغْيًا وَعَدْوًا حَتَّىٰٓ إِذَآ أَدْرَكَهُ ٱلْغَرَقُ قَالَ ءَامَنتُ أَنَّهُۥ لَآ إِلَٰهَ إِلَّا ٱلَّذِىٓ ءَامَنَتْ بِهِۦ بَنُوٓا۟ إِسْرَٰٓءِيلَ وَأَنَا۠ مِنَ ٱلْمُسْلِمِينَ

90 Wajawazna bibanee israeela albahra faatbaAAahum firAAawnu wajunooduhu baghyan waAAadwan hatta itha adrakahu algharaqu qala amantu annahu la ilaha illa allathee amanat bihi banoo israeela waana mina almuslimeena

10:90. And We made the Children of Israel cross the sea. Then Pharaoh and his armies followed them with aggressive and inimical intentions. Until, when about to be drowned, he (Pharaoh) said, "I believe that there is no god but He in Whom the Children of Israel believe, and I am of those who submit."

ءَآلْـَٰنَ وَقَدْ عَصَيْتَ قَبْلُ وَكُنتَ مِنَ ٱلْمُفْسِدِينَ ۞

91 <u>A</u>l<u>a</u>na waqad AAa<u>s</u>ayta qablu wakunta mina almufsideena

---

10:91. "Now! And you did disobey before and you were of those who spread corruption and discord."

فَٱلْيَوْمَ نُنَجِّيكَ بِبَدَنِكَ لِتَكُونَ لِمَنْ خَلْفَكَ ءَايَةً وَإِنَّ كَثِيرًا مِّنَ ٱلنَّاسِ عَنْ ءَايَٰتِنَا لَغَٰفِلُونَ ۞

92 Faalyawma nunajjeeka bibadanika litakoona liman khalfaka <u>a</u>yatan wainna katheeran mina alnn<u>a</u>si AAan <u>a</u>yatin<u>a</u> lagh<u>a</u>filoona

---

10:92. "But then We do, this day, save you in your body so that you become a sign for generations that would come after you. And, indeed, most people are oblivious to Our signs." @

@ **This revelation about the saving of the Pharaoh's body was made in the seventh century A.D. Although the Bible recounts the exodus and the drowning of the Pharaoh, it makes no mention of his body having been saved – nor does the Torah do it. And there is no evidence at all that anyone knew about it when the Qur'aan made this revelation. And except for the believers, no one knew about it as a fact till the nineteenth century when the body was discovered [Watch the YouTube Video]. This is one of the many signs giving clear indication of the Qur'aan being divine. But man, in his self-destuctive obstinacy, believes not!**

وَلَقَدْ بَوَّأْنَا بَنِى إِسْرَآءِيلَ مُبَوَّأَ صِدْقٍ وَرَزَقْنَاهُم مِّنَ ٱلطَّيِّبَاتِ فَمَا ٱخْتَلَفُوا حَتَّىٰ جَآءَهُمُ ٱلْعِلْمُ إِنَّ رَبَّكَ يَقْضِى بَيْنَهُمْ يَوْمَ ٱلْقِيَامَةِ فِيمَا كَانُوا فِيهِ يَخْتَلِفُونَ ۝

93 Walaqad bawwana banee israeela mubawwaa sidqin warazaqnahum mina alttayyibati fama ikhtalafoo hatta jaahumu alAAilmu inna rabbaka yaqdee baynahum yawma alqiyamati feema kanoo feehi yakhtalifoona

---

10:93. And certainly did We settle the Children of Israel in a true settlement and We provided them with good things.[28] And they differed not until the knowledge had come to them![29] Your Lord will indeed settle among them, on the Resurrection Day, the matters in which they differed.

---

28. After the exodus from Egypt under Prophet Moses, the Children of Israel had to lead a nomadic life for some years because of their own intransigent attitude towards Allah and His Messenger, Moses. But thereafter, under Prophets David and Solomon, they enjoyed a settled and a very honourable life.

29. They had then attained to a very high degree of knowledge. The history of the Muslims runs parallel to that of the Children of Israel in many, many ways. Just as the Jews started having differences among themselves after attaining a high degree of knowledge and power and suffered a deep downfall thereafter, so were the Muslims. The Muslims were at the pinnacle of glory during the early years of their history. They had come to acquire immense knowledge, and people from the then backward European nations came to the Muslim universities to learn things. Thereafter, they (Muslims) started having differences among themselves and shunned the divine Guidance of the Qur'aan. And history is witness to their downfall in course of time till the present age.

فَإِن كُنتَ فِى شَكٍّ مِّمَّا أَنزَلْنَا إِلَيْكَ فَسْـَٔلِ ٱلَّذِينَ يَقْرَءُونَ ٱلْكِتَابَ مِن قَبْلِكَ لَقَدْ جَآءَكَ ٱلْحَقُّ مِن رَّبِّكَ فَلَا تَكُونَنَّ مِنَ ٱلْمُمْتَرِينَ ۝

94 Fain kunta fee shakkin mimma anzalnna ilayka faisali allatheena yaqraoona alkitaba min qablika laqad jaaka alhaqqu min rabbika fala takoonanna mina almumtareena

10:94. But if you are in doubt about what We have revealed to you, ask those who read the Book revealed before you. Certainly, the truth has come to you from your Lord. Be not then of those who doubt.

وَلَا تَكُونَنَّ مِنَ ٱلَّذِينَ كَذَّبُواْ بِـَٔايَـٰتِ ٱللَّهِ فَتَكُونَ مِنَ ٱلْخَـٰسِرِينَ ۝

95 Wala takoonanna mina allatheena kaththaboo biayati Allahi fatakoona mina alkhasireena

10:95. And you should not be of those who deny the Verses/signs of Allah; for, then, you should be of those who are doomed.

إِنَّ ٱلَّذِينَ حَقَّتْ عَلَيْهِمْ كَلِمَتُ رَبِّكَ لَا يُؤْمِنُونَ ۝

96 Inna allatheena haqqat AAalayhim kalimatu rabbika la yuminoona

10:96. Indeed, those, upon whom the word of condemnation from your Lord has in truth been decreed, shall not believe,

وَلَوْ جَآءَتْهُمْ كُلُّ ءَايَةٍ حَتَّىٰ يَرَوُاْ ٱلْعَذَابَ ٱلْأَلِيمَ ۝

97 Walaw jaathum kullu ayatin hatta yarawoo alAAathaba alaleema

10:97. Though every sign comes to them, until they witness the painful punishment.

فَلَوْلَا كَانَتْ قَرْيَةٌ ءَامَنَتْ فَنَفَعَهَآ إِيمَـٰنُهَآ إِلَّا قَوْمَ يُونُسَ لَمَّآ ءَامَنُوا۟ كَشَفْنَا عَنْهُمْ عَذَابَ ٱلْخِزْيِ فِى ٱلْحَيَوٰةِ ٱلدُّنْيَا وَمَتَّعْنَـٰهُمْ إِلَىٰ حِينٍ ﴿٩٨﴾

98 Falawla kanat qaryatun amanat fanafaAAaha eemanuha illa qawma yoonusa lamma amanoo kashafna AAanhum AAathaba alkhizyi fee alhayati alddunya wamattaAAnahum ila heenin

10:98. Why then was there no human settlement, other than the people of Jonah, which would believe and then their belief would prove profitable to them? When they (the people of Jonah) believed, We removed from them the punishment of disgrace in this world's life and, for an appointed time, We made their lives comfortable and easy.

وَلَوْ شَآءَ رَبُّكَ لَأَمَنَ مَن فِى ٱلْأَرْضِ كُلُّهُمْ جَمِيعًا أَفَأَنتَ تُكْرِهُ ٱلنَّاسَ حَتَّىٰ يَكُونُوا۟ مُؤْمِنِينَ ﴿٩٩﴾

99 Walaw shaa rabbuka laamana man fee alardi kulluhum jameeAAan afaanta tukrihu alnnasa hatta yakoonoo mumineena

10:99. And if your Lord had so willed, certainly, all on earth would have believed. Could you then make mankind unwillingly to believe?

وَمَا كَانَ لِنَفْسٍ أَن تُؤْمِنَ إِلَّا بِإِذْنِ ٱللَّهِ وَيَجْعَلُ ٱلرِّجْسَ عَلَى ٱلَّذِينَ لَا يَعْقِلُونَ ﴿١٠٠﴾

100 Wama kana linafsin an tumina illa biithni Allahi wayajAAalu alrrijsa AAala allatheena la yaAAqiloona

---

10:100. And it is not possible for anyone to believe except by Allah's leave. And He causes ignominy to befall those who would not use their intelligence.

قُلِ ٱنظُرُواْ مَاذَا فِى ٱلسَّمَـٰوَٰتِ وَٱلْأَرْضِ وَمَا تُغْنِى ٱلْآيَـٰتُ وَٱلنُّذُرُ عَن قَوْمٍ لَّا يُؤْمِنُونَ ﴿١٠١﴾

101 Quli onthuroo matha fee alssamawati waalardi wama tughnee alayatu waalnnuthuru AAan qawmin la yuminoona

---

10:101. Say, "Observe what there is in the heavens and the earth." And signs and warnings do not benefit a people who believe not.

فَهَلْ يَنتَظِرُونَ إِلَّا مِثْلَ أَيَّامِ ٱلَّذِينَ خَلَوْاْ مِن قَبْلِهِمْ قُلْ فَٱنتَظِرُوٓاْ إِنِّى مَعَكُم مِّنَ ٱلْمُنتَظِرِينَ ﴿١٠٢﴾

102 Fahal yantathiroona illa mithla ayyami allatheena khalaw min qablihim qul faintathiroo innee maAAakum mina almuntathireena

10:102. What do they wait for then but the like of the times of those who passed away before them? [30] Say, "Wait then! I too am indeed with you among those who wait."

30. 'Those who passed away before them' connotes people, like Noah's and Lot's, from ancient history who were destroyed because of their deliberate disobedience of divine law. But the examples are not restricted to just ancient history. We have examples from recent history too, like that of Hitler and his Nazis.

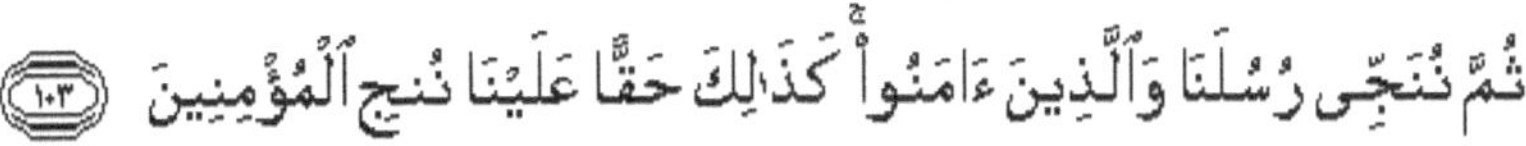

103 Thumma nunajjee rusulana waallatheena amanoo kathalika haqqan AAalayna nunjee almumineena

10:103. We then saved Our Messengers and those who believe. Likewise, it is binding on Us that We save the believers.

104 Qul ya ayyuha alnnasu in kuntum fee shakkin min deenee fala aAAbudu allatheena taAAbudoona min dooni Allahi walakin aAAbudu Allaha allathee yatawaffakum waomirtu an akoona mina almumineena

10:104. Say, "O mankind! If you are in doubt as to my way of life, then know that I do not worship those whom you worship besides Allah; but I do worship Allah, Who causes you to die. And I am commanded that I should be of those who believe."

وَأَنۡ أَقِمۡ وَجۡهَكَ لِلدِّينِ حَنِيفًا وَلَا تَكُونَنَّ مِنَ ٱلۡمُشۡرِكِينَ ۝

105 Waan aqim wajhaka lilddeeni _haneefan wal_a takoonanna mina almushrikeen**a**

10:105. And that "you should keep yourself steadfastly and uprightly on that way of life. And you should not be of those who worship others besides Allah."

وَلَا تَدۡعُ مِن دُونِ ٱللَّهِ مَا لَا يَنفَعُكَ وَلَا يَضُرُّكَ فَإِن فَعَلۡتَ فَإِنَّكَ إِذًا مِّنَ ٱلظَّـٰلِمِينَ ۝

106 Wal_a tadAAu min dooni All_a_hi m_a l_a yanfaAAuka wal_a ya_d_urruka fain faAAalta fainnaka i_th_an mina al_ththa_limeen**a**

10:106. "And pray not, besides Allah, to others who can neither benefit nor harm you. And if you do so, then, indeed, you will in that case be of those who do wrong."

وَإِن يَمۡسَسۡكَ ٱللَّهُ بِضُرٍّ فَلَا كَاشِفَ لَهُۥ إِلَّا هُوَ وَإِن يُرِدۡكَ بِخَيۡرٍ فَلَا رَآدَّ لِفَضۡلِهِۦ يُصِيبُ بِهِۦ مَن يَشَآءُ مِنۡ عِبَادِهِۦ وَهُوَ ٱلۡغَفُورُ ٱلرَّحِيمُ ۝

107 Wain yamsaska All_a_hu bi_d_urrin fal_a k_a_shifa lahu ill_a huwa wain yuridka bikhayrin fal_a _radda lifa_d_lihi yu_s_eebu bihi man yash_a_o min AAib_a_dihi wahuwa alghafooru alrra_h_eem**u**

10:107. And if Allah should afflict you with harm, then there is none to remove it but He. And if He intends doing something good to you, then there is none to cancel His Grace, which He bestows upon whom He wills of His subjects. And He is the One Who forgives, the One Who bestows mercy.

$$\text{قُلْ يَـٰٓأَيُّهَا ٱلنَّاسُ قَدْ جَآءَكُمُ ٱلْحَقُّ مِن رَّبِّكُمْ فَمَنِ ٱهْتَدَىٰ فَإِنَّمَا يَهْتَدِى لِنَفْسِهِۦ وَمَن ضَلَّ فَإِنَّمَا يَضِلُّ عَلَيْهَا وَمَآ أَنَا۠ عَلَيْكُم بِوَكِيلٍ ۝}$$

108 Qul ya ayyuha alnnasu qad jaakumu alhaqqu min rabbikum famani ihtada fainnama yahtadee linafsihi waman dalla fainnama yadillu AAalayha wama ana AAalaykum biwakeelin

10:108. Say, "O mankind! Indeed, there has come to you the Truth from your Lord. So whoever is guided, he is guided only for the good of his own self. And whoever goes astray, he goes astray only to the detriment of his own self. And I am not a guardian over you."

$$\text{وَٱتَّبِعْ مَا يُوحَىٰٓ إِلَيْكَ وَٱصْبِرْ حَتَّىٰ يَحْكُمَ ٱللَّهُ وَهُوَ خَيْرُ ٱلْحَـٰكِمِينَ ۝}$$

109 WaittabiAA ma yooha ilayka waisbir hatta yahkuma Allahu wahuwa khayru alhakimeena

10:109. And follow what is revealed to you and be patient till Allah gives His ruling. And He is the best of the rulers.

Chapter 11: Hood

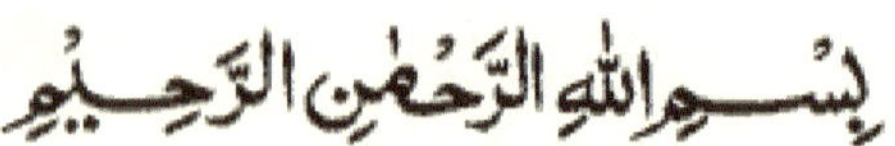

In the Name of Allah, the Gracious, the Merciful

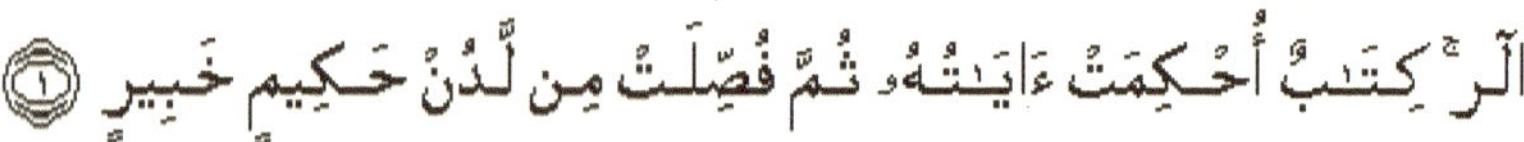

1. Alif-lam-ra kitabun ohkimat ayatuhu thumma fussilat min ladun hakeemin khabeerin

---

11:1. Alif Lam Ra. This is a Book, Verses in which are ordained and then explained from the One Who is Wise and Well-aware.

أَلَّا تَعۡبُدُوٓاْ إِلَّا ٱللَّهَ إِنَّنِى لَكُم مِّنۡهُ نَذِيرٌ وَبَشِيرٌ ۝

2. Alla taAAbudoo illa Allaha innanee lakum minhu natheerun wabasheerun

---

11:2. [And the Messenger proclaims to mankind,] "You shall worship none but Allah. I am indeed from Him a warner for you and a herald of good news."

وَأَنِ ٱسْتَغْفِرُوا۟ رَبَّكُمْ ثُمَّ تُوبُوٓا۟ إِلَيْهِ يُمَتِّعْكُم مَّتَٰعًا حَسَنًا إِلَىٰٓ أَجَلٍ

مُّسَمًّى وَيُؤْتِ كُلَّ ذِى فَضْلٍ فَضْلَهُۥ ۖ وَإِن تَوَلَّوْا۟ فَإِنِّىٓ أَخَافُ عَلَيْكُمْ عَذَابَ

يَوْمٍ كَبِيرٍ ۝

3. Waani istaghfiroo rabbakum thumma tooboo ilayhi yumattiAAkum mataAAan *h*asanan il*a* ajalin musamman wayu/ti kulla *th*ee fa*d*lin fa*d*lahu wa-in tawallaw fa-inee akh*a*fu AAalaykum AAa*th*aba yawmin kabee**rin**

11:3. "And that you ask forgiveness of your Lord, and then turn to Him in repentance. He will provide you with a good provision for an appointed term and give everyone one's dues. And if you turn away, then indeed I fear for you the punishment of a very hard day."

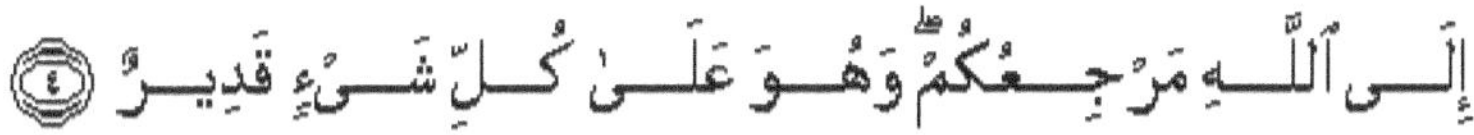

إِلَى ٱللَّهِ مَرْجِعُكُمْ ۖ وَهُوَ عَلَىٰ كُلِّ شَىْءٍ قَدِيرٌ ۝

4. Il*a* All*a*hi marjiAAukum wahuwa AAal*a* kulli shay-in qadee**run**

11:4. To Allah is your return, and He has power over all things.

أَلَآ إِنَّهُمْ يَثْنُونَ صُدُورَهُمْ لِيَسْتَخْفُوا۟ مِنْهُ ۚ أَلَا حِينَ يَسْتَغْشُونَ ثِيَابَهُمْ

يَعْلَمُ مَا يُسِرُّونَ وَمَا يُعْلِنُونَ ۚ إِنَّهُۥ عَلِيمٌۢ بِذَاتِ ٱلصُّدُورِ ۝

5. Al*a* innahum yathnoona *s*udoorahum liyastakhfoo minhu al*a* *h*eena yastaghshoona thiy*a*bahum yaAAlamu m*a* yusirroona wam*a* yuAAlinoona innahu AAaleemun bi*th*ati al*s*sudoori

---

11:5. Do they indeed not shut their minds to conceal their thoughts from Him? Does He not know what they conceal and what they reveal, when they put on their garments? He does indeed know what is in the minds.

وَمَا مِن دَآبَّةٍ فِى ٱلْأَرْضِ إِلَّا عَلَى ٱللَّهِ رِزْقُهَا وَيَعْلَمُ مُسْتَقَرَّهَا وَمُسْتَوْدَعَهَا كُلٌّ فِى كِتَـٰبٍ مُّبِينٍ ۝

6. Wam*a* min *d*abbatin fee al-ar*d*i illa AAala All*a*hi rizquh*a* wayaAAlamu mustaqarrah*a* wamustawdaAAah*a* kullun fee kit*a*bin mubeen**in**

11:6. And no moving creature on earth but on Allah is its sustenance. And He knows where it lives and where its remains are. Everything is in a manifest Record.

وَهُوَ ٱلَّذِى خَلَقَ ٱلسَّمَـٰوَٰتِ وَٱلْأَرْضَ فِى سِتَّةِ أَيَّامٍ وَكَانَ عَرْشُهُۥ عَلَى ٱلْمَآءِ لِيَبْلُوَكُمْ أَيُّكُمْ أَحْسَنُ عَمَلًا وَلَئِن قُلْتَ إِنَّكُم مَّبْعُوثُونَ مِنۢ بَعْدِ ٱلْمَوْتِ لَيَقُولَنَّ ٱلَّذِينَ كَفَرُوٓاْ إِنْ هَـٰذَآ إِلَّا سِحْرٌ مُّبِينٌ ۝

7. Wahuwa alla*th*ee khalaqa al*s*sam*a*w*a*ti waal-ar*d*a fee sittati ayy*a*min wak*a*na AAarshuhu AAala alm*a*-i liyabluwakum ayyukum a*h*sanu AAamalan wala-in qulta innakum mabAAoothoona min baAAdi almawti layaqoolanna alla*th*eena kafaroo in *h*atha illa si*h*run mubeen**un**

11:7. And He it is Who created the heavens and the earth in six periods of time – and His Throne was on ether[1] – that He might test you as to which of you are better in deeds.[2] And if you say, 'You shall indeed be raised up after death', those who suppress the Truth would certainly counter, 'This is nothing but sheer delusion.'

---

1. The Qur'aan informs us here that before the creation of the heavens and the earth, all space was filled with a fluid-like thing, ether, which supports the propagation of electromagnetic waves. Modern science no longer believes in its earlier belief in this 'ether' pervading the universe, but science is not sacrosanct. It is man-made, not divine. It is liable to err and change its theories from time to time. Its task is to discover the secrets of creation; it did not create the universe. It can make mistakes in discovering things.

2. The Qur'aan also reveals here the purpose of creating the heavens and the earth: just to test mankind. And what is this test for? The test is simply whether man recognizes the existence of his Creator without seeing Him. For this purpose, unlike other living creatures on earth, man is endowed with freedom of action. He (man) is given more intelligence, besides being guided through the divine Book, Qur'aan, which is divinely guaranteed to be incorruptible. As the latter part of this very Verse indicates, Allah Almighty will resurrect mankind to reward those who pass His test, and to punish those who do not.

وَلَئِنْ أَخَّرْنَا عَنْهُمُ ٱلْعَذَابَ إِلَىٰ أُمَّةٍ مَّعْدُودَةٍ لَّيَقُولُنَّ مَا يَحْبِسُهُ ۗ

أَلَا يَوْمَ يَأْتِيهِمْ لَيْسَ مَصْرُوفًا عَنْهُمْ وَحَاقَ بِهِم مَّا كَانُوا بِهِۦ

يَسْتَهْزِءُونَ ﴿٨﴾

8. Wala-in akhkharna AAanhumu alAAathaba ila ommatin maAAdoodatin layaqoolunna ma yahbisuhu ala yawma ya/teehim laysa masroofan AAanhum wahaqa bihim ma kanoo bihi yastahzi-oona

---

11:8. And if We put off the punishment from them for a certain period, they will certainly say, "What holds it back?" Verily on the day when it will come to them, nothing can turn it away from them. And that which they scoffed at shall besiege them.

وَلَئِنْ أَذَقْنَا ٱلْإِنسَـٰنَ مِنَّا رَحْمَةً ثُمَّ نَزَعْنَـٰهَا مِنْهُ إِنَّهُۥ لَيَـُٔوسٌ كَفُورٌ ۝

9. Wala-in *ath*aqn*a* al-ins*a*na minn*a* ra*h*matan thumma nazaAAn*a*h*a* minhu innahu layaoosun kafoo**run**

11:9. And, certainly, if We make man taste mercy from Us and then take it off from him, he is indeed sure to despair and be ungrateful.

وَلَئِنْ أَذَقْنَـٰهُ نَعْمَآءَ بَعْدَ ضَرَّآءَ مَسَّتْهُ لَيَقُولَنَّ ذَهَبَ ٱلسَّيِّئَاتُ عَنِّىٓ إِنَّهُۥ

لَفَرِحٌ فَخُورٌ ۝

10. Wala-in *ath*aqn*a*hu naAAm*aa* baAAda *darraa* massat-hu layaqoolanna *th*ahaba al*ss*ayyi-*a*tu AAannee innahu lafari*h*un fakhoo**run**

11:10. And if We make him taste a favour after distress has afflicted him, he will certainly say, "Bad days have gone away from me." He certainly indeed exults, boasts.

إِلَّا ٱلَّذِينَ صَبَرُواْ وَعَمِلُواْ ٱلصَّـٰلِحَـٰتِ أُوْلَـٰٓئِكَ لَهُم مَّغْفِرَةٌ وَأَجْرٌ كَبِيرٌ

11. Ill*a* alla*th*eena *s*abaroo waAAamiloo al*ss*ali*h*ati ol*a*-ika lahum maghfiratun waajrun kabee**run**

11:11. But not those who are patient and do good deeds. For them shall there be forgiveness and a great reward.

فَلَعَلَّكَ تَارِكٌ بَعْضَ مَا يُوحَىٰ إِلَيْكَ وَضَآئِقٌ بِهِ صَدْرُكَ أَن يَقُولُواْ لَوْلَآ أُنزِلَ عَلَيْهِ كَنزٌ أَوْ جَآءَ مَعَهُۥ مَلَكٌ إِنَّمَآ أَنتَ نَذِيرٌ وَٱللَّهُ عَلَىٰ كُلِّ شَىْءٍ وَكِيلٌ ۝

12. FalaAAallaka tarikun baAAda ma yooha ilayka wada-iqun bihi sadruka an yaqooloo lawla onzila AAalayhi kanzun aw jaa maAAahu malakun innama anta natheerun waAllahu AAala kulli shay-in wakeelun

11:12. Then, in order that you abandon part of what is revealed to you and your mind becomes dustressed by it that they say, "Why has not a treasure been sent down upon him or an angel come with him?" You are only a warner; and Allah is the One to take care of all things.

أَمْ يَقُولُونَ ٱفْتَرَىٰهُ قُلْ فَأْتُواْ بِعَشْرِ سُوَرٍ مِّثْلِهِ مُفْتَرَيَٰتٍ وَٱدْعُواْ مَنِ ٱسْتَطَعْتُم مِّن دُونِ ٱللَّهِ إِن كُنتُمْ صَٰدِقِينَ ۝

13. Am yaqooloona iftarahu qul fa/too biAAashri suwarin mithlihi muftarayatin waodAAoo mani istataAAtum min dooni Allahi in kuntum sadiqeena

11:13. Or, they say, "He has forged it." Say, "Then bring ten chapters similarly forged and call for aid from whom you can besides Allah, if what you say is the truth.

فَإِلَّمْ يَسْتَجِيبُواْ لَكُمْ فَاعْلَمُوٓاْ أَنَّمَاۤ أُنزِلَ بِعِلْمِ ٱللَّهِ وَأَن لَّاۤ إِلَـٰهَ إِلَّا هُوَ فَهَلْ أَنتُم مُّسْلِمُونَ ۝

14. Fa-illam yastajeeboo lakum faiAAlamoo annama onzila biAAilmi Allahi waan la ilaha illa huwa fahal antum muslimoona

---

11:14. If they do not respond to you, then know that it (the Qur'aan) is revealed with Allah's knowledge and that there is no god but He. Will you then be the ones who submit?

مَن كَانَ يُرِيدُ ٱلْحَيَوٰةَ ٱلدُّنْيَا وَزِينَتَهَا نُوَفِّ إِلَيْهِمْ أَعْمَـٰلَهُمْ فِيهَا وَهُمْ فِيهَا لَا يُبْخَسُونَ ۝

15. Man kana yureedu alhayata alddunya wazeenataha nuwaffi ilayhim aAAmalahum feeha wahum feeha la yubkhasoona

---

11:15. Whoever desires the life of this world and its charm, We will repay them in full their deeds therein, and therein they shall not be wronged.

أُوْلَـٰۤئِكَ ٱلَّذِينَ لَيْسَ لَهُمْ فِى ٱلْأَخِرَةِ إِلَّا ٱلنَّارُ وَحَبِطَ مَا صَنَعُواْ فِيهَا وَبَـٰطِلٌ مَّا كَانُواْ يَعْمَلُونَ ۝

16. Ola-ika alla*thee*na laysa lahum fee al-*a*khirati ill*a* aln*na*ru wa*h*abi*t*a m*a* *s*anaAAoo fee*h*a waba*t*ilun m*a* k*a*noo yaAAmaloon**a**

11:16. These are they for whom there is nothing but the Fire in the Hereafter. And what they do here, in this world, shall be of no use there. And what they do here is false and futile.

أَفَمَن كَانَ عَلَىٰ بَيِّنَةٍ مِّن رَّبِّهِۦ وَيَتْلُوهُ شَاهِدٌ مِّنْهُ وَمِن قَبْلِهِۦ

كِتَبُ مُوسَىٰ إِمَامًا وَرَحْمَةً أُوْلَٰئِكَ يُؤْمِنُونَ بِهِۦ وَمَن يَكْفُرْ بِهِۦ

مِنَ ٱلْأَحْزَابِ فَٱلنَّارُ مَوْعِدُهُۥ فَلَا تَكُ فِى مِرْيَةٍ مِّنْهُ إِنَّهُ ٱلْحَقُّ مِن

رَّبِّكَ وَلَٰكِنَّ أَكْثَرَ ٱلنَّاسِ لَا يُؤْمِنُونَ ۝

17. Afaman k*a*na AAal*a* bayyinatin min rabbihi wayatloohu sh*a*hidun minhu wamin qablihi kit*a*bu moos*a* im*a*man wara*h*matan ola-ika yu/minoona bihi waman yakfur bihi mina al-a*h*z*a*bi faaln*na*ru mawAAiduhu fal*a* taku fee miryatin minhu innahu al*h*aqqu min rabbika wal*a*kinna akthara aln*na*si l*a* yu/minoon**a**

11:17. What then about the one who stands on clear evidence[3] from his Lord and a witness from Him recites it – and before it, was there the Book of Moses, a precedent and mercy? Such are the ones that believe in it. And whoever, of the tribes, that suppresses the truth in it, the promise to him shall be the Fire. Be not then in doubt about it. It is indeed the Truth from your Lord, but most people believe not.

---

3. The Qur'aan.

وَمَنْ أَظْلَمُ مِمَّنِ ٱفْتَرَىٰ عَلَى ٱللَّهِ كَذِبًا أُوْلَٰٓئِكَ يُعْرَضُونَ عَلَىٰ رَبِّهِمْ وَيَقُولُ ٱلْأَشْهَٰدُ هَٰٓؤُلَاءِ ٱلَّذِينَ كَذَبُواْ عَلَىٰ رَبِّهِمْ أَلَا لَعْنَةُ ٱللَّهِ عَلَى ٱلظَّٰلِمِينَ ۝

18. Waman a*th*lamu mimmani iftar*a* AAal*a* All*a*hi ka*th*iban ol*a*-ika yuAAra*d*oona AAal*a* rabbihim wayaqoolu al-ashh*a*du h*a*ol*a*-i alla*th*eena ka*th*aboo AAal*a* rabbihim al*a* laAAnatu Allahi AAal*a* al*ththa*limeena

---

11:18. And who is more unjust than he who forges a lie against Allah? These shall be brought before their Lord, and the witnesses shall say, "These are they who lied against their Lord." Verily Allah's curse is on the unjust –

ٱلَّذِينَ يَصُدُّونَ عَن سَبِيلِ ٱللَّهِ وَيَبْغُونَهَا عِوَجًا وَهُم بِٱلْأَخِرَةِ هُمْ كَٰفِرُونَ ۝

19. Alla*th*eena ya*s*uddoona AAan sabeeli All*a*hi wayabghoonah*a* AAiwajan wahum bial-*a*khirati hum k*a*firoona

---

11:19. On those that turn people away from Allah's Path and seek to distort it[4] – and those are the ones that believe not in the Hereafter.

---

4. Among the Muslims now, a predominant section has come to believe that the Qur'aan is not self-sufficient in showing Allah's Path. That Path, they say, won't be complete without the *ahaadeeth*. This belief doesn't get any support from Verse 17 above, which requires that people believe in the clear evidence of the Qur'aan. And the Qur'aan repeatedly asserts that it explains in detail all the necessities for the right conduct of human life on this earth and that it has neglected nothing in this regard. [Refer Verses 12:111, 17:89, 18:54, 39:27 and 6:38]. So, if anyone does not believe in this Qur'aanic assertion, it is tantamount to disbelief in the Qur'aan. And the above Verse 17 distinctly declares the destination of

those who do not believe in the Qur'aan. It is sad to note further that there are many Muslims who try to distort the plain meaning of the Qur'aanic Verses in the light of the *ahaadeeth*. Also refer study notes 49 and 50 on Verse 7:145 in this context.

أُوْلَـٰٓئِكَ لَـمْ يَكُونُواْ مُعْجِزِينَ فِى ٱلْأَرْضِ وَمَا كَانَ لَهُـم مِّـن دُونِ ٱللَّـهِ مِنْ أَوْلِيَآءَ يُضَـٰعَفُ لَهُـمُ ٱلْعَـذَابُ مَا كَانُواْ يَسْـتَطِيعُونَ ٱلسَّـمْعَ وَمَا كَانُواْ يُبْصِـرُونَ ﴿٢٠﴾

20. Ola-ika lam yakoonoo muAAjizeena fee al-ar*d*i wam*a* k*a*na lahum min dooni All*a*hi min awliy*a*a yu*da*AAafu lahumu alAAa*th*abu m*a* k*a*noo yasta*t*eeAAoona alssamAAa wam*a* k*a*noo yub*s*iroona

11:20. They are in no position to frustrate Allah's Will on the earth, nor can they have any *awliya*[5] besides Allah. The punishment shall be doubled for them. They could not hear nor see the Truth.

5. Refer study note 154 on Verse 2:107.

أُوْلَـٰٓئِكَ ٱلَّذِينَ خَسِرُوٓاْ أَنفُسَهُمْ وَضَلَّ عَنْهُم مَّا كَانُواْ يَفْتَرُونَ ﴿٢١﴾

21. Ola-ika alla*th*eena khasiroo anfusahum wa*d*alla AAanhum m*a* k*a*noo yaftaroona

11:21. Those are the ones that have doomed themselves. And what they concocted has deserted them.

لَا جَرَمَ أَنَّهُمْ فِى ٱلْأَخِرَةِ هُمُ ٱلْأَخْسَرُونَ ﴿٢٢﴾

22. La jarama annahum fee al-akhirati humu al-akhsaroona

11:22. No doubt, they are the ones that shall in the Hereafter be doomed.

إِنَّ ٱلَّذِينَ ءَامَنُوا۟ وَعَمِلُوا۟ ٱلصَّٰلِحَٰتِ وَأَخْبَتُوٓا۟ إِلَىٰ رَبِّهِمْ أُو۟لَٰٓئِكَ أَصْحَٰبُ ٱلْجَنَّةِ هُمْ فِيهَا خَٰلِدُونَ ﴿٢٣﴾

23. Inna allatheena amanoo waAAamiloo alsalihati waakhbatoo ila rabbihim ola-ika as-habu aljannati hum feeha khalidoona

---

11:23. Indeed, as for those who believe and do good deeds and are humble towards their Lord, they are the dwellers of the Garden. They shall reside therein forever.

۞ مَثَلُ ٱلْفَرِيقَيْنِ كَٱلْأَعْمَىٰ وَٱلْأَصَمِّ وَٱلْبَصِيرِ وَٱلسَّمِيعِ هَلْ يَسْتَوِيَانِ مَثَلًا أَفَلَا تَذَكَّرُونَ ﴿٢٤﴾

24. Mathalu alfareeqayni kaal-aAAma waal-asammi waalbaseeri waalssameeAAi hal yastawiyani mathalan afala tathakkaroona

---

11:24. Are the examples of two persons – one blind and deaf, and the other who sees and hears – the same? Don't you then reflect?

وَلَقَدْ أَرْسَلْنَا نُوحًا إِلَىٰ قَوْمِهِ إِنِّى لَكُمْ نَذِيرٌ مُّبِينٌ ﴿٢٥﴾

25. Walaqad arsal*na* noo*h*an il*a* qawmihi innee lakum na*th*eerun mubeen**un**

11:25. And We did send Noah to his people. He told them, "I have indeed come to give you a plain warning."

أَن لَّا تَعْبُدُوٓاْ إِلَّا ٱللَّهَ إِنِّىٓ أَخَافُ عَلَيْكُمْ عَذَابَ يَوْمٍ أَلِيمٍ ﴿٢٦﴾

26. An l*a* taAAbudoo ill*a* All*a*ha innee akh*a*fu AAalaykum AAa*th*aba yawmin aleem**in**

11:26. "That you shall not worship anyone but Allah. I do indeed fear for you the punishment of a painful day."

فَقَالَ ٱلْمَلَأُ ٱلَّذِينَ كَفَرُواْ مِن قَوْمِهِ مَا نَرَىٰكَ إِلَّا بَشَرًا مِّثْلَنَا وَمَا نَرَىٰكَ ٱتَّبَعَكَ إِلَّا ٱلَّذِينَ هُمْ أَرَاذِلُنَا بَادِىَ ٱلرَّأْيِ وَمَا نَرَىٰ لَكُمْ عَلَيْنَا مِن فَضْلٍ بَلْ نَظُنُّكُمْ كَـٰذِبِينَ ﴿٢٧﴾

27. Faqala almalao alla*th*eena kafaroo min qawmihi m*a* nar*a*ka ill*a* basharan mithlan*a* wam*a* nar*a*ka ittabaAAaka ill*a* alla*th*eena hum ar*ath*ilun*a* b*a*diya alrra/yi wam*a* nar*a* lakum AAalayn*a* min fa*d*lin bal na*th*unnukum k*ath*ibeena

---

11:27. And the chiefs of those who suppressed the Truth from among his people said, "We do not consider you but a man like us, and we do not see any have followed you but those meanest amongst us who have just followed you without conviction[6]. And we do not see in you any excellence over us; nay, we deem you liars."

---

6. The chiefs meant that those who had followed Noah had done so, just superficially, without being convinced of what Noah was telling them.

قَالَ يَـٰقَوْمِ أَرَءَيْتُمْ إِن كُنتُ عَلَىٰ بَيِّنَةٍ مِّن رَّبِّى وَءَاتَىٰنِى رَحْمَةً مِّنْ عِندِهِۦ فَعُمِّيَتْ عَلَيْكُـمْ أَنُلْزِمُكُمُوهَا وَأَنتُـمْ لَهَا كَـٰرِهُـونَ ﴿٢٨﴾

28. Q*a*la y*a* qawmi araaytum in kuntu AAal*a* bayyinatin min rabbee wa*a*t*a*nee ra*h*matan min AAindihi faAAummiyat AAalaykum anulzimukumooh*a* waantum lah*a* k*a*rihoona

---

11:28. He said, "O my people! Do you see that if I have been on clear evidence from my Lord and He has bestowed upon me mercy from Himself, and it is obscure to you, can we force it on you while you are averse to it?"[7]

---

7. Noah, as also other Prophets did, saw for himself the clear signs in Nature unmistakably pointing towards the existence of One Creator. He then, like other Prophets, got divine revelation of being appointed as a Prophet, and started propagating the divine Message to the people. Some of the people, belonging to the lower strata of society, believed him. But the leaders of the higher strata of the society did not believe him and insinuated that the lower people's belief was without conviction. In answer to this insinuation, Noah told them that he had not forced anyone to believe.

وَيَـٰقَوْمِ لَآ أَسْـَٔلُكُمْ عَلَيْهِ مَالًا إِنْ أَجْرِىَ إِلَّا عَلَى ٱللَّهِ وَمَآ أَنَا۠ بِطَارِدِ ٱلَّذِينَ ءَامَنُوٓاْ إِنَّهُم مُّلَـٰقُواْ رَبِّهِمْ وَلَـٰكِنِّىٓ أَرَىٰكُمْ قَوْمًا تَجْهَلُونَ ﴿٢٩﴾

29. Waya qawmi la as-alukum AAalayhi malan in ajriya illa AAala Allahi wama ana bitaridi allatheena amanoo innahum mulaqoo rabbihim walakinnee arakum qawman tajhaloona

---

11:29. "And, O my people! I ask you not for any material compensation for it; my reward is upon none but Allah. And I am not going to drive away those who believe. They shall certainly meet their Lord. And, on the other hand, I see you as an ignorant people.

وَيَـٰقَوْمِ مَن يَنصُرُنِى مِنَ ٱللَّهِ إِن طَرَدتُّهُمْ أَفَلَا تَذَكَّرُونَ ﴿٣٠﴾

30. Waya qawmi man yansurunee mina Allahi in taradtuhum afala tathakkaroona

---

11:30. "And, O my people! Who is there to help me against Allah if I drive them away? Won't you reflect on this?"

وَلَآ أَقُولُ لَكُمْ عِندِى خَزَآئِنُ ٱللَّهِ وَلَآ أَعْلَمُ ٱلْغَيْبَ وَلَآ أَقُولُ إِنِّى مَلَكٌ وَلَآ أَقُولُ لِلَّذِينَ تَزْدَرِىٓ أَعْيُنُكُمْ لَن يُؤْتِيَهُمُ ٱللَّهُ خَيْرًا ٱللَّهُ أَعْلَمُ بِمَا فِىٓ أَنفُسِهِمْ إِنِّىٓ إِذًا لَّمِنَ ٱلظَّـٰلِمِينَ ﴿٣١﴾

31. Wal*a* aqoolu lakum AAindee khaz*a*-inu All*a*hi wal*a* aAAlamu alghayba wal*a* aqoolu innee malakun wal*a* aqoolu lill*a*theena tazdaree aAAyunukum lan yu/tiyahumu All*a*hu khayran All*a*hu aAAlamu bim*a* fee anfusihim innee i*th*an lamina al*ththa*limeen**a**

11:31. "And I do not say to you that I have the treasures of Allah. And I do not know the unseen, and I do not say I am an angel, nor do I say that Allah will never grant any good things to those who are mean in your eyes. Allah knows well what is there in them. I would indeed be of the unjust, otherwise."

قَالُواْ يَـٰنُوحُ قَدْ جَـٰدَلْتَنَا فَأَكْثَرْتَ جِدَٰلَنَا فَأْتِنَا بِمَا تَعِدُنَآ إِن كُنتَ مِنَ
ٱلصَّـٰدِقِينَ ﴿٣٢﴾

32. *Q*aloo *ya* noo*h*u qad *j*adaltan*a* faaktharta jid*a*lan*a* fa/tin*a* bim*a* taAAidun*a* in kunta mina al*ss*adiqeen*a*

11:32. They said, "O Noah! You did argue with us a great deal. Now bring us what you threaten us with, if what you say is the truth."

قَالَ إِنَّمَا يَأْتِيكُم بِهِ ٱللَّهُ إِن شَآءَ وَمَآ أَنتُم بِمُعْجِزِينَ ﴿٣٣﴾

33. *Q*al*a* innam*a* ya/teekum bihi All*a*hu in sh*a*a wam*a* antum bimuAAjizeen**a**

11:33. He said, "Only Allah will bring it to you if He wills, and you won't be able to do anything to prevent it."

$$\text{وَلَا يَنفَعُكُمْ نُصْحِىٓ إِنْ أَرَدتُّ أَنْ أَنصَحَ لَكُمْ إِن كَانَ ٱللَّهُ}$$

$$\text{يُرِيدُ أَن يُغْوِيَكُمْ هُوَ رَبُّكُمْ وَإِلَيْهِ تُرْجَعُونَ ﴿٣٤﴾}$$

34. Wal*a* yanfaAAukum nu*sh*ee in aradtu an an*sah*a lakum in k*a*na All*a*hu yureedu an yughwiyakum huwa rabbukum wa-ilayhi turjaAAoon**a**

11:34. "And if I intend to give you advice, my advice will not profit you if Allah intended that He should leave you go astray. He is your Lord, and to Him shall you be returned."

$$\text{أَمْ يَقُولُونَ ٱفْتَرَىٰهُ قُلْ إِنِ ٱفْتَرَيْتُهُۥ فَعَلَىَّ إِجْرَامِى وَأَنَا۠ بَرِىٓءٌ}$$

$$\text{مِّمَّا تُجْرِمُونَ ﴿٣٥﴾}$$

35. Am yaqooloona iftar*a*hu qul ini iftaraytuhu faAAalayya ijr*a*mee waan*a* baree-on mimm*a* tujrimoona

---

11:35. They do say, "He has concocted it." Say, "If I have concocted it, then it is my sin and I shall be punished for it. But the responsibility for the sin you commit shall not be on me."[8]

---

8. About this parenthetic Verse placed in the midst of a narrative about Prophet Noah, please refer study note 6 on Verse 5:3**. The Verse here (11:35) of course refers to Prophet Muhammad and the unbelieving Makkans who alleged that the Qur'aan and/or the on-going narrative about Noah was a concoction by Muhammad.**

وَأُوحِىَ إِلَىٰ نُوحٍ أَنَّهُۥ لَن يُؤْمِنَ مِن قَوْمِكَ إِلَّا مَن قَدْ ءَامَنَ فَلَا تَبْتَئِسْ بِمَا كَانُواْ يَفْعَلُونَ ﴿٣٦﴾

36. Waoohiya ila noohin annahu lan yu/mina min qawmika illa man qad amana fala tabta-is bima kanoo yafAAaloona

---

11:36. And it was revealed to Noah, "None of your people will believe except those who have already believed. So, grieve not at what they do."

وَٱصْنَعِ ٱلْفُلْكَ بِأَعْيُنِنَا وَوَحْيِنَا وَلَا تُخَٰطِبْنِى فِى ٱلَّذِينَ ظَلَمُوٓاْ إِنَّهُم مُّغْرَقُونَ ﴿٣٧﴾

37. WaisnaAAi alfulka bi-aAAyunina wawahyina wala tukhatibnee fee allatheena thalamoo innahum mughraqoona

---

11:37. "And construct the ark under Our supervision and guidance, and do not address Me for those who are unjust. They shall indeed be drowned."

وَيَصْنَعُ ٱلْفُلْكَ وَكُلَّمَا مَرَّ عَلَيْهِ مَلَأٌ مِّن قَوْمِهِۦ سَخِرُواْ مِنْهُ قَالَ إِن تَسْخَرُواْ مِنَّا فَإِنَّا نَسْخَرُ مِنكُمْ كَمَا تَسْخَرُونَ ﴿٣٨﴾

38. WayasnaAAu alfulka wakullama marra AAalayhi malaon min qawmihi sakhiroo minhu qala in taskharoo minna fa-inna naskharu minkum kama taskharoona

11:38. And he began constructing the ark. And whenever the chiefs from among his people passed by him, they laughed at him. He said, "If you laugh at us, we too indeed laugh at you as you laugh at us."

$$\text{فَسَوْفَ تَعْلَمُونَ مَن يَأْتِيهِ عَذَابٌ يُخْزِيهِ وَيَحِلُّ عَلَيْهِ عَذَابٌ مُّقِيمٌ ﴿٣٩﴾}$$

39. Fasawfa taAAlamoona man ya/teehi AAa*tha*bun yukhzeehi waya*h*illu AAalayhi AAa*tha*bun muqeem**un**

11:39. "So you shall soon come to know on whom a punishment will come that will disgrace him, and on whom will the lasting punishment be imposed."

$$\text{حَتَّىٰ إِذَا جَاءَ أَمْرُنَا وَفَارَ ٱلتَّنُّورُ قُلْنَا ٱحْمِلْ فِيهَا مِن كُلٍّ زَوْجَيْنِ ٱثْنَيْنِ}$$
$$\text{وَأَهْلَكَ إِلَّا مَن سَبَقَ عَلَيْهِ ٱلْقَوْلُ وَمَنْ ءَامَنَ وَمَا ءَامَنَ مَعَهُ إِلَّا قَلِيلٌ ﴿٤٠﴾}$$

40. *Hatta itha* jaa amrun*a* wafa*ra* alttannooru quln*a* i*h*mil feeh*a* min kullin zawjayni ithnayni waahlaka il*la* man sabaqa AAalayhi alqawlu waman *a*mana wam*a a*mana maAAahu il*la* qaleel**un**

11:40. Until when Our command came to be executed and the oven boiled over[9], We said, "Carry in it two of every pair, your own family – except those against whom the divine decree has already come – and those who believe." And only a few had believed with him.

9. The meaning of this obviously idiomatic phrase is given in Verses 54:11 and 54:12. There it is explained that the gates of heaven were opened with water pouring down, and the earth gushed forth with springs. In other words, the land area of the earth was overwhelmed with floods.

۞ وَقَالَ ٱرْكَبُواْ فِيهَا بِسْمِ ٱللَّهِ مَجْرٜىٰهَا وَمُرْسَىٰهَآ إِنَّ رَبِّى لَغَفُورٌ رَّحِيمٌ

41. Waqala irkaboo feeha bismi Allahi majraha wamursaha inna rabbee laghafoorun raheemun

11:41. And he said, "Get on board! In the name of Allah are its sailing and its anchoring. My Lord is indeed Forgiving, Merciful."

وَهِىَ تَجْرِى بِهِمْ فِى مَوْجٍ كَٱلْجِبَالِ وَنَادَىٰ نُوحٌ ٱبْنَهُۥ وَكَانَ فِى مَعْزِلٍ يَٰبُنَىَّ ٱرْكَب مَّعَنَا وَلَا تَكُن مَّعَ ٱلْكَٰفِرِينَ

42. Wahiya tajree bihim fee mawjin kaaljibali wanada noohunu ibnahu wakana fee maAAzilin ya bunayya irkab maAAana wala takun maAAa alkafireena

11:42. And it moved on with them amid waves like mountains, and Noah called out to his son, and he was isolated from others, "O my son! Get on board with us and be not with those who suppress the Truth."

قَالَ سَـَٔاوِىٓ إِلَىٰ جَبَلٍ يَعْصِمُنِى مِنَ ٱلْمَآءِ قَالَ لَا عَاصِمَ ٱلْيَوْمَ مِنْ أَمْرِ ٱللَّهِ إِلَّا مَن رَّحِمَ وَحَالَ بَيْنَهُمَا ٱلْمَوْجُ فَكَانَ مِنَ ٱلْمُغْرَقِينَ

43. Q*a*la sa*a*wee il*a* jabalin yaAA*a*simunee mina alm*a*-i q*a*la la AA*a*sima alyawma min amri All*a*hi illa man ra*h*ima wa*h*ala baynahum*a* almawju fak*a*na mina almughraqeena

---

11:43. He said, "I will take shelter on a mountain that shall protect me from the water." Noah said, "There is no protection today from Allah's command but for him on whom He shows mercy." And a wave intervened between them, and he (the son) was drowned.

$$ \text{وَقِيلَ يَٰٓأَرۡضُ ٱبۡلَعِى مَآءَكِ وَيَٰسَمَآءُ أَقۡلِعِى وَغِيضَ ٱلۡمَآءُ وَقُضِىَ ٱلۡأَمۡرُ} $$

$$ \text{وَٱسۡتَوَتۡ عَلَى ٱلۡجُودِىِّ وَقِيلَ بُعۡدًا لِّلۡقَوۡمِ ٱلظَّٰلِمِينَ ﴿٤٤﴾} $$

44. Waqeela *ya* ar*d*u iblaAAee m*a*aki way*a* sam*a*o aqliAAee waghee*d*a alm*a*o waqu*d*iya al-amru waistawat AAal*a* aljoodiyyi waqeela buAAdan lilqawmi al*ththa*limeena

---

11:44. And it was decreed, "O earth, swallow down your water, and O sky, stop!" And the water was made to abate and the divine Will, accomplished. And the Ark came to rest on the Judi[10], and it was proclaimed, "Away with the unjust people."

---

10. This is a mountain on the southern borders of Turkey. Watch YouTube Video claiming that the remains of an ancient boat (Noah's Ark) have been found there.

$$ \text{وَنَادَىٰ نُوحٌ رَّبَّهُۥ فَقَالَ رَبِّ إِنَّ ٱبۡنِى مِنۡ أَهۡلِى وَإِنَّ وَعۡدَكَ ٱلۡحَقُّ} $$

$$ \text{وَأَنتَ أَحۡكَمُ ٱلۡحَٰكِمِينَ ﴿٤٥﴾} $$

45. Wan*a*d*a* noo*h*un rabbahu faq*a*la rabbi inna ibnee min ahlee wa-inna waAAdaka al*h*aqqu waanta a*h*kamu al*h*akimeen**a**

11:45. And Noah called upon his Lord and said, "My Lord! My son indeed is a member of my family, and Your promise is indeed true, and You are the best Judge."

قَالَ يَـٰنُوحُ إِنَّهُۥ لَيْسَ مِنْ أَهْلِكَ إِنَّهُۥ عَمَلٌ غَيْرُ صَـٰلِحٍ فَلَا تَسْـَٔلْنِ مَا لَيْسَ لَكَ بِهِۦ عِلْمٌ إِنِّىٓ أَعِظُكَ أَن تَكُونَ مِنَ ٱلْجَـٰهِلِينَ ﴿٤٦﴾

46. Qala ya noohu innahu laysa min ahlika innahu AAamalun ghayru salihin fala tas-alni ma laysa laka bihi AAilmun innee aAAithuka an takoona mina aljahileena

11:46. He said, "O Noah! He is indeed not of your family. His deeds indeed are not good. Put Me no questions then about things of which you are given no knowledge. I do indeed admonish you lest you be of those who do things ignorantly."

قَالَ رَبِّ إِنِّىٓ أَعُوذُ بِكَ أَنْ أَسْـَٔلَكَ مَا لَيْسَ لِى بِهِۦ عِلْمٌ وَإِلَّا تَغْفِرْ لِى وَتَرْحَمْنِىٓ أَكُن مِّنَ ٱلْخَـٰسِرِينَ ﴿٤٧﴾

47. Qala rabbi innee aAAoothu bika an as-alaka ma laysa lee bihi AAilmun wa-illa taghfir lee watarhamnee akun mina alkhasireena

11:47. He said, "My Lord! I seek refuge in You lest I again put questions to You about things of which I am given no knowledge. And should You forgive me not and have no mercy on me, I should then be of those who are doomed."

قِيلَ يَٰنُوحُ ٱهۡبِطۡ بِسَلَٰمٍ مِّنَّا وَبَرَكَٰتٍ عَلَيۡكَ وَعَلَىٰٓ أُمَمٍ مِّمَّن مَّعَكَ وَأُمَمٌ سَنُمَتِّعُهُمۡ ثُمَّ يَمَسُّهُم مِّنَّا عَذَابٌ أَلِيمٌ ۝

48. Qeela ya noohu ihbit bisalamin minna wabarakatin AAalayka waAAala omamin mimman maAAaka waomamun sanumattiAAuhum thumma yamassuhum minna AAathabun aleemun

---

11:48. It was said, "O Noah! Disembark, with peace from Us and blessings on you and on those of the communities, who are with you. And there will be communities whom We shall provide for, and then a painful punishment from Us shall afflict them.

تِلۡكَ مِنۡ أَنۢبَآءِ ٱلۡغَيۡبِ نُوحِيهَآ إِلَيۡكَ مَا كُنتَ تَعۡلَمُهَآ أَنتَ وَلَا قَوۡمُكَ مِن قَبۡلِ هَٰذَا فَٱصۡبِرۡ إِنَّ ٱلۡعَٰقِبَةَ لِلۡمُتَّقِينَ ۝

49. Tilka min anba-i alghaybi nooheeha ilayka ma kunta taAAlamuha anta wala qawmuka min qabli hatha faisbir inna alAAaqibata lilmuttaqeena

---

11:49. Those are narratives relating to the unseen which We reveal to you. You did not know them – neither you nor your people – before this. Do have patience then! The end shall indeed be in favour of those who fear Allah.

وَإِلَىٰ عَادٍ أَخَاهُمۡ هُودٗا قَالَ يَٰقَوۡمِ ٱعۡبُدُواْ ٱللَّهَ مَا لَكُم مِّنۡ إِلَٰهٍ غَيۡرُهُۥٓ إِنۡ أَنتُمۡ إِلَّا مُفۡتَرُونَ ۝

50. Wa-ila AAadin akhahum hoodan qala ya qawmi oAAbudoo Allaha ma lakum min ilahin ghayruhu in antum illa muftaroona

---

11:50. And to the people of AAad We sent their brother Hood. He said, "O my people! Worship Allah. You have no god other than Him. You do not but fabricate lies[11]."

---

11. In other words, Prophet Hood told his people AAad that they were worshipping false gods.

يَـٰقَوْمِ لَآ أَسْـَٔلُكُمْ عَلَيْهِ أَجْرًا إِنْ أَجْرِىَ إِلَّا عَلَى ٱلَّذِى فَطَرَنِىٓ أَفَلَا تَعْقِلُونَ ﴿٥١﴾

51. Ya qawmi la as-alukum AAalayhi ajran in ajriya illa AAala allathee fataranee afala taAAqiloona

---

11:51. "O my people! I do not ask of you any reward for it. My reward is only with Him Who created me. Don't you understand?"

وَيَـٰقَوْمِ ٱسْتَغْفِرُوا۟ رَبَّكُمْ ثُمَّ تُوبُوٓا۟ إِلَيْهِ يُرْسِلِ ٱلسَّمَآءَ عَلَيْكُم مِّدْرَارًا وَيَزِدْكُمْ قُوَّةً إِلَىٰ قُوَّتِكُمْ وَلَا تَتَوَلَّوْا۟ مُجْرِمِينَ ﴿٥٢﴾

52. Waya qawmi istaghfiroo rabbakum thumma tooboo ilayhi yursili alssamaa AAalaykum midraran wayazidkum quwwatan ila quwwatikum wala tatawallaw mujrimeena

---

11:52 "And, O my people! Ask forgiveness of your Lord and then turn to Him in repentance. He will send down on you, abundant rain and add strength to your strength. And do not turn back to sin.

قَالُواْ يَـٰهُودُ مَا جِئْتَنَا بِبَيِّنَةٍ وَمَا نَحْنُ بِتَارِكِىٓ ءَالِهَتِنَا عَن قَوْلِكَ وَمَا نَحْنُ لَكَ بِمُؤْمِنِينَ ۝

53. Qaloo ya hoodu ma ji/tana bibayyinatin wama nahnu bitarikee alihatina AAan qawlika wama nahnu laka bimu/mineena

11:53. They said, "O Hood! You have not brought to us any clear sign and we are not going to desert our gods on your word, and we do not believe in you."

إِن نَّقُولُ إِلَّا ٱعْتَرَىٰكَ بَعْضُ ءَالِهَتِنَا بِسُوٓءٍ قَالَ إِنِّىٓ أُشْهِدُ ٱللَّهَ وَٱشْهَدُوٓاْ أَنِّى بَرِىٓءٌ مِّمَّا تُشْرِكُونَ ۝

54. In naqoolu illa iAAtaraka baAAdu alihatina bisoo-in qala innee oshhidu Allaha waishhadoo annee baree-on mimma tushrikoona

11:54. "We do not but say that some of our gods have worked evil on you." He said, "I do indeed call Allah to witness – and you do bear witness – that I am absolutely free of the sin you commit of worshipping anyone..."

مِن دُونِهِۦ فَكِيدُونِى جَمِيعًا ثُمَّ لَا تُنظِرُونِ ۝

55. Min doonihi fakeedoonee jameeAAan thumma la tun*th*iroon**i**

11:55. "… other than Him. All of you do together scheme against me then and give me no respite."

إِنِّى تَوَكَّلْتُ عَلَى ٱللَّهِ رَبِّى وَرَبِّكُم مَّا مِن دَآبَّةٍ إِلَّا هُوَ ءَاخِذٌۢ بِنَاصِيَتِهَآ إِنَّ رَبِّى عَلَىٰ صِرَاطٍ مُّسْتَقِيمٍ ۝

56. Innee tawakkaltu AAal*a* All*a*hi rabbee warabbikum m*a* min d*a*bbatin ill*a* huwa akhi*th*un binasiyatih*a* inna rabbee AAal*a* sira*t*in mustaqeem**in**

11:56. "I do indeed have trust in Allah, my Lord and your Lord. There is no living creature, but He holds it by its forelock.[12] My Lord is indeed on the Straight Path."

---

12. I.e., Allah has absolute control over every creature.

فَإِن تَوَلَّوْا۟ فَقَدْ أَبْلَغْتُكُم مَّآ أُرْسِلْتُ بِهِۦٓ إِلَيْكُمْ وَيَسْتَخْلِفُ رَبِّى قَوْمًا غَيْرَكُمْ وَلَا تَضُرُّونَهُۥ شَيْئًا إِنَّ رَبِّى عَلَىٰ كُلِّ شَىْءٍ حَفِيظٌ ۝

57. Fa-in tawallaw faqad ablaghtukum m*a* orsiltu bihi ilaykum wayastakhlifu rabbee qawman ghayrakum wal*a* ta*d*urroonahu shay-an inna rabbee AAal*a* kulli shay-in hafee*th***un**

11:57. "And if you turn away, then indeed I have delivered to you what I have been sent to you with. And my Lord will bring another people in your place, and you can do Him no harm. My Lord is indeed the Guardian over all things."

وَلَمَّا جَآءَ أَمْرُنَا نَجَّيْنَا هُودًا وَٱلَّذِينَ ءَامَنُواْ مَعَهُۥ بِرَحْمَةٍ مِّنَّا وَنَجَّيْنَٰهُم مِّنْ عَذَابٍ غَلِيظٍ ﴿٥٨﴾

58. Walamma *jaa* amrun*a* najjayn*a* hoodan waalla*theena* *a*manoo maAAahu bira*h*matin minn*a* wanajjayn*a*hum min AAa*th*abin ghalee*th*in

11:58. And when Our decree came to pass, We saved Hood, and those who believed with him, as a mercy from Us. And We saved them from a hard punishment.

وَتِلْكَ عَادٌ جَحَدُواْ بِـَٔايَٰتِ رَبِّهِمْ وَعَصَوْاْ رُسُلَهُۥ وَٱتَّبَعُوٓاْ أَمْرَ كُلِّ جَبَّارٍ عَنِيدٍ ﴿٥٩﴾

59. Watilka AA*a*dun ja*h*adoo bi-*a*y*a*ti rabbihim waAA*a*saw rusulahu waittabaAAoo amra kulli jabb*a*rin AAaneed*in*

11:59. And those were the people of AA*a*d! They disputed the Verses/signs of their Lord, disobeyed His Messengers and followed the bidding of anyone obstinately strong and powerful.[13]

13. That is, unfortunately, the general tendency of every human being now. He bends before anyone strong and powerful in this world, although the latter may be manifestly treading the path of iniquity and insolence.

وَأُتْبِعُواْ فِى هَـٰذِهِ ٱلدُّنْيَا لَعْنَةً وَيَوْمَ ٱلْقِيَـٰمَةِ أَلَآ إِنَّ عَادًا كَفَرُواْ رَبَّهُمْ أَلَا بُعْدًا لِّعَادٍ قَوْمِ هُودٍ ۝

60. WaotbiAAoo fee ha*th*ihi alddunya laAAnatan wayawma alqiy*a*mati al*a* inna AA*a*dan kafaroo rabbahum al*a* buAAdan liAA*a*din qawmi hood**in**

11:60. And they were pursued by curse in this world and so will they be, on the Resurrection Day. Verily, AA<u>a</u>d suppressed the Truth about their Lord! Verily, indeed, AA<u>a</u>d, the people of Hood perished!

۞ وَإِلَىٰ ثَمُودَ أَخَاهُمْ صَـٰلِحًا قَالَ يَـٰقَوْمِ ٱعْبُدُواْ ٱللَّهَ مَا لَكُم مِّنْ إِلَـٰهٍ غَيْرُهُۥ هُوَ أَنشَأَكُم مِّنَ ٱلْأَرْضِ وَٱسْتَعْمَرَكُمْ فِيهَا فَٱسْتَغْفِرُوهُ ثُمَّ تُوبُوٓاْ إِلَيْهِ إِنَّ رَبِّى قَرِيبٌ مُّجِيبٌ ۝

61. Wa-il*a* thamooda akha*h*um *salihan* qala ya qawmi oAAbudoo All*a*ha m*a* lakum min il*a*hin ghayruhu huwa anshaakum mina al-ar*d*i waistaAAmarakum feeh*a* faistaghfiroohu thumma tooboo ilayhi inna rabbee qareebun mujee**bun**

11:61. And to the people of Thamood[14] We sent their brother Salih. He said, "O my people! Worship Allah, you have no god other than He. He brought you into being from the earth, and made you dwell on it. Ask forgiveness of Him then and turn to Him in repentance. My Lord is indeed close, and He does respond!

14. The story of Thamood (Thamood) is also narrated in <u>Verses 7:73 to 7:79</u>.

قَالُواْ يَـٰصَـٰلِحُ قَدْ كُنتَ فِينَا مَرْجُوًّا قَبْلَ هَـٰذَآ أَتَنْهَىٰنَآ أَن نَّعْبُدَ مَا يَعْبُدُ
ءَابَآؤُنَا وَإِنَّنَا لَفِى شَكٍّ مِّمَّا تَدْعُونَآ إِلَيْهِ مُرِيبٍ ۝

62. Qaloo ya salihu qad kunta feena marjuwwan qabla hatha atanhana an naAAbuda ma yaAAbudu abaona wa-innana lafee shakkin mimma tadAAoona ilayhi mureebun

11:62. They said, "O Salih! Before this, we did have great expectations in you. Do you now forbid us from worshipping what our fathers worshipped? And we are indeed in great doubt in that which you call us to.

قَالَ يَـٰقَوْمِ أَرَءَيْتُمْ إِن كُنتُ عَلَىٰ بَيِّنَةٍ مِّن رَّبِّى وَءَاتَنِى مِنْهُ رَحْمَةً
فَمَن يَنصُرُنِى مِنَ ٱللَّهِ إِنْ عَصَيْتُهُ فَمَا تَزِيدُونَنِى غَيْرَ تَخْسِيرٍ ۝

63. Qala ya qawmi araaytum in kuntu AAala bayyinatin min rabbee waatanee minhu rahmatan faman yansurunee mina Allahi in AAasaytuhu fama tazeedoonanee ghayra takhseerin

11:63. He said, "O my people! Do you see that if I have been on clear evidence from my Lord and He has bestowed upon me mercy from Himself, who will then help me against Allah if I disobey Him? You would then cause no increase in anything for me, other than in loss."

وَيَـٰقَوْمِ هَـٰذِهِ نَاقَةُ ٱللَّهِ لَكُمْ ءَايَةً فَذَرُوهَا تَأْكُلْ فِىٓ أَرْضِ ٱللَّهِ وَلَا تَمَسُّوهَا بِسُوٓءٍ فَيَأْخُذَكُمْ عَذَابٌ قَرِيبٌ ۝

64. Way*a* qawmi h*a*th*i*hi n*a*qatu All*a*hi lakum *a*yatan fa*t*haroo*ha* ta/kul fee ar*d*i All*a*hi wal*a* tamassoo*ha* bisoo-in faya/khu*th*akum AAa*th*abun qareeb**un**

11:64. "And, O my people, this is Allah's she-camel for you – a sign. So, leave her free to pasture on Allah's earth. And do her no harm, for then, soon, a punishment will seize you."

فَعَقَرُوهَا فَقَالَ تَمَتَّعُوا۟ فِى دَارِكُمْ ثَلَـٰثَةَ أَيَّامٍ ذَٰلِكَ وَعْدٌ غَيْرُ مَكْذُوبٍ

65. FaAAaqaroo*ha* faq*a*la tamattaAAoo fee d*a*rikum thala*th*ata ayy*a*min *th*alika waAAdun ghayru mak*th*oob**in**

11:65. But they crippled her. Then he said, "Enjoy in your abode just for three days. That is a promise that shall not prove to be false."

فَلَمَّا جَآءَ أَمْرُنَا نَجَّيْنَا صَـٰلِحًا وَٱلَّذِينَ ءَامَنُوا۟ مَعَهُۥ بِرَحْمَةٍ مِّنَّا وَمِنْ خِزْيِ يَوْمِئِذٍ إِنَّ رَبَّكَ هُوَ ٱلْقَوِىُّ ٱلْعَزِيزُ ۝

66. Falamm*a* j*a*a amrun*a* najjayn*a* *s*alihan waalla*th*eena *a*manoo maAAahu bira*h*matin minn*a* wamin khizyi yawmi-i*th*in inna rabbaka huwa alqawiyyu alAAazeez**u**

11:66. So when Our decree came to pass, We saved Salih, and those who believed with him, by mercy from Us and from the disgrace of that day. Your Lord indeed is the One Strong and Omnipotent.

وَأَخَذَ ٱلَّذِينَ ظَلَمُواْ ٱلصَّيْحَةُ فَأَصْبَحُواْ فِى دِيَـٰرِهِمْ جَـٰثِمِينَ ۝

67. Waakha*tha* alla*theena thalamoo* al*s*sayhatu faa*s*ba*h*oo fee diy*a*rihim j*a*thimeen**a**

11:67. And the terribly rumbling sound[15] struck those who were unjust, and they lay prostrate in their houses.

15. In <u>Verse 7:78</u>**, the Arabic word used is** *a*l*rrajfatu* **(shaking). Therefore, what struck those people appears to be a severe earthquake.**

كَأَن لَّمْ يَغْنَوْاْ فِيهَآ أَلَا إِنَّ ثَمُودَا۟ كَفَرُواْ رَبَّهُمْ أَلَا بُعْدًا لِّثَمُودَ ۝

68. Kaan lam yaghnaw feeh*a* al*a* inna thamooda kafaroo rabbahum al*a* buAAdan lithamood**a**

11:68. As though they had never flourished in them. Verily, Thamood suppressed the Truth about their Lord! Verily, Thamood perished.

وَلَقَدْ جَآءَتْ رُسُلُنَآ إِبْرَٰهِيمَ بِٱلْبُشْرَىٰ قَالُواْ سَلَـٰمًا قَالَ سَلَـٰمٌ فَمَا لَبِثَ أَن جَآءَ بِعِجْلٍ حَنِيذٍ ۞

69. Walaqad jaat rusuluna ibraheema bialbushra qaloo salaman qala salamun fama labitha an jaa biAAijlin haneethin

---

11:69. And certainly Our messengers came to Abraham with good news. They said, "Peace." "Peace." said he, and he made no delay in bringing a roasted calf.

فَلَمَّا رَءَآ أَيْدِيَهُمْ لَا تَصِلُ إِلَيْهِ نَكِرَهُمْ وَأَوْجَسَ مِنْهُمْ خِيفَةً قَالُواْ لَا تَخَفْ إِنَّآ أُرْسِلْنَآ إِلَىٰ قَوْمِ لُوطٍ ۞

70. Falamma raa aydiyahum la tasilu ilayhi nakirahum waawjasa minhum kheefatan qaloo la takhaf inna orsilna ila qawmi lootin

---

11:70. But when he saw that their hands were not extended towards it, he had misgivings about them and became fearful of them. They said, "Fear not, we are sent but for people of Lot."

وَٱمْرَأَتُهُۥ قَآئِمَةٌ فَضَحِكَتْ فَبَشَّرْنَٰهَا بِإِسْحَـٰقَ وَمِن وَرَآءِ إِسْحَـٰقَ يَعْقُوبَ ۞

71. Waimraatuhu qa-imatun fadahikat fabashsharnaha bi-ishaqa wamin wara-i ishaqa yaAAqooba

11:71. And his wife, standing by, laughed. Then We gave her the good news of Isaac, and of Jacob after Isaac.

قَـــالَتْ يَـــوَيْلَتَىٰٓ ءَأَلِـــدُ وَأَنَـــاْ عَجُـــوزٌ وَهَـــٰذَا بَعْلِـــى شَـــيْخًا إِنَّ هَـــٰذَا لَشَـــىْءٌ عَجِـــيبٌ ۝

72. *Q*alat *ya* waylat*a* aalidu waan*a* AAajoozun wah*atha* baAAlee shaykhan inna *hatha* lashay-on AAajeeb**un**

11:72. She said, "Alas! Shall I bear a son when I am an old woman and this my husband an old man? This is indeed a strange thing!"

قَـــالُوٓاْ أَتَعْجَـــبِينَ مِـــنْ أَمْـــرِ ٱللَّـــهِ رَحْـــمَتُ ٱللَّـــهِ وَبَرَكَـٰتُـــهُۥ عَلَيْكُمْ أَهْلَ ٱلْبَيْتِ إِنَّهُۥ حَمِيدٌ مَّجِيدٌ ۝

73. *Q*aloo ataAAajabeena min amri All*a*hi ra*h*matu All*a*hi wabarak*a*tuhu AAalaykum ahla albayti innahu *h*ameedun majeed**un**

11:73. They said, "Do you consider it strange that Allah does what He wills? Allah's mercy and His blessings are on you, O members of this household! He is indeed Praiseworthy, Glorious."

فَلَمَّا ذَهَبَ عَنْ إِبْرَاهِيمَ ٱلرَّوْعُ وَجَاءَتْهُ ٱلْبُشْرَىٰ يُجَادِلُنَا فِى قَوْمِ لُوطٍ

74. Falamm*a* *th*ahaba AAan ibr*a*heema alrrawAAu waj*a*at-hu albushr*a* yuj*a*dilun*a* fee qawmi loo*t*in

11:74. And when the fear was gone from Abraham and the good news came to him, he began pleading with Us for the people of Lot!

إِنَّ إِبْرَاهِيمَ لَحَلِيمٌ أَوَّاهٌ مُنِيبٌ

75. Inna ibr*a*heema la*h*aleemun aww*a*hun muneeb**un**

11:75. Abraham was indeed considerate and tender-hearted, often turning to Allah in repentance.

يَٰإِبْرَاهِيمُ أَعْرِضْ عَنْ هَٰذَآ إِنَّهُۥ قَدْ جَاءَ أَمْرُ رَبِّكَ وَإِنَّهُمْ ءَاتِيهِمْ عَذَابٌ غَيْرُ مَرْدُودٍ

76. Y*a* ibr*a*heemu aAAri*d* AAan h*atha* innahu qad j*a*a amru rabbika wa-innahum *a*teehim AAa*tha*bun ghayru mardood**in**

11:76. "O Abraham! Forget it. The decree of your Lord on this has indeed come to pass. And a punishment, that cannot be undone, is indeed coming to them."

وَلَمَّا جَآءَتْ رُسُلُنَا لُوطًا سِيٓءَ بِهِمْ وَضَاقَ بِهِمْ ذَرْعًا وَقَالَ هَـٰذَا يَوْمٌ عَصِيبٌ ۝

77. Walamma jaat rusuluna lootan see-a bihim wadaqa bihim tharAAan waqala hatha yawmun AAaseebun

11:77. And when Our Messengers came to Lot, he was worried about them, and he felt powerless to protect them. And he said, "This is a dreadful day!"

وَجَآءَهُۥ قَوْمُهُۥ يُهْرَعُونَ إِلَيْهِ وَمِن قَبْلُ كَانُوا۟ يَعْمَلُونَ ٱلسَّيِّئَاتِ قَالَ يَـٰقَوْمِ هَـٰٓؤُلَآءِ بَنَاتِى هُنَّ أَطْهَرُ لَكُمْ فَٱتَّقُوا۟ ٱللَّهَ وَلَا تُخْزُونِ فِى ضَيْفِىٓ أَلَيْسَ مِنكُمْ رَجُلٌ رَّشِيدٌ ۝

78. Wajaahu qawmuhu yuhraAAoona ilayhi wamin qablu kanoo yaAAmaloona alssayyi-ati qala ya qawmi haola-i banatee hunna atharu lakum faittaqoo Allaha wala tukhzooni fee dayfee alaysa minkum rajulun rasheedun

11:78. And his people came rushing towards him, and they had indulged in evil deeds before. He said, "O my people! These, my daughters[16], are purer for you. So, fear Allah and do not disgrace me about my guests. Is there no rightly-guided man amongst you?"

16. Lot could well have meant daughters of his community.

قَالُوا۟ لَقَدْ عَلِمْتَ مَا لَنَا فِى بَنَاتِكَ مِنْ حَقٍّ وَإِنَّكَ لَتَعْلَمُ مَا نُرِيدُ ۝

79. Qaloo laqad AAalimta ma lana fee banatika min haqqin wa-innaka lataAAlamu ma nureedu

11:79. They said, "You do certainly know that we have nothing to do with your daughters. And you do indeed know what we want."

قَالَ لَوْ أَنَّ لِى بِكُمْ قُوَّةً أَوْ ءَاوِىٓ إِلَىٰ رُكْنٍ شَدِيدٍ ۝

80. Qala law anna lee bikum quwwatan aw awee ila ruknin shadeedin

11:80. He said, "I wish I had power to resist you, or had recourse to a strong support."

قَالُوا۟ يَٰلُوطُ إِنَّا رُسُلُ رَبِّكَ لَن يَصِلُوٓا۟ إِلَيْكَ فَأَسْرِ بِأَهْلِكَ بِقِطْعٍ مِّنَ ٱلَّيْلِ وَلَا يَلْتَفِتْ مِنكُمْ أَحَدٌ إِلَّا ٱمْرَأَتَكَ إِنَّهُ مُصِيبُهَا مَآ أَصَابَهُمْ إِنَّ مَوْعِدَهُمُ ٱلصُّبْحُ أَلَيْسَ ٱلصُّبْحُ بِقَرِيبٍ ۝

81. Qaloo ya lootu inna rusulu rabbika lan yasiloo ilayka faasri bi-ahlika biqitAAin mina allayli wala yaltafit minkum ahadun illa imraataka innahu museebuha ma asabahum inna mawAAidahumu alssubhu alaysa alssubhu biqareebin

11:81. They said, "O Lot! We are the Messengers of your Lord. They won't reach you. So leave this place, with your family, sometime in the night. And let none of you tarry, except for your wife. What happens to them shall indeed happen to her. The appointed time for them is the morning indeed. Is not the morning nigh?"

82. Falamma jaa amruna jaAAalna AAaliyaha safilaha waamtarna AAalayha hijaratan min sijjeelin mandoodin

11:82. And when Our decree came to pass, We turned them upside down and rained down upon them layer over layer of stones of dry and hardened mud.

83. Musawwamatan AAinda rabbika wama hiya mina alththalimeena bibaAAeedin

11:83. These, stand targeted with your Lord and never far from the unjust.[17]

17. The general assumption about natural calamities like earthquakes, hurricanes, floods etc. is that these occur because of geophysical reasons and not because the Intelligent Creator of the universe intentionally directs these against peoples to punish them. Many Qur'aanic Verses, like this one, negates this assumption.

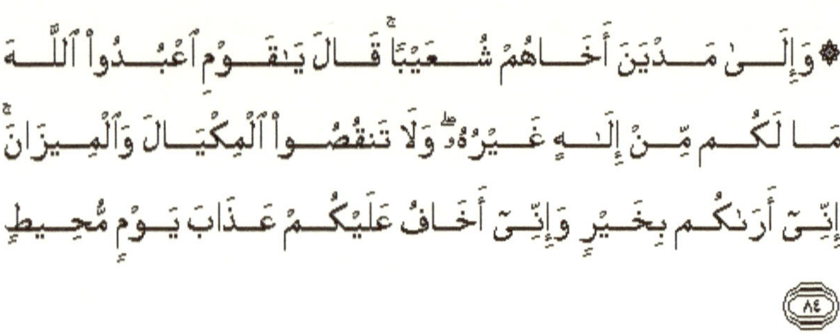

84. Wa-il*a* madyana akh*a*hum shuAAayban q*a*la y*a* qawmi oAAbudoo All*a*ha m*a* lakum min il*a*hin ghayruhu wal*a* tanqu*s*oo almiky*a*la wa*a*lmeez*a*na innee ar*a*kum bikhayrin wa-innee akh*a*fu AAalaykum AAa*th*aba yawmin mu*h*ee*t*in

---

11:84. And to the people of Midian, We sent their brother Shu'aib. He said, "O my people! Worship Allah. You have no god other than Him. And cheat not in measure and weight. I do indeed see you that you are in prosperity, and I do indeed fear for you the punishment of a Day that will not leave out anything."

---

85. Way*a* qawmi awfoo almiky*a*la wa*a*lmeez*a*na bialqis*t*i wal*a* tabkhasoo a*l*n*a*sa ashy*a*ahum wal*a* taAAthaw fee al-ar*d*i mufsideena

---

11:85. "And, O my people! Give full and fair measure and weight and defraud not people of their things. And make no mischief on earth, spreading corruption."

بَقِيَّتُ ٱللَّهِ خَيْرٌ لَّكُمْ إِن كُنتُم مُّؤْمِنِينَ وَمَآ أَنَا۠ عَلَيْكُم بِحَفِيظٍ ﴿٨٦﴾

86. Baqiyyatu Allahi khayrun lakum in kuntum mu/mineena wama ana AAalaykum bihafeethin

11:86. "What lawful gain Allah keeps back for you is better, if you but believe! And I am not a guardian over you."

قَالُوا۟ يَٰشُعَيْبُ أَصَلَوٰتُكَ تَأْمُرُكَ أَن نَّتْرُكَ مَا يَعْبُدُ ءَابَآؤُنَآ أَوْ أَن نَّفْعَلَ فِىٓ أَمْوَٰلِنَا مَا نَشَٰٓؤُا۟ إِنَّكَ لَأَنتَ ٱلْحَلِيمُ ٱلرَّشِيدُ ﴿٨٧﴾

87. Qaloo ya shuAAaybu asalatuka ta/muruka an natruka ma yaAAbudu abaona aw an nafAAala fee amwalina ma nashao innaka laanta alhaleemu alrrasheedu

11:87. They said, "O Shu'aib! Does the code of your worship enjoin you that we should forsake what our fathers worshipped, or that we should not do what we please with our property? You have indeed been the considerate and right-thinking person."

قَالَ يَٰقَوْمِ أَرَءَيْتُمْ إِن كُنتُ عَلَىٰ بَيِّنَةٍ مِّن رَّبِّى وَرَزَقَنِى مِنْهُ رِزْقًا حَسَنًا وَمَآ أُرِيدُ أَنْ أُخَالِفَكُمْ إِلَىٰ مَآ أَنْهَٰكُمْ عَنْهُ إِنْ أُرِيدُ إِلَّا ٱلْإِصْلَٰحَ مَا ٱسْتَطَعْتُ وَمَا تَوْفِيقِىٓ إِلَّا بِٱللَّهِ عَلَيْهِ تَوَكَّلْتُ وَإِلَيْهِ أُنِيبُ ﴿٨٨﴾

88. Qala ya qawmi araaytum in kuntu AAala bayyinatin min rabbee warazaqanee minhu rizqan hasanan wama oreedu an okhalifakum ila ma anhakum AAanhu in oreedu illa al-islaha ma istataAAtu wama tawfeeqee illa biAllahi AAalayhi tawakkaltu wa-ilayhi oneebu

11:88. He said, "O my people! Do you see that, if I have been on clear evidence from my Lord and He has given me a good providence from Him Himself, and I do not wish to do, behind your backs, the very thing that I forbid you from, I desire nothing but reform so far as I am able to? And I get inspiration from none but Allah. On Him do I place my trust and to Him do I turn:"

وَيَٰقَوْمِ لَا يَجْرِمَنَّكُمْ شِقَاقِىٓ أَن يُصِيبَكُم مِّثْلُ مَآ أَصَابَ قَوْمَ نُوحٍ أَوْ قَوْمَ هُودٍ أَوْ قَوْمَ صَٰلِحٍ وَمَا قَوْمُ لُوطٍ مِّنكُم بِبَعِيدٍ ۝

89. Waya qawmi la yajrimannakum shiqaqee an yuseebakum mithlu ma asaba qawma noohin aw qawma hudin aw qawma salihin wama qawmu lootin minkum bibaAAeedin

11:89. "And, O my people, let not hostility to me make you commit sin so that there may befall on you the like of what befell the peoples of Noah, Hood or Salih. And the people of Lot were not very far in the past from you."

وَٱسْتَغْفِرُوا۟ رَبَّكُمْ ثُمَّ تُوبُوٓا۟ إِلَيْهِ إِنَّ رَبِّى رَحِيمٌ وَدُودٌ ۝

90. Waistaghfiroo rabbakum thumma tooboo ilayhi inna rabbee raheemun wadoodun

11:90. "And ask forgiveness of your Lord and turn to Him in repentance. My Lord is indeed Merciful, Loving."

قَالُواْ يَٰشُعَيْبُ مَا نَفْقَهُ كَثِيرًا مِّمَّا تَقُولُ وَإِنَّا لَنَرَىٰكَ فِينَا ضَعِيفًا وَلَوْلَا رَهْطُكَ لَرَجَمْنَٰكَ وَمَآ أَنتَ عَلَيْنَا بِعَزِيزٍ ﴿٩١﴾

91. Q*a*loo y*a* shuAAaybu m*a* nafqahu katheeran mimm*a* taqoolu wa-inn*a* lanar*a*ka feen*a* *d*aAAeefan walawl*a* rah*t*uka larajamn*a*ka wam*a* anta AAalayn*a* biAAazeez*in*

11:91. They said, "O Shu'aib! We do not understand much of what you say, and we do indeed consider you weak amongst us. And were it not for your family we would surely have stoned you to death. And you have no power over us."

قَالَ يَٰقَوْمِ أَرَهْطِيٓ أَعَزُّ عَلَيْكُم مِّنَ ٱللَّهِ وَٱتَّخَذْتُمُوهُ وَرَآءَكُمْ ظِهْرِيًّا إِنَّ رَبِّى بِمَا تَعْمَلُونَ مُحِيطٌ ﴿٩٢﴾

92. Q*a*la y*a* qawmi arah*t*ee aAAazzu AAalaykum mina All*a*hi waittakha*th*tumoohu war*a*akum *th*ihriyy*a*n inna rabbee bim*a* taAAmaloona mu*h*ee*t*un

11:92. He said, "O my people! Is my family more powerful for you than Allah? And you put Him behind your backs? What you do is indeed under the ever-vigilant purview of my Lord."[18]

18. Those pre-historic people of Midian put Allah behind their backs and thus got destroyed (see Verse 94 below), but what about us now? Most of the mankind (Muslims included) today has also put Allah behind its back. So, what are we waiting for (refer Verse 93 below): the Last Day?

وَيَٰقَوْمِ ٱعْمَلُواْ عَلَىٰ مَكَانَتِكُمْ إِنِّى عَٰمِلٌ سَوْفَ تَعْلَمُونَ مَن يَأْتِيهِ عَذَابٌ يُخْزِيهِ وَمَنْ هُوَ كَٰذِبٌ وَٱرْتَقِبُوٓاْ إِنِّى مَعَكُمْ رَقِيبٌ ۝

93. Way*a* qawmi iAAmaloo AAal*a* mak*a*natikum innee AA*a*milun sawfa taAAlamoona man ya/teehi AAa*th*abun yukhzeehi waman huwa k*ath*ibun wairtaqiboo inne maAAakum raqeeb**un**

11:93. "And, O my people! Do what you can. I do what I do. You will soon come to know upon whom the disgracing punishment shall come and who the liar is. And you do wait! Indeed! I too am waiting with you."

وَلَمَّا جَآءَ أَمْرُنَا نَجَّيْنَا شُعَيْبًا وَٱلَّذِينَ ءَامَنُواْ مَعَهُۥ بِرَحْمَةٍ مِّنَّا وَأَخَذَتِ ٱلَّذِينَ ظَلَمُواْ ٱلصَّيْحَةُ فَأَصْبَحُواْ فِى دِيَٰرِهِمْ جَٰثِمِينَ ۝

94. Walamm*a* jaa amrun*a* najjayn*a* shuAAayban waalla*th*eena *a*manoo maAAahu bira*h*matin minn*a* waakha*th*ati alla*th*eena *th*alamoo al*s*say*h*atu faa*s*bahoo fee diy*a*rihim j*a*thimeen**a**

11:94. And when did Our decree come to pass, We saved, by mercy from Us, Shu'aib and those who believed with him. And the terribly rumbling sound[19] struck those who were unjust, and they lay prostrate in their homes.

---

19. It could be the sound that is generated when an earthquake occurs.

كَأَن لَّمْ يَغْنَوْاْ فِيهَآ أَلَا بُعْدًا لِّمَدْيَنَ كَمَا بَعِدَتْ ثَمُودُ ﴿٩٥﴾

95. Kaan lam yaghnaw feeha ala buAAdan limadyana kama baAAidat thamoodu

11:95. As though they had never dwelt in them! Verily, the people of Midian perished just as the people of Thamood[20] had perished.

20. The people of Thamood too were destroyed by an earthquake (see Verse 67 above**).**

وَلَقَدْ أَرْسَلْنَا مُوسَىٰ بِآيَٰتِنَا وَسُلْطَٰنٍ مُّبِينٍ ﴿٩٦﴾

96. Walaqad arsalna moosa bi-ayatina wasultanin mubeenin

11:96. And certainly We did send Moses with Our signs/Verses and clear authority.

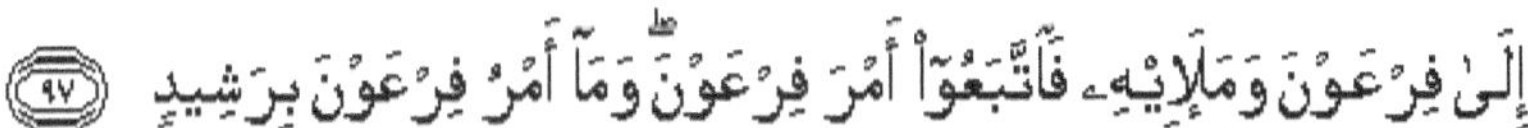

إِلَىٰ فِرْعَوْنَ وَمَلَإِيْهِ فَٱتَّبَعُوٓاْ أَمْرَ فِرْعَوْنَ وَمَآ أَمْرُ فِرْعَوْنَ بِرَشِيدٍ ﴿٩٧﴾

97. Ila firAAawna wamala-ihi faittabaAAoo amra firAAawna wama amru firAAawna birasheedin

11:97. To Pharaoh and his chieftains who followed his rule. And Pharaoh's rule was not good.

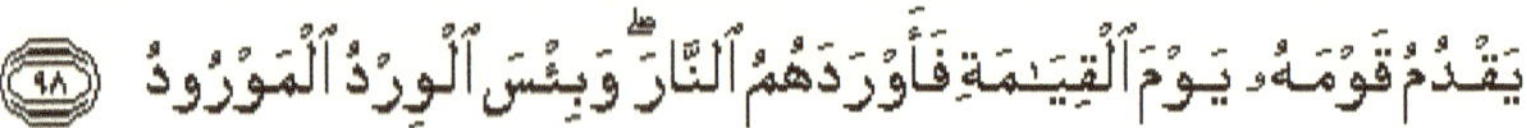

98. Yaqdumu qawmahu yawma alqiy*a*mati faawradahumu alnn*a*ra wabi/sa alwirdu almawrood**u**

11:98. He (Pharaoh) shall lead his people, on the Resurrection Day, to the Fire. And bad is the place which they shall be led to.

99. WaotbiAAoo fee h*ath*ihi laAAnatan wayawma alqiy*a*mati bi/sa alrrifdu almarfood**u**

11:99. And curse followed them in this world and shall follow them on the Resurrection Day. Bad would be the gift they shall be given!

100. *Tha*lika min anb*a*-i alqur*a* naqu*ss*uhu AAalayka minh*a* q*a*-imun wa*h*aseed**un**

11:100. That is an account, We relate to you, of the peoples that inhabited this earth. Of them are some that still exist and others, destroyed.

وَمَا ظَلَمْنَـٰهُمْ وَلَـٰكِن ظَلَمُوٓا۟ أَنفُسَهُمْ ۖ فَمَآ أَغْنَتْ عَنْهُمْ ءَالِهَتُهُمُ

ٱلَّتِى يَدْعُونَ مِن دُونِ ٱللَّهِ مِن شَىْءٍ لَّمَّا جَآءَ أَمْرُ رَبِّكَ ۖ وَمَا زَادُوهُمْ

غَيْرَ تَتْبِيبٍ ﴿١٠١﴾

101. Wam*a* *th*alamn*a*hum wal*a*kin *th*alamoo anfusahum fam*a* aghnat AAanhum *a*lihatuhumu allatee yadAAoona min dooni All*a*hi min shay-in lamm*a* j*a*a amru rabbika wam*a* zadoohum ghayra tatbeeb**in**

11:101. And We wronged them not, but they wronged themselves. And their gods, whom they invoked besides Allah, did avail them nothing when the decree of your Lord came to pass. And they but added to their ruin.

وَكَذَٰلِكَ أَخْذُ رَبِّكَ إِذَآ أَخَذَ ٱلْقُرَىٰ وَهِىَ ظَـٰلِمَةٌ ۚ إِنَّ أَخْذَهُۥٓ أَلِيمٌ شَدِيدٌ

﴿١٠٢﴾

102. Waka*th*alika akh*th*u rabbika i*th*a akha*th*a alqur*a* wahiya *th*alimatun inna akh*th*ahu aleemun shadeed**un**

11:102. And such was the seizure of your Lord when He seized the inhabitants of the earth while they did wrong. His seizure is indeed painful, severe!

إِنَّ فِى ذَٰلِكَ لَآيَةً لِّمَنْ خَافَ عَذَابَ ٱلْأَخِرَةِ ۚ ذَٰلِكَ يَوْمٌ مَّجْمُوعٌ لَّهُ ٱلنَّاسُ وَذَٰلِكَ يَوْمٌ مَّشْهُودٌ ۝١٠٣

103. Inna fee *tha*lika la*a*yatan liman kh*a*fa AAa*tha*ba al-*a*khirati *tha*lika yawmun majmooAAun lahu alnn*a*su wa*tha*lika yawmun mashhoodun

---

11:103. There is indeed in that a sign for him who fears the punishment in the Hereafter. That is the day for the gathering together of mankind and that is the day for production of evidence[21].

---

21. Before the divine Judgment is pronounced, everyone will get the complete and irrefutable evidence of how he or she fared in the great test of his/her worldly life.

وَمَا نُؤَخِّرُهُۥ إِلَّا لِأَجَلٍ مَّعْدُودٍ ۝١٠٤

104. Wam*a* nu-akhkhiruhu ill*a* li-ajalin maAAdood*in*

11:104. And We won't convene the Hereafter till an appointed time.

يَوْمَ يَأْتِ لَا تَكَلَّمُ نَفْسٌ إِلَّا بِإِذْنِهِۦ ۚ فَمِنْهُمْ شَقِىٌّ وَسَعِيدٌ ۝١٠٥

105. Yawma ya/ti l*a* takallamu nafsun ill*a* bi-i*th*nihi faminhum shaqiyyun wasaAAeed*in*

11:105. The day when it is convened, no one shall speak except with His permission. Some of them then shall be miserable, and some happy.

فَأَمَّا ٱلَّذِينَ شَقُوا۟ فَفِى ٱلنَّارِ لَهُمْ فِيهَا زَفِيرٌ وَشَهِيقٌ ۝

106. Faamma allatheena shaqoo fafee alnnari lahum feeha zafeerun washaheequn

11:106. The miserable ones, then, shall be in the Fire. For them there shall be sighing and groaning in it.

خَـٰلِدِينَ فِيهَا مَا دَامَتِ ٱلسَّمَـٰوَٰتُ وَٱلْأَرْضُ إِلَّا مَا شَآءَ رَبُّكَ إِنَّ رَبَّكَ فَعَّالٌ لِّمَا يُرِيدُ ۝

107. Khalideena feeha ma damati alssamawatu waal-ardu illa ma shaa rabbuka inna rabbaka faAAAAalun lima yureedu

11:107. They shall abide therein so long as the heavens and the earth last, unless your Lord wills otherwise. Your Lord does indeed do what He wills.[22]

22. Allah Almighty wills that those sho suppressed the Truth in this world and rebelled against His laws should suffer for ever in Hell-fire. HE does what He wills. If He wills to terminate their suffering, it will indeed be terminated. But, as indicated in this Verse and in many other Verses of the Qur'aan, the suffering in the Hell shall be ever-lasting. And as explained in Verse 14:48, the heavens and the earth as we understand these today, will not be destroyed to nothingness in the Hereafter, but will be changed. See also Verse 108 below in this context.

وَأَمَّا ٱلَّذِينَ سُعِدُواْ فَفِى ٱلْجَنَّةِ خَـٰلِدِينَ فِيهَا مَا دَامَتِ ٱلسَّمَـٰوَٰتُ وَٱلْأَرْضُ إِلَّا مَا شَاءَ رَبُّكَ عَطَآءً غَيْرَ مَجْذُوذٍ ۝

108. Waamma allatheena suAAidoo fafee aljannati khalideena feeha ma damati alssamawatu waal-ardu illa ma shaa rabbuka AAataan ghayra majthoothin

---

11:108. And the happy ones, then, shall be in the Paradise. They shall abide therein till the heavens and the earth last, unless your Lord wills otherwise. It's a gift that shall never be terminated.

فَلَا تَكُ فِى مِرْيَةٍ مِّمَّا يَعْبُدُ هَـٰٓؤُلَآءِ مَا يَعْبُدُونَ إِلَّا كَمَا يَعْبُدُ ءَابَآؤُهُم مِّن قَبْلُ وَإِنَّا لَمُوَفُّوهُمْ نَصِيبَهُمْ غَيْرَ مَنقُوصٍ

109. Fala taku fee miryatin mimma yaAAbudu haola-i ma yaAAbudoona illa kama yaAAbudu abaohum min qablu wa-inna lamuwaffoohum naseebahum ghayra manqoosin

---

11:109. Be not then in doubt as to what these people worship: they do not worship but as their fathers did before. And indeed, We will pay them back in full their due, undiminished.

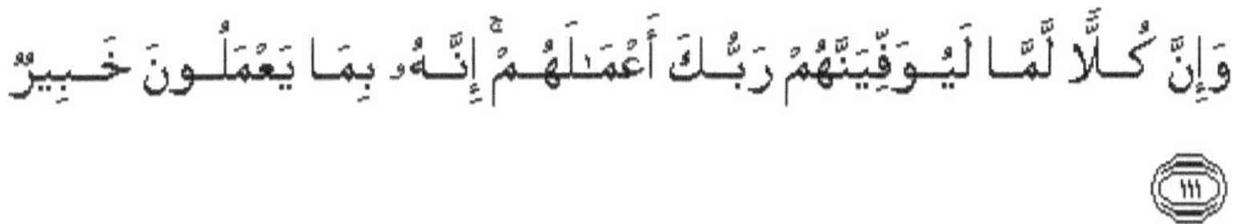

110. Walaqad *atayna moosa* alkitaba faikhtulifa feehi walawla kalimatun sabaqat min rabbika laqud*i*ya baynahum wa-innahum lafee shakkin minhu mureeb**un**

11:110. And certainly, did We give the Book to Moses, and disputes were raised therein. And had not a Word already gone forth from your Lord[23], the matter would surely·have been decided between them. And the sceptics are indeed in doubt over it.

23. I.e., had not the Lord fixed an appropriate time for His decision on the disputes. And one may take a serious note of the fact that just as the Jews had differences over their Torah, the Muslims have differences over the Qur'aan.

111. Wa-inna kullan lamm*a* layuwaffiyannahum rabbuka aAAm*a*lahum innahu bim*a* yaAAmaloona khabeer**un**

11:111. And your Lord will indeed pay back to them all for their deeds in full. He is indeed aware of what they do.

فَٱسْتَقِمْ كَمَآ أُمِرْتَ وَمَن تَابَ مَعَكَ وَلَا تَطْغَوْاْ إِنَّهُۥ بِمَا تَعْمَلُونَ بَصِيرٌ

112. Faistaqim kam*a* omirta waman t*a*ba maAAaka wal*a* ta*t*ghaw innahu bim*a* taAAmaloona ba*s*eer**un**

11:112. Stand firm then, you and those who have turned to Allah with you, on what you are commanded with, and transgress not. HE does indeed see what you do.

وَلَا تَرْكَنُوٓاْ إِلَى ٱلَّذِينَ ظَلَمُواْ فَتَمَسَّكُمُ ٱلنَّارُ وَمَا لَكُم مِّن دُونِ ٱللَّهِ مِنْ أَوْلِيَآءَ ثُمَّ لَا تُنصَرُونَ

113. Wal*a* tarkanoo il*a* alla*th*eena *th*alamoo fatamassakumu al*nna*ru wam*a* lakum min dooni All*a*hi min awliy*a*a thumma l*a* tun*s*aroon**a**

11:113. And do not incline towards those who are unjust, lest the Fire catches you. And you have no *awliya*[24] other than Allah, and you shall not be helped.

---

24. Refer study note 2:154 on <u>Verse 2:107</u>.

وَأَقِمِ ٱلصَّلَوٰةَ طَرَفَيِ ٱلنَّهَارِ وَزُلَفًا مِّنَ ٱلَّيْلِ إِنَّ ٱلْحَسَنَٰتِ يُذْهِبْنَ ٱلسَّيِّئَاتِ ذَٰلِكَ ذِكْرَىٰ لِلذَّٰكِرِينَ

114. Waaqimi al*s*sal*a*ta *t*arafayi alnnah*a*ri wazulafan mina allayli inna al*h*asan*a*ti yu*t*hhibna alssayyi-*a*ti *th*alika *th*ikr*a* lil*thth*akir*e*ena

---

11:114. And establish prayer at the two ends of the day and proximities of the night.[25] Good deeds do indeed eradicate the evil. That is a reminder to those who remember Allah much.

---

25. In the chronological order of revelation, this is the second divine command, after Verse 17:78, specifying the times for ritual prayers at dawn and dusk. The third is 2:238. Please see study notes 451 to 455 on that Verse in this context. I may add here that 'two ends of the day' and 'proximities of the night' both indicate only the periods of dawn and dusk together. The two groups of words do not indicate two different timings other than dawn and dusk.

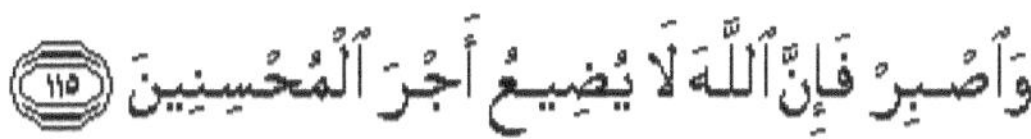

115. Wai*s*bir fa-inna All*a*ha l*a* yu*d*eeAAu ajra almu*h*sin*e*ena

---

11:115. And be patient; for, Allah does indeed not let the good people do, go unrewarded! [26]

---

26. If only we would adhere to this golden principle! We could have the best of this world and the next. We do not adhere to this principle because we do not believe that just being good will give us good rewards. Most of us believe that we get nothing for our good deeds. In the ultimate analysis, we do not have a strong, unshakable faith in Allah.

فَلَوْلَا كَانَ مِنَ ٱلْقُرُونِ مِن قَبْلِكُمْ أُوْلُواْ بَقِيَّةٍ يَنْهَوْنَ عَنِ ٱلْفَسَادِ فِى ٱلْأَرْضِ إِلَّا قَلِيلًا مِّمَّنْ أَنجَيْنَا مِنْهُمْ وَٱتَّبَعَ ٱلَّذِينَ ظَلَمُواْ مَآ أُتْرِفُواْ فِيهِ وَكَانُواْ مُجْرِمِينَ ۝

116. Falawla kana mina alqurooni min qablikum oloo baqiyyatin yanhawna AAani alfasadi fee al-ardi illa qaleelan mimman anjayna minhum waittabaAAa allatheena thalamoo ma otrifoo feehi wakanoo mujrimeena

---

11:116. If only there were, among the generations before you, more men of understanding forbidding mischief on earth! There were but a few men of understanding of those whom We saved from among them. And those who were unjust were preoccupied with the luxuries they were given. And they sinned.

وَمَا كَانَ رَبُّكَ لِيُهْلِكَ ٱلْقُرَىٰ بِظُلْمٍ وَأَهْلُهَا مُصْلِحُونَ ۝

117. Wama kana rabbuka liyuhlika alqura bithulmin waahluha muslihoona

---

11:117. And your Lord could not have unjustly destroyed habitations, while the people living there were good.

وَلَوْ شَآءَ رَبُّكَ لَجَعَلَ ٱلنَّاسَ أُمَّةً وَاحِدَةً وَلَا يَزَالُونَ مُخْتَلِفِينَ ۝

118. Walaw shaa rabbuka lajaAAala alnnasa ommatan wahidatan wala yazaloona mukhtalifeena

---

11:118. And if your Lord had so willed, He would certainly have made mankind a single community. And they shall not cease to differ.

إِلَّا مَن رَّحِمَ رَبُّكَ وَلِذَلِكَ خَلَقَهُمْ وَتَمَّتْ كَلِمَةُ رَبِّكَ لَأَمْلَأَنَّ جَهَنَّمَ مِنَ الْجِنَّةِ وَالنَّاسِ أَجْمَعِينَ ۝

119. Illa man rahima rabbuka walithalika khalaqahum watammat kalimatu rabbika laamlaanna jahannama mina aljinnati waalnnasi ajmaAAeena

---

11:119. Except for those to whom your Lord turns with mercy. And for that[27] did He create them. And the statement of your Lord is bound to be fulfilled, "I will certainly fill Hell with the jinn and the human beings, together."[28]

---

27. I.e., for bestowing mercy upon the human beings.

28. But most of mankind disqualify themselves by disobeying Allah Almighty. And in His infinite knowledge, He knows this in advance. Hence is this dreadful divine prediction.

وَكُلًّا نَّقُصُّ عَلَيْكَ مِنْ أَنبَاءِ الرُّسُلِ مَا نُثَبِّتُ بِهِ فُؤَادَكَ وَجَاءَكَ فِي هَذِهِ الْحَقُّ وَمَوْعِظَةٌ وَذِكْرَى لِلْمُؤْمِنِينَ ۝

120. Wakullan naqussu AAalayka min anba-i alrrusuli ma nuthabbitu bihi fu-adaka wajaaka fee hathihi alhaqqu wamawAAithatun wathikra lilmu/mineena

---

11:120. All that we relate to you of the accounts of the Messengers is to strengthen your mind therewith. And in this[29] have come to you the Truth, Admonition and a Book, for being frequently referred to, for the believers.

---

29. I.e., the Qur'aan. This Verse is a divine confirmation of the fact that the Qur'aan contains all the truth and admonition for man to conduct his life on this earth, and it should serve him frequently as a Reference Book for trouble-shooting problems encountered.

وَقُل لِّلَّذِينَ لَا يُؤْمِنُونَ ٱعْمَلُواْ عَلَىٰ مَكَانَتِكُمْ إِنَّا عَٰمِلُونَ ﴿١٢١﴾

121. Waqul lilla*theena* la yu/minoona iAAmaloo AAal*a* mak*a*natikum inn*a* AAamiloon**a**

11:121. And tell those who do not believe "You act your way; we act ours."

وَٱنتَظِرُوٓاْ إِنَّا مُنتَظِرُونَ ﴿١٢٢﴾

122. Wainta*th*iroo inn*a* munta*th*iroon**a**

11:122. "And you wait. We too indeed wait."

وَلِلَّهِ غَيْبُ ٱلسَّمَٰوَٰتِ وَٱلْأَرْضِ وَإِلَيْهِ يُرْجَعُ ٱلْأَمْرُ كُلُّهُۥ فَٱعْبُدْهُ وَتَوَكَّلْ عَلَيْهِ وَمَا رَبُّكَ بِغَٰفِلٍ عَمَّا تَعْمَلُونَ ﴿١٢٣﴾

123. Walill*a*hi ghaybu alssam*a*w*a*ti wa*a*l-ar*d*i wa-ilayhi yurjaAAu al-amru kulluhu faoAAbudhu watawakkal AAalayhi wam*a* rabbuka bigh*a*filin AAamm*a* taAAmaloon**a**

11:123. And Allah's are the secrets of the heavens and the earth and to Him are all matters returned. Do worship Him then and do put your trust in Him! And your Lord is not unaware of what you do.

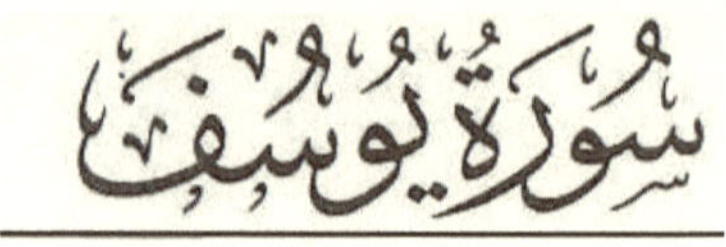

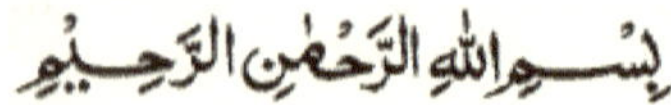

In the Name of Allah, the Gracious, the Merciful

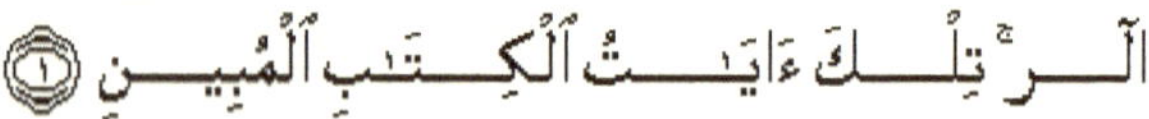

1. Alif-lam-ra tilka *ay*a*t*u alkit*a*bi almubeen**u**

12:1. Alif Lam Ra. Those are the Verses of the clear and self-explanatory Book.

2. Inn*a* anzaln*a*hu qur-*a*nan AAarabiyyan laAAallakum taAAqiloona

---

12:2. We have indeed sent it down as an Arabic Qur'aan in order that you understand it.[1]

---

1. The Qur'aan was revealed for all the peoples of the entire world. And it was to be revealed through one human Messenger to emphasise the unity of religion for mankind. And since the All-knowing Allah had chosen an Arab to be that Messenger, the language of the divine Message had necessarily to be in Arabic. It is therefore the bounden duty of every Muslim living anywhere in the world to learn Arabic. Failure to learn it betrays a grave lack of faith in Islam on the part of the Muslims.

نَحْنُ نَقُصُّ عَلَيْكَ أَحْسَنَ ٱلْقَصَصِ بِمَآ أَوْحَيْنَآ إِلَيْكَ هَـٰذَا ٱلْقُرْءَانَ وَإِن كُنتَ مِن قَبْلِهِۦ لَمِنَ ٱلْغَـٰفِلِينَ ۝

3. Nahnu naqussu AAalayka ahsana alqasasi bima awhayna ilayka hatha alqur-ana wa-in kunta min qablihi lamina alghafileena

---

12:3. We narrate to you the best of narratives by Our revealing to you this Qur'aan. And, before this, you were indeed among those who did not know.[2]

---

2. The addressee in this Verse is in the 2nd person singular. Therefore, it was the Prophet (peace on him) who was the addressee initially, but every other Muslim is also implied.

إِذْ قَالَ يُوسُفُ لِأَبِيهِ يَـٰٓأَبَتِ إِنِّى رَأَيْتُ أَحَدَ عَشَرَ كَوْكَبًا وَٱلشَّمْسَ وَٱلْقَمَرَ رَأَيْتُهُمْ لِى سَـٰجِدِينَ ۝

4. Ith qala yoosufu li-abeehi ya abati innee raaytu ahada AAashara kawkaban waalshshamsa waalqamara raaytuhum lee sajideena

---

12:4. When Joseph said to his father, "O my father! I did indeed see eleven stars and the sun and the moon. I saw them prostrating to me."

قَالَ يَـٰبُنَيَّ لَا تَقْصُصْ رُءْيَاكَ عَلَىٰٓ إِخْوَتِكَ فَيَكِيدُوا۟ لَكَ كَيْدًا إِنَّ ٱلشَّيْطَـٰنَ لِلْإِنسَـٰنِ عَدُوٌّ مُّبِينٌ ۝

5. Qala ya bunayya la taqsus ru/yaka AAala ikhwatika fayakeedoo laka kaydan inna alshshaytana lil-insani AAaduwwun mubeenun

---

12:5. He said, "O my son! Do not relate your dream to your brothers, lest they devise a plan against you. The Satan is indeed an open enemy to man."

وَكَذَٰلِكَ يَجْتَبِيكَ رَبُّكَ وَيُعَلِّمُكَ مِن تَأْوِيلِ ٱلْأَحَادِيثِ وَيُتِمُّ نِعْمَتَهُۥ عَلَيْكَ وَعَلَىٰٓ ءَالِ يَعْقُوبَ كَمَآ أَتَمَّهَا عَلَىٰٓ أَبَوَيْكَ مِن قَبْلُ إِبْرَٰهِيمَ وَإِسْحَـٰقَ إِنَّ رَبَّكَ عَلِيمٌ حَكِيمٌ ۝

6. Wakathalika yajtabeeka rabbuka wayuAAallimuka min ta/weeli al-ahadeethi wayutimmu niAAmatahu AAalayka waAAala ali yaAAqooba kama atammaha AAala abawayka min qablu ibraheema wa-ishaqa inna rabbaka AAaleemun hakeemun

---

12:6. "And accordingly [according to interpretation of the dream, that is,] your Lord will choose you and teach you the interpretation of events and complete His favour upon you and upon the children of Jacob, as He did complete it, before, upon your fathers, Abraham and Isaac. Your Lord is indeed Knowledgeable, Wise."

۞ لَّقَدْ كَانَ فِى يُوسُفَ وَإِخْوَتِهِۦٓ ءَايَـٰتٌ لِّلسَّآئِلِينَ ۝

7. Laqad *ka*na fee yoosufa wa-ikhwatihi *aya*tun lilss*a*-ilee**na**

12:7. Certainly in Joseph and his brothers there are signs for the seekers.

$$\text{إِذْ قَالُوا۟ لَيُوسُفُ وَأَخُوهُ أَحَبُّ إِلَىٰٓ أَبِينَا مِنَّا وَنَحْنُ عُصْبَةٌ إِنَّ أَبَانَا لَفِى}$$

$$\text{ضَلَـٰلٍ مُّبِينٍ ﴿٨﴾}$$

8. I*th* q*a*loo layoosufu waakhoohu a*h*abbu il*a* abee*na* minn*a* wana*h*nu AAu*s*batun inna ab*a*na lafee *d*al*a*lin mubeen**in**

12:8. When they said, "Certainly Joseph and his brother are dearer to our father than we. And we are more in number and strength.[3] Our father is indeed making a manifest mistake."

---

3. The elder brothers were envious of their two youngest ones being doted on by their father. The youngest ones, being weak, needed more attention, and the father was naturally more protective of those two. But the elder brothers could not understand this. It was the usual sibling rivalry, which in this case had gone too far.

$$\text{ٱقْتُلُوا۟ يُوسُفَ أَوِ ٱطْرَحُوهُ أَرْضًا يَخْلُ لَكُمْ وَجْهُ أَبِيكُمْ وَتَكُونُوا۟}$$

$$\text{مِنْ بَعْدِهِۦ قَوْمًا صَـٰلِحِينَ ﴿٩﴾}$$

9. Oqtuloo yoosufa awi i*trah*oohu ar*d*an yakhlu lakum wajhu abeekum watakoonoo min baAAdihi qawman *s*ali*h*ee**na**

12:9. "Kill Joseph or abandon him into a distant land, so that your father dotes on you exclusively. And thereafter you can become righteous people."

قَـالَ قَـآئِلٌ مِّنْهُـمْ لَا تَقْتُلُـواْ يُوسُـفَ وَأَلْقُـوهُ فِـى غَيَـبَتِ ٱلْجُـبِّ يَلْتَقِطْهُ بَعْضُ ٱلسَّـيَّارَةِ إِن كُنتُمْ فَـعِلِيـنَ ۝

10. Qala qa-ilun minhum la taqtuloo yoosufa waalqoohu fee ghayabati aljubbi yaltaqithu baAAdu alssayyarati in kuntum faAAileena

12:10. One of them said, "Do not kill Joseph, but, if you must do something about him, put him down into the bottom of a well so that some travellers may pick him up."

قَالُواْ يَتَأَبَانَا مَا لَكَ لَا تَأْمَنَّا عَلَىٰ يُوسُفَ وَإِنَّا لَهُ لَنَصِحُونَ ۝

11. Qaloo ya abana ma laka la ta/manna AAala yoosufa wa-inna lahu lanasihoona

12:11. They said, "O our father! Why do you not trust us about Joseph? And we are indeed his sincere well-wishers!"

أَرْسِـلْهُ مَعَنَـا غَـدًا يَـرْتَعْ وَيَلْعَـبْ وَإِنَّا لَـهُ لَحَـفِظُونَ ۝

12. Arsilhu maAAana ghadan yartaAA wayalAAab wa-inna lahu lahafithoona

12:12. "Send him with us tomorrow that he may eat, drink and play. And we will indeed guard him well."

قَالَ إِنِّى لَيَحْزُنُنِىٓ أَن تَذْهَبُوا۟ بِهِۦ وَأَخَافُ أَن يَأْكُلَهُ ٱلذِّئْبُ وَأَنتُمْ عَنْهُ غَٰفِلُونَ ﴿١٣﴾

13. Qala innee laya*h*zununee an tha*thth*aboo bihi waakh*a*fu an ya/kulahu al*thth*i/bu waantum AAanhu gh*a*filoon**a**

12:13. Their father said, "It does indeed grieve me that you should take him away. And I fear lest the wolf devour him while your attention is diverted from him."

قَالُوا۟ لَئِنْ أَكَلَهُ ٱلذِّئْبُ وَنَحْنُ عُصْبَةٌ إِنَّآ إِذًا لَّخَٰسِرُونَ ﴿١٤﴾

14. Qaloo la-in akalahu al*thth*i/bu wana*h*nu AAu*s*batun inn*a* i*th*an lakh*a*siroon**a**

12:14. They said, "Surely if the wolf should devour him even when we are a strong group, we should then indeed be the doomed ones!"

فَلَمَّا ذَهَبُوا۟ بِهِۦ وَأَجْمَعُوٓا۟ أَن يَجْعَلُوهُ فِى غَيَٰبَتِ ٱلْجُبِّ وَأَوْحَيْنَآ إِلَيْهِ لَتُنَبِّئَنَّهُم بِأَمْرِهِمْ هَٰذَا وَهُمْ لَا يَشْعُرُونَ ﴿١٥﴾

15. Falamm*a* *th*ahaboo bihi waajmaAAoo an yajAAaloohu fee ghay*a*bati aljubbi waaw*h*ayn*a* ilayhi latunabi-annahum bi-amrihim *hatha* wahum l*a* yashAAuroon**a**

12:15. So then they went off with him and mutually agreed that they should put him down at the bottom of a well. And We revealed to him, "They know it not, but you shall one day certainly tell them of this act of theirs."[4]

---

4. The little Joseph was thus divinely reassured, while he was at the bottom of the well, that he will overcome the difficult situation he was in at that particular time and will live to tell his brothers about their nefarious act.

16. Waj*a*oo ab*a*hum AAish*a*an yabkoon**a**

12:16. And they came to their father in the evening, weeping.

---

17. Q*a*loo y*a* ab*a*na inn*a* *th*ahabn*a* nastabiqu watarakn*a* yoosufa AAinda mat*a*AAin*a* faakalahu al*thth*i/bu wam*a* anta bimu/minin lan*a* walaw kunn*a* *s*adiqeen**a**

12:17. They said, "O our father! We did indeed get ourselves engaged in the racing game and left Joseph behind with our goods. Then, the wolf ate him. And you will not believe us though we do tell you the truth."

وَجَآءُو عَلَىٰ قَمِيصِهِۦ بِدَمٍ كَذِبٍ قَالَ بَلْ سَوَّلَتْ لَكُمْ أَنفُسُكُمْ أَمْرًا فَصَبْرٌ جَمِيلٌ وَٱللَّهُ ٱلْمُسْتَعَانُ عَلَىٰ مَا تَصِفُونَ ۝

18. Waj*a*oo AA*a*l*a* qamee*s*ihi bidamin ka*th*ibin q*a*la bal sawwalat lakum anfusukum amran fa*s*abrun jameelun waAll*a*hu almustaAA*a*nu AA*a*l*a* m*a* ta*s*ifoon**a**

12:18. And they brought his shirt with fake blood thereon. He said, "Nay, you yourselves have contrived this tale. All I can do is resort to graceful patience. And it is Allah's help that is sought, against what you tell me."

وَجَآءَتْ سَيَّارَةٌ فَأَرْسَلُواْ وَارِدَهُمْ فَأَدْلَىٰ دَلْوَهُۥ قَالَ يَٰبُشْرَىٰ هَٰذَا غُلَٰمٌ وَأَسَرُّوهُ بِضَٰعَةً وَٱللَّهُ عَلِيمٌۢ بِمَا يَعْمَلُونَ ۝

19. Waj*a*at sayy*a*ratun f*a*arsaloo w*a*ridahum f*a*adl*a* dalwahu q*a*la y*a* bushr*a* h*atha* ghul*a*mun waasarroohu bi*da*AAatan waAll*a*hu AA*a*leemun bim*a* yaAAmaloon**a**

12:19. And a caravan of travellers did come there and they sent their man to draw water from the well and he let down his bucket. He exclaimed, "O goodness! There is a boy there." And they took him along as an article of merchandise. And Allah knew what they did.

وَشَرَوْهُ بِثَمَنٍ بَخْسٍ دَرَاهِمَ مَعْدُودَةٍ وَكَانُوا فِيهِ مِنَ ٱلزَّاهِدِينَ ﴿٢٠﴾

20. Washarawhu bithamanin bakhsin dar*a*hima maAAdoodatin wak*a*noo feehi mina alzz*a*hideena

12:20. And they sold him for a paltry price – a few dirhams – and they had been eager to get rid of him.

وَقَالَ ٱلَّذِى ٱشْتَرَاهُ مِن مِّصْرَ لِٱمْرَأَتِهِ أَكْرِمِى مَثْوَاهُ عَسَىٰ أَن يَنفَعَنَا أَوْ نَتَّخِذَهُ وَلَدًا وَكَذَٰلِكَ مَكَّنَّا لِيُوسُفَ فِى ٱلْأَرْضِ وَلِنُعَلِّمَهُ مِن تَأْوِيلِ ٱلْأَحَادِيثِ وَٱللَّهُ غَالِبٌ عَلَىٰ أَمْرِهِ وَلَٰكِنَّ أَكْثَرَ ٱلنَّاسِ لَا يَعْلَمُونَ ﴿٢١﴾

21. Waq*a*la alla*th*ee ishtar*a*hu min mi*s*ra liimraatihi akrimee math*wa*hu AAas*a* an yanfaAAan*a* aw natta*kh*i*th*ahu waladan waka*th*alika makkann*a* liyoosufa fee al-ar*d*i walinuAAallimahu min ta/weeli al-a*h*adeethi waAll*a*hu *gh*alibun AAal*a* amrihi walakinna akthara aln*a*si l*a* yaAAlamoon*a*

12:21. And the man from the city who bought him said to his wife, "Make his stay comfortable. Maybe he will be useful to us, or we may adopt him as a son." And thus, did We establish Joseph in the land and taught him the interpretation of events. And Allah is in complete control of what He does, but most people know not.

وَلَمَّا بَلَغَ أَشُدَّهُ ءَاتَيْنَاهُ حُكْمًا وَعِلْمًا وَكَذَٰلِكَ نَجْزِى ٱلْمُحْسِنِينَ ﴿٢٢﴾

22. Walamm*a* balagha ashuddahu *a*tayn*a*hu *h*ukman waAAilman waka*th*alika najzee almu*h*sineena

12:22. And when he attained his maturity, We gave him authority and knowledge. And thus, do We reward those who are good.

وَرَٰوَدَتْهُ ٱلَّتِى هُوَ فِى بَيْتِهَا عَن نَّفْسِهِۦ وَغَلَّقَتِ ٱلْأَبْوَٰبَ وَقَالَتْ هَيْتَ لَكَ ۚ قَالَ مَعَاذَ ٱللَّهِ ۖ إِنَّهُۥ رَبِّىٓ أَحْسَنَ مَثْوَاىَ ۖ إِنَّهُۥ لَا يُفْلِحُ ٱلظَّٰلِمُونَ ﴿٢٣﴾

23. War*a*wadat-hu allatee huwa fee baytih*a* AAan nafsihi waghallaqati al-abw*a*ba waq*a*lat hayta laka q*a*la maAA*ath*a All*a*hi innahu rabbee a*h*sana mathw*a*ya innahu l*a* yufli*h*u al*ththa*limoon**a**

12:23. And she, in whose house he lived, solicited him, closed the doors and said, "Come on!" He said, "I seek Allah's protection. My master has indeed given me good shelter. Those who do wrong shall indeed not prosper."

وَلَقَدْ هَمَّتْ بِهِۦ ۖ وَهَمَّ بِهَا لَوْلَآ أَن رَّءَا بُرْهَٰنَ رَبِّهِۦ ۚ كَذَٰلِكَ لِنَصْرِفَ عَنْهُ ٱلسُّوٓءَ وَٱلْفَحْشَآءَ ۚ إِنَّهُۥ مِنْ عِبَادِنَا ٱلْمُخْلَصِينَ ﴿٢٤﴾

24. Walaqad hammat bihi wahamma bih*a* lawl*a* an ra*a* burh*a*na rabbihi ka*tha*lika lina*s*rifa AAanhu alssoo-a w*a*alfa*h*sh*a*a innahu min AAib*a*din*a* almukhla*s*eena

12:24. And she did desire him. And he would have desired her too, had he not seen a clear sign from his Lord. Thus, did We turn evil and indecency away from him. He was indeed one of Our sincere worshippers.

وَٱسْتَبَقَا ٱلْبَابَ وَقَدَّتْ قَمِيصَهُۥ مِن دُبُرٍ وَأَلْفَيَا سَيِّدَهَا لَدَا ٱلْبَابِ قَالَتْ مَا جَزَآءُ مَنْ أَرَادَ بِأَهْلِكَ سُوٓءًا إِلَّآ أَن يُسْجَنَ أَوْ عَذَابٌ أَلِيمٌ ۝

25. Wa*i*stab*a*q*a* alb*a*ba waqaddat qamee*s*ahu min duburin waalfay*a* sayyidah*a* lad*a* alb*a*bi q*a*lat m*a* jaz*a*o man ar*a*da bi-ahlika soo-an ill*a* an yusjana aw AAa*th*abun aleem**un**

12:25. And they both hastened to the door, and she tore off his shirt from behind and they met her husband at the door. She said, "What is to be done to him who wanted to molest your wife except to imprison him or give him some other painful punishment?"

قَالَ هِىَ رَٰوَدَتْنِى عَن نَّفْسِى وَشَهِدَ شَاهِدٌ مِّنْ أَهْلِهَآ إِن كَانَ قَمِيصُهُۥ قُدَّ مِن قُبُلٍ فَصَدَقَتْ وَهُوَ مِنَ ٱلْكَٰذِبِينَ ۝

26. Q*a*la hiya r*a*wadatnee AAan nafsee washahida sh*a*hidun min ahlih*a* in k*a*na qamee*s*uhu qudda min qubulin fa*s*adaqat wahuwa mina alk*ath*ibeen**a**

12:26. He [Joseph] said, "It was she who tried to seduce me." And a witness from her own family said, "If his shirt is torn off from the front, she speaks the truth and he is the liar."

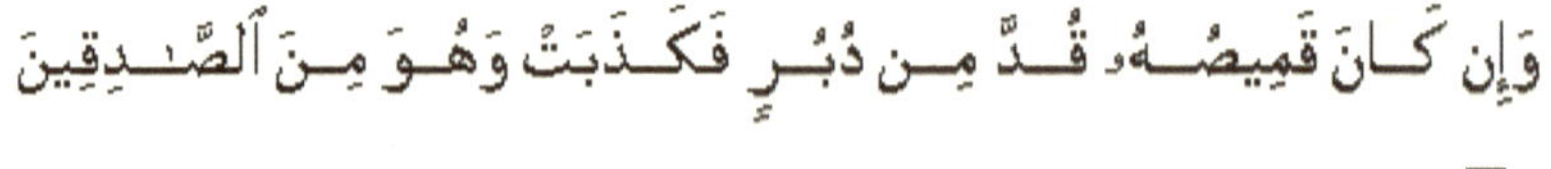

27. Wa-in kana qameesuhu qudda min duburin fakathabat wahuwa mina alssadiqeena

---

12:27. "And if his shirt is torn off from behind, she is telling a lie and he is telling the truth."

فَلَمَّا رَءَا قَمِيصَهُۥ قُدَّ مِن دُبُرٍ قَالَ إِنَّهُۥ مِن كَيۡدِكُنَّ إِنَّ كَيۡدَكُنَّ عَظِيمٌ ﴿٢٨﴾

28. Falamma raa qameesahu qudda min duburin qala innahu min kaydikunna inna kaydakunna AAatheemun

---

12:28. So when he (husband of the woman) saw his (Joseph's) shirt torn off from behind, he (the husband) said, "It is indeed an instance of female cunningness. You women are indeed great at being cunning."

يُوسُفُ أَعۡرِضۡ عَنۡ هَـٰذَا وَٱسۡتَغۡفِرِى لِذَنۢبِكِ إِنَّكِ كُنتِ مِنَ ٱلۡخَاطِئِينَ ﴿٢٩﴾

29. Yoosufu aAArid AAan hatha waistaghfiree lithanbiki innaki kunti mina alkhati-eena

---

12:29. "Joseph! You stay away from this; and (to his wife) you ask forgiveness for your sin, you are indeed the one at fault."

وَقَالَ نِسْوَةٌ فِى ٱلْمَدِينَةِ ٱمْرَأَتُ ٱلْعَزِيزِ تُرَاوِدُ فَتَىٰهَا عَن نَّفْسِهِۦ قَدْ شَغَفَهَا حُبًّا إِنَّا لَنَرَىٰهَا فِى ضَلَٰلٍ مُّبِينٍ ۝

30. Waqala niswatun fee almadeenati imraatu alAAazeezi turawidu fataha AAan nafsihi qad shaghafaha hubban inna lanaraha fee dalalin mubeenin

---

12:30. And the city women gossiped, "The nobleman's wife has tried to seduce her young slave. She is surely overcome with love for him. We do indeed see her going manifestly astray."

فَلَمَّا سَمِعَتْ بِمَكْرِهِنَّ أَرْسَلَتْ إِلَيْهِنَّ وَأَعْتَدَتْ لَهُنَّ مُتَّكَأً وَءَاتَتْ كُلَّ وَٰحِدَةٍ مِّنْهُنَّ سِكِّينًا وَقَالَتِ ٱخْرُجْ عَلَيْهِنَّ فَلَمَّا رَأَيْنَهُۥ أَكْبَرْنَهُۥ وَقَطَّعْنَ أَيْدِيَهُنَّ وَقُلْنَ حَٰشَ لِلَّهِ مَا هَٰذَا بَشَرًا إِنْ هَٰذَآ إِلَّا مَلَكٌ كَرِيمٌ ۝

31. Falamma samiAAat bimakrihinna arsalat ilayhinna waaAAtadat lahunna muttakaan waatat kulla wahidatin minhunna sikkeenan waqalati okhruj AAalayhinna falamma raaynahu akbarnahu waqattaAAna aydiyahunna waqulna hasha lillahi ma hatha basharan in hatha illa malakun kareemun

---

12:31. So when she heard of their malicious talk, she sent for them and arranged comfortable seats for them. And she gave everyone of them a knife, and asked Joseph to come out before them. So, when they saw him, they were so much stunned by his personality that they cut their hands, and said, "Glory to Allah! This is not a man; this is none but a noble angel."

$$\text{قَالَتْ فَذَلِكُنَّ ٱلَّذِى لُمْتُنَّنِى فِيهِ وَلَقَدْ رَاوَدتُّهُ عَن نَّفْسِهِ فَٱسْتَعْصَمَ}$$
$$\text{وَلَئِن لَّمْ يَفْعَلْ مَآ ءَامُرُهُ لَيُسْجَنَنَّ وَلَيَكُونًا مِّنَ ٱلصَّاغِرِينَ ﴿٣٢﴾}$$

32. Qalat fathalikunna allathee lumtunnanee feehi walaqad rawadtuhu AAan nafsihi faistAAsama wala-in lam yafAAal ma amuruhu layusjananna walayakoonan mina alssaghireena

---

12:32. She said, "This is the man whom you blamed me about. And I did certainly seek to seduce him, but he resisted. And if he does not do my bidding, he shall certainly be imprisoned, and he shall certainly suffer the ignominy."

$$\text{قَالَ رَبِّ ٱلسِّجْنُ أَحَبُّ إِلَىَّ مِمَّا يَدْعُونَنِىٓ إِلَيْهِ وَإِلَّا تَصْرِفْ عَنِّى كَيْدَهُنَّ}$$
$$\text{أَصْبُ إِلَيْهِنَّ وَأَكُن مِّنَ ٱلْجَاهِلِينَ ﴿٣٣﴾}$$

33. Qala rabbi alssijnu ahabbu ilayya mimma yadAAoonanee ilayhi wa-illa tasrif AAannee kaydahunna asbu ilayhinna waakun mina aljahileena

---

12:33. He said, "My Lord! I would prefer to go to jail rather than do what they invite me to. And unless You make their scheme against me ineffective, I will be tempted towards them and behave as one ignorant."

$$\text{فَٱسْتَجَابَ لَهُ رَبُّهُ فَصَرَفَ عَنْهُ كَيْدَهُنَّ إِنَّهُ هُوَ ٱلسَّمِيعُ ٱلْعَلِيمُ ﴿٣٤﴾}$$

34. Faistajaba lahu rabbuhu fasarafa AAanhu kaydahunna innahu huwa alssameeAAu alAAaleemu

---

12:34. His Lord then accepted his prayer and made their scheme against him ineffective. He (Allah) does indeed hear, know!

ثُمَّ بَدَا لَهُم مِّنْ بَعْدِ مَا رَأَوُا الْآيَٰتِ لَيَسْجُنُنَّهُۥ حَتَّىٰ حِينٍ ۝

35. Thumma bada lahum min baAAdi ma raawoo al-ayati layasjununnahu hatta heenin

12:35. Then, after weighing the pros and cons of the matter, they thought it advisable to keep him in the prison for the time being.

وَدَخَلَ مَعَهُ السِّجْنَ فَتَيَانِ قَالَ أَحَدُهُمَآ إِنِّى أَرَىٰنِىٓ أَعْصِرُ خَمْرًا وَقَالَ الْآخَرُ إِنِّىٓ أَرَىٰنِىٓ أَحْمِلُ فَوْقَ رَأْسِى خُبْزًا تَأْكُلُ الطَّيْرُ مِنْهُ نَبِّئْنَا بِتَأْوِيلِهِۦٓ إِنَّا نَرَىٰكَ مِنَ الْمُحْسِنِينَ ۝

36. Wadakhala maAAahu alssijna fatayani qala ahaduhuma innee aranee aAAsiru khamran waqala al-akharu innee aranee ahmilu fawqa ra/see khubzan ta/kulu alttayru minhu nabbi/na bita/weelihi inna naraka mina almuhsineena

12:36. And two youngsters entered the prison with him. One of them said, "I saw myself making wine." And the other said, "I saw myself carrying bread on my head, birds eating wherefrom. Tell us what it means. We do indeed see you as a good man."

قَالَ لَا يَأْتِيكُمَا طَعَامٌ تُرْزَقَانِهِ إِلَّا نَبَّأْتُكُمَا بِتَأْوِيلِهِ قَبْلَ أَن يَأْتِيَكُمَا ذَلِكُمَا مِمَّا عَلَّمَنِى رَبِّى إِنِّى تَرَكْتُ مِلَّةَ قَوْمٍ لَّا يُؤْمِنُونَ بِٱللَّهِ وَهُم بِٱلْأَخِرَةِ هُمْ كَافِرُونَ ۝

37. Qala la ya/teekuma taAAamun turzaqanihi illa nabba/tukuma bita/weelihi qabla an ya/tiyakuma thalikuma mimma AAallamanee rabbee innee taraktu millata qawmin la yu/minoona biAllahi wahum bial-akhirati hum kafiroona

---

12:37. He said, "I shall tell you both what the dreams mean before the food you eat is brought to you. This is one of the things my Lord has taught me. I have indeed forsaken the lifestyle of people who do not believe in Allah, and who deny the Hereafter."

وَٱتَّبَعْتُ مِلَّةَ ءَابَآءِى إِبْرَاهِيمَ وَإِسْحَقَ وَيَعْقُوبَ مَا كَانَ لَنَآ أَن نُّشْرِكَ بِٱللَّهِ مِن شَىْءٍ ذَلِكَ مِن فَضْلِ ٱللَّهِ عَلَيْنَا وَعَلَى ٱلنَّاسِ وَلَكِنَّ أَكْثَرَ ٱلنَّاسِ لَا يَشْكُرُونَ ۝

38. WaittabaAAtu millata aba-ee ibraheema wa-ishaqa wayaAAqooba ma kana lana an nushrika biAllahi min shay-in thalika min fadli Allahi AAalayna waAAala alnnasi walakinna akthara alnnasi la yashkuroona

---

12:38. "And I follow the lifestyle of my forefathers, Abraham, Isaac and Jacob. We do not have to worship anything other than Allah. That[5] is by Allah's grace upon us and on mankind, but most people are ungrateful."

---

5. I.e., the fact that we are not to worship anything other than Allah. Monotheism is Allah's grace upon mankind, but most people spurn the divine grace and take upon themselves the abomination of polytheism.

يَـٰصَـٰحِبَيِ ٱلسِّجْنِ ءَأَرْبَابٌ مُّتَفَرِّقُونَ خَيْرٌ أَمِ ٱللَّهُ ٱلْوَٰحِدُ ٱلْقَهَّارُ ۝٣٩

39. Ya sahibayi alssijni aarbabun mutafarriqoona khayrun ami Allahu alwahidu alqahharu

12:39. "O my two prison mates! Are sundry lords better or Allah the One, the Almighty?"

مَا تَعْبُدُونَ مِن دُونِهِۦٓ إِلَّآ أَسْمَآءً سَمَّيْتُمُوهَآ أَنتُمْ وَءَابَآؤُكُم مَّآ أَنزَلَ ٱللَّهُ بِهَا مِن سُلْطَـٰنٍ إِنِ ٱلْحُكْمُ إِلَّا لِلَّهِ أَمَرَ أَلَّا تَعْبُدُوٓاْ إِلَّآ إِيَّاهُ ذَٰلِكَ ٱلدِّينُ ٱلْقَيِّمُ وَلَـٰكِنَّ أَكْثَرَ ٱلنَّاسِ لَا يَعْلَمُونَ ۝٤٠

40. Ma taAAbudoona min doonihi illa asmaan sammaytumooha antum waabaokum ma anzala Allahu biha min sultanin ini alhukmu illa lillahi amara alla taAAbudoo illa iyyahu thalika alddeenu alqayyimu walakinna akthara alnnasi la yaAAlamoona

12:40. "What you worship besides Him are but fictitious things to which you and your fathers have given names. Allah has not sent down any authority for them. The absolute authority is with Allah alone. He has commanded that you shall not worship[6] anything or anybody but Him. That is the established way of life, but most people know not."

6. To worship is to obey unquestioningly all commands of the authority in question. As this Verse proclaims, this authority is none other than Allah, the one and only Creator and Sustainer of the entire

universe and of everything therein. But by treating the *ahaadeeth* to be as sacrosanct as the Qur'aanic Verses, many Muslims are guilty of contravening the dictum of this Verse. Unlike for the Qur'aan, there is no divine guarantee of genuineness for the *ahaadeeth*. By following and thus obeying the *ahaadeeth* that are contradictory to Qur'aanic teachings, the Muslims are unquestioningly obeying and thus worshipping the narrators and writers of the *ahaadeeth*, besides Allah Almighty.

يَـٰصَـٰحِبَىِ ٱلسِّجْنِ أَمَّآ أَحَدُكُمَا فَيَسْقِى رَبَّهُۥ خَمْرًا ۖ وَأَمَّا ٱلْءَاخَرُ فَيُصْلَبُ فَتَأْكُلُ ٱلطَّيْرُ مِن رَّأْسِهِۦ ۚ قُضِىَ ٱلْأَمْرُ ٱلَّذِى فِيهِ تَسْتَفْتِيَانِ ﴿٤١﴾

41. Ya *sah*ibayi alssijni amm*a a*hadukum*a* fayasqee rabbahu khamran waamm*a* al-*a*kharu fayu*s*labu fata/kulu al*tt*ayru min ra/sihi qu*d*iya al-amru alla*thee* feehi tastaftiy*a*ni

12:41. "O my two prison mates! As for the first one of you, he shall serve wine to his lord. And as for the other, he shall be crucified, and the birds shall peck from his head. The matter you inquired about is so decreed."

وَقَالَ لِلَّذِى ظَنَّ أَنَّهُۥ نَاجٍ مِّنْهُمَا ٱذْكُرْنِى عِندَ رَبِّكَ فَأَنسَىٰهُ ٱلشَّيْطَـٰنُ ذِكْرَ رَبِّهِۦ فَلَبِثَ فِى ٱلسِّجْنِ بِضْعَ سِنِينَ ﴿٤٢﴾

42. Waq*a*la lilla*thee thanna* annahu n*a*jin minhum*a* o*th*kurnee AAinda rabbika faans*a*hu alshshay*ta*nu *th*ikra rabbihi falabitha fee alssijni bi*d*AAa sineena

12:42. And he (Joseph) said to the one of the two, whom he thought was indeed going to be saved, "Mention me to your lord." But the Satan caused him to forget mentioning him to his lord, so he remained in the prison for a few years.

وَقَالَ ٱلْمَلِكُ إِنِّى أَرَىٰ سَبْعَ بَقَرَٰتٍ سِمَانٍ يَأْكُلُهُنَّ سَبْعٌ عِجَافٌ وَسَبْعَ سُنۢبُلَٰتٍ خُضْرٍ وَأُخَرَ يَابِسَٰتٍ يَٰٓأَيُّهَا ٱلْمَلَأُ أَفْتُونِى فِى رُءْيَٰىَ إِن كُنتُمْ لِلرُّءْيَا تَعْبُرُونَ ﴿٤٣﴾

43. Waqala almaliku innee ara sabAAa baqaratin simanin ya/kuluhunna sabAAun AAijafun wasabAAa sunbulatin khudrin waokhara yabisatin ya ayyuha almalao aftoonee fee ru/yaya in kuntum lilrru/ya taAAburoona

---

12:43. And the king said, "I saw seven fat cows, but seven lean cows ate them up! And I saw seven ears of corn that were green and other ears that were withered and dry. O chieftains! Explain to me my dream, if you do know how to interpret dreams."

قَالُوٓاْ أَضْغَٰثُ أَحْلَٰمٍ وَمَا نَحْنُ بِتَأْوِيلِ ٱلْأَحْلَٰمِ بِعَٰلِمِينَ ﴿٤٤﴾

44. Qaloo adghathu ahlamin wama nahnu bita/weeli al-ahlami biAAalimeena

---

12:44. They said, "Dreams are jumbled, and we do not know the interpretation of dreams."

وَقَالَ ٱلَّذِى نَجَا مِنْهُمَا وَٱدَّكَرَ بَعْدَ أُمَّةٍ أَنَا۠ أُنَبِّئُكُم بِتَأْوِيلِهِۦ فَأَرْسِلُونِ ﴿٤٥﴾

45. Waq*a*la alla*thee* naj*a* minhum*a* waiddakara baAAda ommatin an*a* onabbi-okum bita/weelihi faarsiloon*i*

12:45. And of the two prisoners, the one, who survived, recollected after a long time Joseph's request to him and said, "I will give you its interpretation, and let me go out now to get it."

يُوسُفُ أَيُّهَا ٱلصِّدِّيقُ أَفْتِنَا فِى سَبْعِ بَقَرَٰتٍ سِمَانٍ يَأْكُلُهُنَّ سَبْعٌ عِجَافٌ وَسَبْعِ سُنۢبُلَٰتٍ خُضْرٍ وَأُخَرَ يَابِسَٰتٍ لَّعَلِّىٓ أَرْجِعُ إِلَى ٱلنَّاسِ لَعَلَّهُمْ يَعْلَمُونَ ۝

46. Yoosufu ayyuh*a* al*s*siddeequ aftin*a* fee sabAAi baqar*a*tin sim*a*nin ya/kuluhunna sabAAun AAij*a*fun wasabAAi sunbul*a*tin khu*d*rin waokhara y*a*bis*a*tin laAAall*ee* arjiAAu il*a* alnn*a*si laAAallahum yaAAlamoon*a*

12:46. "Joseph! O truthful one! Explain to us the dream in which there were seven fat cows, but seven lean cows ate them up! Besides, there were seven ears of corn that were green and other ears that were withered and dry. Explain, so that I may go back to those people and let them know."

قَالَ تَزْرَعُونَ سَبْعَ سِنِينَ دَأَبًا فَمَا حَصَدتُّمْ فَذَرُوهُ فِى سُنۢبُلِهِۦٓ إِلَّا قَلِيلًا مِّمَّا تَأْكُلُونَ ۝

47. Q*a*la tazraAAoona sabAAa sineena daaban fam*a* *h*asadtum fa*th*aroohu fee sunbulihi ill*a* qaleelan mimm*a* ta/kuloon**a**

12:47. Joseph explained, "You shall sow for seven years continuously, then leave what you reap in ears, except the little that you need for immediate consumption."

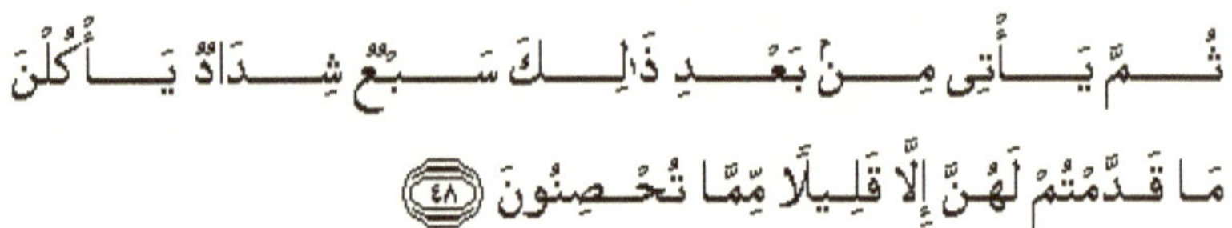

48. Thumma ya/tee min baAAdi *tha*lika sabAAun shid*a*dun ya/kulna m*a* qaddamtum lahunna ill*a* qaleelan mimm*a* tu*h*sinoon**a**

12:48. "Then there shall come thereafter seven years of hardship which shall eat away all that you would have preserved for those years, except for a little thereof."

49. Thumma ya/tee min baAAdi *tha*lika AA*a*mun feehi yughathu alnn*a*su wafeehi yaAA*a*siroon**a**

12:49. "Then there will come after that a year in which people shall have rain and in which they shall produce wine/oil."

وَقَالَ ٱلْمَلِكُ ٱئْتُونِى بِهِ ۖ فَلَمَّا جَآءَهُ ٱلرَّسُولُ قَالَ ٱرْجِعْ إِلَىٰ رَبِّكَ فَسْـَٔلْهُ مَا بَالُ ٱلنِّسْوَةِ ٱلَّٰتِى قَطَّعْنَ أَيْدِيَهُنَّ إِنَّ رَبِّى بِكَيْدِهِنَّ عَلِيمٌ

50. Waqala almaliku i/toonee bihi falamma jaahu alrrasoolu qala irjiAA ila rabbika fais-alhu ma balu alnniswati allatee qattaAAna aydiyahunna inna rabbee bikaydihinna AAaleemun

---

12:50. And the king said, "Bring him (Joseph) to me." So, when the messenger came to him, he said, "Go back to your lord and ask him about the case of the women who cut their hands. My Lord does indeed know their guile."

قَالَ مَا خَطْبُكُنَّ إِذْ رَاوَدتُّنَّ يُوسُفَ عَن نَّفْسِهِ ۚ قُلْنَ حَاشَ لِلَّهِ مَا عَلِمْنَا عَلَيْهِ مِن سُوٓءٍ ۚ قَالَتِ ٱمْرَأَتُ ٱلْعَزِيزِ ٱلْـَٰٔنَ حَصْحَصَ ٱلْحَقُّ أَنَا۠ رَاوَدتُّهُ عَن نَّفْسِهِ ۚ وَإِنَّهُ لَمِنَ ٱلصَّٰدِقِينَ

51. Qala ma khatbukunna ith rawadtunna yoosufa AAan nafsihi qulna hasha lillahi ma AAalimna AAalayhi min soo-in qalati imraatu alAAazeezi al-ana hashasa alhaqqu ana rawadtuhu AAan nafsihi wa-innahu lamina alssadiqeena

---

12:51. The king called for the women and asked them, "What have you to say on the affair when you sought to seduce Joseph?" They said, "Glory to Allah! We knew of no evil on his part." And the chieftain's wife said, "Now that the truth has come out, it was I who tried to seduce him, and he is indeed the truthful one."

ذَٰلِكَ لِيَعْلَمَ أَنِّى لَمْ أَخُنْهُ بِالْغَيْبِ وَأَنَّ ٱللَّهَ لَا يَهْدِى كَيْدَ
ٱلْخَآئِنِينَ ﴿٥٢﴾

52. *Tha*lika liyaAAlama annee lam akhunhu bialghaybi waanna All*a*ha l*a* yahdee kayda alkh*a*-ineena

---

12:52. "That is to let him (Joseph) know that I have not betrayed him behind his back and that Allah guides not the scheme of the betrayers."

۞ وَمَآ أُبَرِّئُ نَفْسِىٓ إِنَّ ٱلنَّفْسَ لَأَمَّارَةٌ بِٱلسُّوٓءِ إِلَّا مَا رَحِمَ رَبِّىٓ إِنَّ رَبِّى
غَفُورٌ رَّحِيمٌ ﴿٥٣﴾

53. Wam*a* obarri-o nafsee inna alnnafsa laamm*a*ratun bialssoo-i ill*a* m*a* ra*h*ima rabbee inna rabbee ghafoorun ra*h*eem**un**

12:53. The Chieftain's wife[7] continued, "And I do not claim to be innocent. The self is indeed prone to evil, except for such as my Lord has had mercy on. Indeed! My Lord is Forgiving, Merciful."

---

7. Please see preceding Verses 51 and 52.

وَقَالَ ٱلْمَلِكُ ٱئْتُونِى بِهِۦٓ أَسْتَخْلِصْهُ لِنَفْسِى فَلَمَّا كَلَّمَهُۥ قَالَ إِنَّكَ ٱلْيَوْمَ لَدَيْنَا مَكِينٌ أَمِينٌ ۝

54. Waq*a*la almaliku i/toonee bihi astakhli*sh*u linafsee falamm*a* kallamahu q*a*la innaka alyawma ladayn*a* makeenun ameen**un**

12:54. And the king said, "Bring him to me. I will make him my personal aide." So, when Joseph was brought to him, the king said, "You are indeed from today a trusted person in an honourable position with us."

قَالَ ٱجْعَلْنِى عَلَىٰ خَزَآئِنِ ٱلْأَرْضِ إِنِّى حَفِيظٌ عَلِيمٌ ۝

55. Q*a*la ijAAalnee AAal*a* khaz*a*-ini al-ar*d*i innee *h*afee*th*un AAaleem**un**

12:55. Joseph said, "Place me in authority over the treasures of the land. I know how to keep them well preserved."

وَكَذَٰلِكَ مَكَّنَّا لِيُوسُفَ فِى ٱلْأَرْضِ يَتَبَوَّأُ مِنْهَا حَيْثُ يَشَآءُ نُصِيبُ بِرَحْمَتِنَا مَن نَّشَآءُ وَلَا نُضِيعُ أَجْرَ ٱلْمُحْسِنِينَ ۝

56. Waka*tha*lika makann*a* liyoosufa fee al-ar*d*i yatabawwao minh*a* *h*aythu yash*a*o nu*s*eebu bira*h*matin*a* man nash*a*o wal*a* nu*d*eeAAu ajra almu*h*sineen**a**

12:56. And thus did We give Yusuf an honourable position in the land. He could settle therein in whatever way he liked. We bestow Our mercy upon whom We please. And We do not let good people go unrewarded.

وَلَأَجْرُ ٱلْأَخِرَةِ خَيْرٌ لِّلَّذِينَ ءَامَنُوا۟ وَكَانُوا۟ يَتَّقُونَ ۝

57. Walaajru al-*akhirati khayrun lilla*theena *a*manoo wak*a*noo yattaqoon**a**

12:57. And certainly the reward of the Hereafter is much better for those who believe and fear Allah.

وَجَآءَ إِخْوَةُ يُوسُفَ فَدَخَلُوا۟ عَلَيْهِ فَعَرَفَهُمْ وَهُمْ لَهُۥ مُنكِرُونَ ۝

58. Waj*a*a ikhwatu yoosufa fadakhaloo AAalayhi faAAarafahum wahum lahu munkiroon**a**

12:58. And Joseph's brothers came[8] and went in to him, when he recognised them and they did not recognise him.

8. The narrative skips the gap of several years during which the granaries were filled under the wise counsel of Joseph with the produce of good years, and the drought had set in just as predicted in the king's dream [Verse 12.43 as decodified by Joseph (Verses 12:47 to 12:49)]. It was to get grains from the State granaries that Joseph's brothers had come there during the drought years.

وَلَمَّا جَهَّزَهُم بِجَهَازِهِمْ قَالَ ائْتُونِى بِأَخٍ لَّكُم مِّنْ أَبِيكُمْ أَلَا تَرَوْنَ أَنِّى أُوفِى الْكَيْلَ وَأَنَا خَيْرُ الْمُنزِلِينَ ۝

59. Walamma jahhazahum bijahazihim qala i/toonee bi-akhin lakum min abeekum ala tarawna annee oofee alkayla waana khayru almunzileena

12:59. And when he furnished them their provision, Joseph said, "Bring to me the other brother you have from your father! Do you not see that I give you your full ration and offer you hospitality at its best?"

فَإِن لَّمْ تَأْتُونِى بِهِ فَلَا كَيْلَ لَكُمْ عِندِى وَلَا تَقْرَبُونِ ۝

60. Fa-in lam ta/toonee bihi fala kayla lakum AAindee wala taqrabooni

12:60. "But if you do not bring him to me, you shall have no ration from me, nor shall you come near me."

قَالُوا سَنُرَاوِدُ عَنْهُ أَبَاهُ وَإِنَّا لَفَاعِلُونَ ۝

61. Qaloo sanurawidu AAanhu abahu wa-inna lafaAAiloona

12:61. They said, "We will plead for him with his father, and we will most certainly do that."

وَقَالَ لِفِتْيَنِهِ اجْعَلُواْ بِضَعَتَهُمْ فِى رِحَالِهِمْ لَعَلَّهُمْ يَعْرِفُونَهَآ إِذَا
انقَلَبُوٓاْ إِلَىٰٓ أَهْلِهِمْ لَعَلَّهُمْ يَرْجِعُونَ ﴿٦٢﴾

62. Waq*a*la lifity*a*nihi ijAAaloo bi*da*AAatahum fee ri*h*alihim laAAallahum yaAArifoonah*a* *itha* inqalaboo il*a* ahlihim laAAallahum yarjiAAoon*a*

12:62. And Joseph told his men, "Put back their payments secretly in their bags so that they come to know about it only when they go back to their family. It may induce them to come back here."

فَلَمَّا رَجَعُوٓاْ إِلَىٰٓ أَبِيهِمْ قَالُواْ يَتَأَبَانَا مُنِعَ مِنَّا الْكَيْلُ فَأَرْسِلْ
مَعَنَآ أَخَانَا نَكْتَلْ وَإِنَّا لَهُۥ لَحَٰفِظُونَ ﴿٦٣﴾

63. Falamm*a* rajaAAoo il*a* abeehim qaloo y*a* ab*a*n*a* muniAAa minn*a* alkaylu faarsil maAAan*a* akh*a*n*a* naktal wa-inn*a* lahu la*h*afi*th*oon*a*

12:63. So when they returned to their father, they said, "O our father, our ration would be denied to us. Therefore, send our brother with us. We may then get our ration, and we will most certainly take care of him."

قَالَ هَلْ ءَامَنُكُمْ عَلَيْهِ إِلَّا كَمَا أَمِنتُكُمْ عَلَىٰ أَخِيهِ مِن قَبْلُ فَاللَّهُ خَيْرٌ حَافِظًا وَهُوَ أَرْحَمُ الرَّاحِمِينَ ۝

64. Qala hal amanukum AAalayhi illa kama amintukum AAala akheehi min qablu faAllahu khayrun hafithan wahuwa arhamu alrrahimeena

---

12:64. He said, "Shall I entrust him to you just as I entrusted to you his brother before? But Allah is the best Protector, and He is the most Merciful."

وَلَمَّا فَتَحُواْ مَتَاعَهُمْ وَجَدُواْ بِضَاعَتَهُمْ رُدَّتْ إِلَيْهِمْ قَالُواْ يَتَأَبَانَا مَا نَبْغِى هَٰذِهِ بِضَاعَتُنَا رُدَّتْ إِلَيْنَا وَنَمِيرُ أَهْلَنَا وَنَحْفَظُ أَخَانَا وَنَزْدَادُ كَيْلَ بَعِيرٍ ذَٰلِكَ كَيْلٌ يَسِيرٌ ۝

65. Walamma fatahoo mataAAahum wajadoo bidaAAatahum ruddat ilayhim qaloo ya abana ma nabghee hathihi bidaAAatuna ruddat ilayna wanameeru ahlana wanahfathu akhana wanazdadu kayla baAAeerin thalika kaylun yaseerun

---

12:65. And when they opened their goods, they found returned to them what they had paid therefor! They said, "O our father, what more can we desire? Here is our capital returned to us! Now we can feed our family, take care of our brother, and have a surplus of a camel load of grains. That would make our problem of getting sufficient ration easy."

قَالَ لَنْ أُرْسِلَهُ مَعَكُمْ حَتَّىٰ تُؤْتُونِ مَوْثِقًا مِّنَ ٱللَّهِ لَتَأْتُنَّنِى بِهِ إِلَّا أَن يُحَاطَ بِكُمْ فَلَمَّا ءَاتَوْهُ مَوْثِقَهُمْ قَالَ ٱللَّهُ عَلَىٰ مَا نَقُولُ وَكِيلٌ ۝

66. Q*a*la lan orsilahu maAAakum *h*att*a* tu/tooni mawthiqan mina All*a*hi lata/tunnanee bihi ill*a* an yu*h*a*t*a bikum falamm*a a*tawhu mawthiqahum q*a*la All*a*hu AAal*a* m*a* naqoolu wakeel**un**

12:66. He said, "I will not send him with you until you give me a pledge, in Allah's name, that you will most certainly bring him back to me unless in the circumstance that you are besieged. And when they gave him their pledge, he said, "Allah is Witness and Trustee to what we say."

وَقَالَ يَٰبَنِىَّ لَا تَدْخُلُوا۟ مِنۢ بَابٍ وَٰحِدٍ وَٱدْخُلُوا۟ مِنْ أَبْوَابٍ مُّتَفَرِّقَةٍ وَمَا أُغْنِى عَنكُم مِّنَ ٱللَّهِ مِن شَىْءٍ إِنِ ٱلْحُكْمُ إِلَّا لِلَّهِ عَلَيْهِ تَوَكَّلْتُ وَعَلَيْهِ فَلْيَتَوَكَّلِ ٱلْمُتَوَكِّلُونَ ۝

67. Waq*a*la *ya* baniyya l*a* tadkhuloo min b*a*bin w*ah*idin waodkhuloo min abw*a*bin mutafarriqatin wam*a* oghnee AAankum mina All*a*hi min shay-in ini al*h*ukmu ill*a* lill*a*hi AAalayhi tawakkaltu waAAalayhi falyatawakkali almutawakkiloon**a**

12:67. And he said, "O my sons! Do not enter by one gate and enter by different gates. And I can avail you nothing against Allah. The absolute authority is with none but Allah. On Him I do trust. And on Him then let those who trust, put their trust."[9]

---

9. The father's advice to his numerous sons not to enter all together by one gate was just a human strategy to avoid undue attention. As he later explains, no human strategy can withstand Allah's Will. There's a lesson here for mankind that they may take all precautions against perceived troubles, but, ultimately, it is Allah they should rely on.

وَلَمَّا دَخَلُواْ مِنْ حَيْثُ أَمَرَهُمْ أَبُوهُم مَّا كَانَ يُغْنِى عَنْهُم مِّنَ ٱللَّهِ مِن شَىْءٍ إِلَّا حَاجَةً فِى نَفْسِ يَعْقُوبَ قَضَىٰهَا وَإِنَّهُ لَذُو عِلْمٍ لِّمَا عَلَّمْنَـٰهُ وَلَـٰكِنَّ أَكْثَرَ ٱلنَّاسِ لَا يَعْلَمُونَ ﴿٦٨﴾

68. Walamma dakhaloo min *h*aythu amarahum aboohum m*a* k*a*na yughnee AAanhum mina All*a*hi min shay-in ill*a* *h*ajatan fee nafsi yaAAqooba qa*dah*a wa-innahu la*th*oo AAilmin lim*a* AAallamn*a*hu wal*a*kinna akthara alnn*a*si l*a* yaAAlamoon**a**

12:68. And when they entered as their father had bidden them, it availed them nothing against Allah. It was an act deemed prudent by Jacob and he expressed it. And indeed, he had the knowledge We taught him, but most people know not.[10]

10. Jacob was a Prophet, and he knew certain things from Allah, which other people are not privy to.

وَلَمَّا دَخَلُواْ عَلَىٰ يُوسُفَ ءَاوَىٰ إِلَيْهِ أَخَاهُ قَالَ إِنِّى أَنَا۠ أَخُوكَ فَلَا تَبْتَئِسْ بِمَا كَانُواْ يَعْمَلُونَ ﴿٦٩﴾

69. Walamma dakhaloo AAal*a* yoosufa *a*w*a* ilayhi akh*a*hu q*a*la innee an*a* akhooka fal*a* tabta-is bim*a* k*a*noo yaAAmaloon**a**

12:69. And when they went in to Joseph, he took his brother[11] to stay with himself, and told him, "I am your brother, therefore grieve not at what they do."

11. From the context of this and the preceding Verses, it is apparent that Joseph and the youngest brother brought to him now were born to one wife, while the other brothers were born to another wife of Jacob.

فَلَمَّا جَهَّزَهُم بِجَهَازِهِمْ جَعَلَ ٱلسِّقَايَةَ فِى رَحْلِ أَخِيهِ ثُمَّ أَذَّنَ مُؤَذِّنٌ أَيَّتُهَا ٱلْعِيرُ إِنَّكُمْ لَسَٰرِقُونَ ۝

70. Falamm*a* jahhazahum bijah*a*zihim jaAAala alssiq*a*yata fee ra*h*li akheehi thumma a*thth*ana mu-a*thth*inun ayyatuh*a* alAAeeru innakum las*a*riqoona

---

12:70. So when he gave them their provisions, he placed a cup in his brother's bag. Then someone cried out, "O people of the caravan! You are most surely thieves."

قَالُواْ وَأَقْبَلُواْ عَلَيْهِم مَّاذَا تَفْقِدُونَ ۝

71. Q*a*loo waaqbaloo AAalayhim m*atha* tafqidoona

12:71. Joseph's brothers in the caravan came forward and asked, "What is it that you find missing?"

قَالُواْ نَفْقِدُ صُوَاعَ ٱلْمَلِكِ وَلِمَن جَآءَ بِهِۦ حِمْلُ بَعِيرٍ وَأَنَا۠ بِهِۦ زَعِيمٌ ۝

72. Q*a*loo nafqidu *s*uw*a*AAa almaliki waliman j*a*a bihi *h*imlu baAAeerin waan*a* bihi zaAAeem**un**

12:72. Joseph's men replied, "We find the king's cup missing, and he, who comes up with it, shall get a camel-load of extra grains." And Joseph added, "I am guarantor of this."

قَـالُواْ تَٱللَّـهِ لَقَـدْ عَلِمْتُـم مَّـا جِئْنَـا لِنُفْسِـدَ فِـى ٱلْأَرْضِ وَمَـا كُنَّـا سَـٰرِقِينَ ۝٧٣

73. Q*a*loo taAll*a*hi laqad AAalimtum m*a* ji/n*a* linufsida fee al-ar*d*i wam*a* kunn*a* s*a*riqeen**a**

12:73. Joseph's brothers said, "By Allah! You know for certain that we have not come to make mischief in the land, and we are not thieves."

قَالُواْ فَمَا جَزَآؤُهُۥٓ إِن كُنتُمْ كَـٰذِبِيـنَ ۝٧٤

74. Q*a*loo fam*a* jaz*a*ohu in kuntum k*ath*ibeen**a**

12:74. The men asked, "But what should be the punishment for this, if you happen to be lying?"

قَالُواْ جَزَآؤُهُ مَن وُجِدَ فِى رَحْلِهِۦ فَهُوَ جَزَآؤُهُۥ كَذَٰلِكَ نَجْزِى الظَّٰلِمِينَ ﴿٧٥﴾

75. Qaloo jazaohu man wujida fee ra*h*lihi fahuwa jazaohu ka*tha*lika najzee al*ththa*limeen**a**

12:75. The brothers said, "The punishment for this is that the person in whose bag it is found shall himself suffer it. Thus, we do punish the wrongdoers."

فَبَدَأَ بِأَوْعِيَتِهِمْ قَبْلَ وِعَآءِ أَخِيهِ ثُمَّ ٱسْتَخْرَجَهَا مِن وِعَآءِ أَخِيهِ كَذَٰلِكَ كِدْنَا لِيُوسُفَ مَا كَانَ لِيَأْخُذَ أَخَاهُ فِى دِينِ ٱلْمَلِكِ إِلَّا أَن يَشَآءَ ٱللَّهُ نَرْفَعُ دَرَجَٰتٍ مَّن نَّشَآءُ وَفَوْقَ كُلِّ ذِى عِلْمٍ عَلِيمٌ ﴿٧٦﴾

76. Fabadaa bi-aw*AA*iyatihim qabla wi*AAa*-i akheehi thumma istakhrajaha min wi*AAa*-i akheehi ka*tha*lika kidn*a* liyoosufa m*a* k*a*na liya/khu*th*a akhahu fee deeni almaliki ill*a* an yashaa Allahu narfa*AA*u daraj*a*tin man nash*a*o wafawqa kulli *thee* *AA*ilmin *AA*aleem**un**

12:76. So he (Joseph) began the search with their (his step-brothers') packs before searching the pack of his brother, and then he brought it (the king's cup) out from his brother's pack. Thus did We plan a stratagem for the sake of Joseph. He could not legally take and keep his brother with him under the king's laws, unless Allah pleased.[12] We raise the ranks of whomsoever We please. And over every person of knowledge, there is one having better knowledge.[13]

---

12. Apparently, Joseph acted against the laws of the country in which he himself was in an executive position. But Joseph was a Prophet; and, what he did was under the direct direction of the highest

Authority, Allah. So, Joseph's act of manipulating his younger brother continuing to stay with him, against the laws of the country, should not be taken as a precedent for such acts by other human beings.

13. No human being, at any point of time, could ever claim that he was the most knowledgeable or had all the knowledge. There could always be someone with better knowledge on some or the other subject. It is Allah alone Who can possess all knowledge far above any of His created beings could or can ever possess.

77. Qaloo in yasriq faqad saraqa akhun lahu min qablu faasarraha yoosufu fee nafsihi walam yubdiha lahum qala antum sharrun makanan waAllahu aAAlamu bima tasifoona

12:77. They said, "If he has stolen, a brother of his did indeed steal before." And Joseph kept his secret with himself and did not disclose it to them. He said, "You have been in a wicked state of mind and Allah knows the truth about the clarification you have given."

78. Qaloo ya ayyuha alAAazeezu inna lahu aban shaykhan kabeeran fakhuth ahadana makanahu inna naraka mina almuhsineena

12:78. They said, "Sir! He has a very old father; so, retain one of us in his place. We do indeed see you as a good man."

قَالَ مَعَاذَ ٱللَّهِ أَن نَّأْخُذَ إِلَّا مَن وَجَدْنَا مَتَـٰعَنَا عِندَهُۥٓ إِنَّآ إِذًا لَّظَـٰلِمُونَ ۝

79. Qala maAAatha Allahi an na/khutha illa man wajadna mataAAana AAindahu inna ithan lathalimoona

---

12:79. He said, "Allah forbid that we seize a man other than him with whom we found our property. We would indeed then be doing a very wrong thing."

فَلَمَّا ٱسْتَيْـَٔسُوا۟ مِنْهُ خَلَصُوا۟ نَجِيًّا قَالَ كَبِيرُهُمْ أَلَمْ تَعْلَمُوٓا۟ أَنَّ أَبَاكُمْ قَدْ أَخَذَ عَلَيْكُم مَّوْثِقًا مِّنَ ٱللَّهِ وَمِن قَبْلُ مَا فَرَّطتُمْ فِى يُوسُفَ فَلَنْ أَبْرَحَ ٱلْأَرْضَ حَتَّىٰ يَأْذَنَ لِىٓ أَبِىٓ أَوْ يَحْكُمَ ٱللَّهُ لِىۖ وَهُوَ خَيْرُ ٱلْحَـٰكِمِينَ ۝

80. Falamma istay-asoo minhu khalasoo najiyyan qala kabeeruhum alam taAAalamoo anna abakum qad akhatha AAalaykum mawthiqan mina Allahi wamin qablu ma farrattum fee yoosufa falan abraha al-arda hatta ya/thana lee abee aw yahkuma Allahu lee wahuwa khayru alhakimeena

---

12:80. Then when they got despaired of him, they conferred among themselves. The eldest of them said, "Do you not know that your father took from you a pledge in Allah's name, and that you committed excesses in respect of Joseph, before? Therefore, I will not leave this place until my father permits me, or Allah otherwise decrees for me. And He is the best Ruler."

ٱرْجِعُوٓا۟ إِلَىٰٓ أَبِيكُمْ فَقُولُوا۟ يَٰٓأَبَانَآ إِنَّ ٱبْنَكَ سَرَقَ وَمَا
شَهِدْنَآ إِلَّا بِمَا عَلِمْنَا وَمَا كُنَّا لِلْغَيْبِ حَٰفِظِينَ ﴿٨١﴾

81. IrjiAAoo il*a* abeekum faqooloo y*a* ab*ana* inna ibnaka saraqa wam*a* shahidn*a* ill*a* bim*a* AAalimn*a* wam*a* kunn*a* lilghaybi *ha*fi*th*eena

---

12:81. “Go back to your father.” They went back and said, “O our father! Your son did indeed commit theft, and we do not bear witness except to what we have known. And we could not keep watch over the unseen.”

وَسْـَٔلِ ٱلْقَرْيَةَ ٱلَّتِى كُنَّا فِيهَا وَٱلْعِيرَ ٱلَّتِىٓ أَقْبَلْنَا فِيهَا ۖ وَإِنَّا لَصَٰدِقُونَ ﴿٨٢﴾

82. Wais-ali alqaryata allatee kunn*a* feeh*a* waalAAeera allatee aqbaln*a* feeh*a* wa-inn*a* la*s*adiqoona

---

12:82. “And make enquiries at the place in which we had been to and with the caravan with which we had proceeded. And what we say is most certainly true.”

قَالَ بَلْ سَوَّلَتْ لَكُمْ أَنفُسُكُمْ أَمْرًا ۖ فَصَبْرٌ جَمِيلٌ ۖ عَسَى ٱللَّهُ أَن يَأْتِيَنِى
بِهِمْ جَمِيعًا ۚ إِنَّهُۥ هُوَ ٱلْعَلِيمُ ٱلْحَكِيمُ ﴿٨٣﴾

83. Q*a*la bal sawwalat lakum anfusukum amran fa*s*abrun jameelun AAas*a* All*a*hu an ya/tiyanee bihim jameeAAan innahu huwa alAAaleemu al*h*akeemu

---

12:83. He (Jacob) said, "Nay, you have made up a convenient story for yourselves! So, it is better for me to be patient. Maybe, Allah will bring them all together to me. He is indeed Knowledgeable, Wise."

84. Watawall*a* AAanhum waq*a*la ya asaf*a* AAal*a* yoosufa waibya*dd*at AAayn*a*hu mina al*h*uzni fahuwa ka*th*eem**un**

12:84. And, turning away from them, he silently cried, "Alas for Joseph!" And his eyes turned white with grief, and he did control his emotions.

85. Q*a*loo taAll*a*hi taftao ta*th*kuru yoosufa *h*att*a* takoona *h*ara*d*an aw takoona mina al*h*alikeena

12:85. They (Joseph's brothers) said to him, "By Allah! You will cease not remembering Joseph until you get severely ill or get perished."

86. Q*a*la innam*a* ashkoo baththee wa*h*uznee il*a* All*a*hi waaAAlamu mina All*a*hi m*a* l*a* taAAlamoon**a**

12:86. He said, "I complain of my distress and grief only to Allah. And I know from Allah what you do not know."

يَـٰبَنِىَّ ٱذْهَبُواْ فَتَحَسَّسُواْ مِن يُوسُفَ وَأَخِيهِ وَلَا تَاْيْـَٔسُواْ مِن رَّوْحِ ٱللَّهِ إِنَّهُۥ لَا يَاْيْـَٔسُ مِن رَّوْحِ ٱللَّهِ إِلَّا ٱلْقَوْمُ ٱلْكَـٰفِرُونَ ۝

87. Y*a* baniyya i*thh*aboo fata*h*assasoo min yoosufa waakheehi wal*a* tay-asoo min raw*h*i All*a*hi innahu l*a* yay-asu min raw*h*i All*a*hi ill*a* alqawmu alk*a*firoon**a**

12:87. "O my sons! Go and make enquiries about Joseph and his brother, and despair not of getting relief from Allah. Indeed, none but the people who suppress the Truth despair of getting relief from Allah."

فَلَمَّا دَخَلُواْ عَلَيْهِ قَالُواْ يَـٰٓأَيُّهَا ٱلْعَزِيزُ مَسَّنَا وَأَهْلَنَا ٱلضُّرُّ وَجِئْنَا بِبِضَـٰعَةٍ مُّزْجَىٰةٍ فَأَوْفِ لَنَا ٱلْكَيْلَ وَتَصَدَّقْ عَلَيْنَآ إِنَّ ٱللَّهَ يَجْزِى ٱلْمُتَصَدِّقِينَ ۝

88. Falamm*a* dakhaloo AAalayhi q*a*loo y*a* ayyuh*a* alAAazeezu massan*a* waahlan*a* al*dd*urru waji/n*a* bibi*da*AAatin muzj*a*tin faawfi lan*a* alkayla wata*s*addaq AAalayn*a* inna All*a*ha yajzee almuta*s*addiqeen**a**

12:88. So when the brothers came back to Joseph, they said, "Sir! Distress has afflicted us, and our family and we have brought but little capital to pay for the rations. Give us the full ration and be charitable to us. Allah does indeed reward those that are charitable."

قَالَ هَلْ عَلِمْتُم مَّا فَعَلْتُم بِيُوسُفَ وَأَخِيهِ إِذْ أَنتُمْ جَـٰهِلُونَ ﴿٨٩﴾

89. Q*a*la hal AAalimtum m*a* faAAaltum biyoosufa waakheehi i*th* antum j*a*hiloon*a*

12:89. He said, "Do you know how you treated Joseph and his brother in your ignorance?"

قَالُوٓاْ أَءِنَّكَ لَأَنتَ يُوسُفُ قَالَ أَنَا۠ يُوسُفُ وَهَـٰذَآ أَخِى قَدْ مَنَّ ٱللَّهُ عَلَيْنَآ إِنَّهُۥ مَن يَتَّقِ وَيَصْبِرْ فَإِنَّ ٱللَّهَ لَا يُضِيعُ أَجْرَ ٱلْمُحْسِنِينَ ﴿٩٠﴾

90. Q*a*loo a-innaka laanta yoosufa q*a*la an*a* yoosufu wah*atha* akhee qad manna All*a*hu AAalayn*a* innahu man yattaqi waya*s*bir fa-inna All*a*ha l*a* yudeeAAu ajra almu*h*sineen*a*

12:90. They said, "Are you indeed Joseph?" He said, "I am Joseph, and this is my brother. Allah has certainly been gracious to us. Indeed, such is the reward for him who fears Allah and exercises patience. And, indeed, Allah does not let the reward, of those who do good, go waste."

قَالُوا۟ تَٱللَّهِ لَقَدْ ءَاثَرَكَ ٱللَّهُ عَلَيْنَا وَإِن كُنَّا لَخَـٰطِئِينَ ﴿٩١﴾

91. Q*a*loo taAll*a*hi laqad *a*tharaka All*a*hu AAalayn*a* wa-in kunn*a* lakha*ti*-een*a*

12:91. They said, "By Allah! HE has certainly chosen you over us, and we were indeed the sinners."

قَـالَ لَا تَـثْرِيبَ عَلَيْكُـمُ ٱلْيَـوْمَ يَغْفِرُ ٱللَّـهُ لَكُـمْ وَهُـوَ أَرْحَـمُ ٱلرَّاحِمِينَ ۝

92. Qala la tathreeba AAalaykumu alyawma yaghfiru Allahu lakum wahuwa arhamu alrrahimeena

12:92. He said, "No reproof against you this day. Allah may forgive you, and He is the most Merciful."

ٱذْهَبُواْ بِقَمِيصِى هَـذَا فَأَلْقُوهُ عَلَىٰ وَجْهِ أَبِى يَأْتِ بَصِيرًا وَأْتُونِى بِأَهْلِكُمْ أَجْمَعِينَ ۝

93. Ithhaboo biqameesee hatha faalqoohu AAala wajhi abee ya/ti baseeran wa/toonee bi-ahlikum ajmaAAeena

12:93. "Take this shirt of mine and put it on my father's face. He will be able to see. And then come back to me with your entire family."

وَلَمَّا فَصَلَتِ ٱلْعِيرُ قَالَ أَبُوهُمْ إِنِّى لَأَجِدُ رِيحَ يُوسُفَ لَوْلَا أَن تُفَنِّدُونِ

94. Walamm*a* fasalati alAAeeru *q*ala aboohum innee laajidu ree*h*a yoosufa lawl*a* an tufannidooni

---

12:94. And when the caravan had set out, their father said, "I do indeed get the smell of Joseph, unless you consider me delirious."

قَالُوا۟ تَٱللَّهِ إِنَّكَ لَفِى ضَلَـٰلِكَ ٱلْقَدِيمِ ﴿٩٥﴾

95. *Q*aloo taAll*a*hi innaka lafee *d*al*a*lika alqadeem*i*

12:95. Those who were there with him said, "By Allah, you are indeed in your old error."[14]

---

14. It may well be remembered that at that stage Joseph's brothers had not yet returned to their father; they were still on their way back. It was the other people with him then saying this to him. They thought that the old man had become senile in his remembrance of the long-lost Joseph.

فَلَمَّآ أَن جَآءَ ٱلْبَشِيرُ أَلْقَىٰهُ عَلَىٰ وَجْهِهِۦ فَٱرْتَدَّ بَصِيرًا ۖ قَالَ أَلَمْ أَقُل لَّكُمْ إِنِّىٓ أَعْلَمُ مِنَ ٱللَّهِ مَا لَا تَعْلَمُونَ ﴿٩٦﴾

96. Falamm*a* an j*a*a albasheeru alq*a*hu AAal*a* wajhihi fairtadda ba*s*eeran *q*ala alam aqul lakum innee aAAlamu mina All*a*hi m*a* l*a* taAAlamoona

---

12:96. And when the bearer of good news (Joseph's brother with Joseph's shirt) did arrive, he put the shirt on the face of Jacob, who then got back his sight. Jacob said, "Did I not tell you that I know from Allah what you know not?"

قَالُوا۟ يَـٰٓأَبَانَا ٱسْتَغْفِرْ لَنَا ذُنُوبَنَآ إِنَّا كُنَّا خَـٰطِـِٔينَ ۝

97. Q*a*loo *ya* ab*a*na istaghfir lan*a* *th*unoobana inn*a* kunn*a* kh*a*ti-een**a**

12:97. They said, "O our father! Pray for forgiveness of our sins. We indeed did wrong."

قَالَ سَوْفَ أَسْتَغْفِرُ لَكُمْ رَبِّىٓ إِنَّهُۥ هُوَ ٱلْغَفُورُ ٱلرَّحِيمُ ۝

98. Q*a*la sawfa astaghfiru lakum rabbee innahu huwa alghafooru alrra*h*eem**u**

12:98. The father said, "I will pray to my Lord to forgive you. He is indeed Forgiving, Merciful.

فَلَمَّا دَخَلُوا۟ عَلَىٰ يُوسُفَ ءَاوَىٰٓ إِلَيْهِ أَبَوَيْهِ وَقَالَ ٱدْخُلُوا۟ مِصْرَ إِن شَآءَ ٱللَّهُ ءَامِنِينَ ۝

99. Falamm*a* dakhaloo AAal*a* yoosufa *a*wa ilayhi abawayhi waq*a*la odkhuloo mi*s*ra in sh*a*a All*a*hu *a*mineen**a**

12:99. When they then came to Joseph, he got his parents to stay with him and said, "Welcome to Egypt. You will, Allah willing, be safe here."

وَرَفَعَ أَبَوَيْهِ عَلَى ٱلْعَرْشِ وَخَرُّواْ لَهُۥ سُجَّدًا ۖ وَقَالَ يَتَأَبَتِ هَٰذَا تَأْوِيلُ رُءْيَٰىَ مِن قَبْلُ قَدْ جَعَلَهَا رَبِّى حَقًّا ۖ وَقَدْ أَحْسَنَ بِىٓ إِذْ أَخْرَجَنِى مِنَ ٱلسِّجْنِ وَجَآءَ بِكُم مِّنَ ٱلْبَدْوِ مِنۢ بَعْدِ أَن نَّزَغَ ٱلشَّيْطَٰنُ بَيْنِى وَبَيْنَ إِخْوَتِىٓ ۚ إِنَّ رَبِّى لَطِيفٌ لِّمَا يَشَآءُ ۚ إِنَّهُۥ هُوَ ٱلْعَلِيمُ ٱلْحَكِيمُ

100. WarafaAAa abawayhi AAal*a* alAAarshi wakharroo lahu sujjadan waq*a*la *ya* abati *ha*tha ta/weelu ru/*ya*ya min qablu qad jaAAalah*a* rabbee *h*aqqan waqad a*h*sana bee i*th* akhrajanee mina alssijni waj*a*a bikum mina albadwi min baAAdi an nazagha alshshay*ta*nu baynee wabayna ikhwatee inna rabbee la*t*eefun lim*a* yash*a*o innahu huwa alAAaleemu al*h*akeem*u*

12:100. And Joseph raised his parents upon the throne; and they fell in prostration before him.[15] And he said, "O my father! This is the interpretation of the dream I had seen before.[16] My Lord has indeed made it come true. And He was indeed kind to me when He brought me out from the prison and brought you from the desert after the Satan had fomented discord between me and my brothers. My Lord is indeed benevolent to whom He pleases. He is indeed Knowledgeable, Wise."

---

15. Apparently, Joseph arranged for a sort of ceremony to welcome his parents and brothers to Egypt, and in that ceremony, he gave his parents the highest honour – a ceremonial throne to sit on. There the parents and the brothers fell in prostration before Joseph in recognition of the high position he had acquired, by Allah's grace, despite the brothers treating him very cruelly in his childhood. About prostration per se, refer study notes 2:27 and 2:28 on Qur'aanic Chapter 2.

16. Refer <u>Verse 12:4</u>.

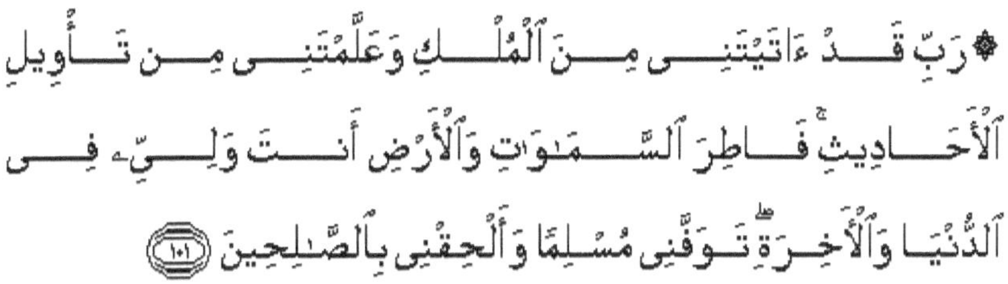

101. Rabbi qad *a*taytanee mina almulki waAAAallamtanee min ta/weeli al-a*h*adeethi fa*t*ira alssam*a*w*a*ti waal-ar*d*i anta waliyyee fee aldduny*a* waal-*a*khirati tawaffanee musliman waal*h*iqnee bial*s*sali*h*eena

---

12:101. "My Lord! You have given me some political power and taught me some knowledge on interpretation of events. Originator of the heavens and the earth! You are my *wali*[17] in this world and the Hereafter. Make me die as one who willingly submits to You and make me join the ranks of the righteous people."

---

17. Refer study note 2:154 on Chapter 2 for the comprehensive Qur'aanic meaning of this term.

---

102. *Th*alika min anb*a*-i alghaybi noo*h*eehi ilayka wam*a* kunta ladayhim i*th* ajmaAAoo amrahum wahum yamkuroona

---

12:102. That is from annals of the unseen past which We reveal to you. And you were not with them[18] when they got together to act, and they conspired.

---

18. Brothers of Joseph.

وَمَآ أَكْثَرُ ٱلنَّاسِ وَلَوْ حَرَصْتَ بِمُؤْمِنِينَ ۝

103. Wam*a* aktharu alnn*a*si walaw *h*arasta bimu/mineena

12:103. And most men will not believe, though you desire eagerly that they believe.

وَمَا تَسْـَٔلُهُمْ عَلَيْهِ مِنْ أَجْرٍ إِنْ هُوَ إِلَّا ذِكْرٌ لِّلْعَٰلَمِينَ ۝

104. Wam*a* tas-aluhum AAalayhi min ajrin in huwa ill*a* *th*ikrun lilAA*a*lameena

12:104. And you ask them not for any reward for this[19]. It is nothing but that which all human beings need to constantly refer to for rightful decisions and actions in their respective worlds[20].

19. The Qur'aan.

20. Refer study note 1:5 on Chapter 1.

وَكَأَيِّن مِّنْ ءَايَةٍ فِى ٱلسَّمَٰوَٰتِ وَٱلْأَرْضِ يَمُرُّونَ عَلَيْهَا وَهُمْ عَنْهَا مُعْرِضُونَ ۝

105. Wakaayyin min *a*yatin fee alssam*awa*ti waal-ar*d*i yamurroona AAalayh*a* wahum AAanh*a* muAAari*d*oona

---

12:105. And how many a sign, in the heavens and the earth, do they pass by? And yet they turn aside from it! [21]

---

21. The very tips of our fingers and everything, little or big, around us in this world and in the unimaginably vast universe over us provide irrefutable signs of the existence of an Unseen, but All powerful, Being, Who can do and undo anything. And there are signs that provide proof that the Qur'aan is a Message of Guidance from that Being to the entire mankind. It is a pity that most of mankind remains blind to these signs galore.

وَمَا يُؤْمِنُ أَكْثَرُهُم بِاللَّهِ إِلَّا وَهُم مُّشْرِكُونَ ﴿١٠٦﴾

106. Wam*a* yu/minu aktharuhum biAll*a*hi ill*a* wahum mushrikoona

---

12:106. And most of them do not believe in Allah without worshipping others besides Him.

أَفَأَمِنُوٓا۟ أَن تَأْتِيَهُمْ غَاشِيَةٌ مِّنْ عَذَابِ اللَّهِ أَوْ تَأْتِيَهُمُ السَّاعَةُ بَغْتَةً وَهُمْ لَا يَشْعُرُونَ ﴿١٠٧﴾

107. Afaaminoo an ta/tiyahum gh*a*shiyatun min AAa*tha*bi All*a*hi aw ta/tiyahumu alss*a*AAatu baghtatan wahum l*a* yashAAuroon*a*

12:107. Do they then feel secure that some punishment from Allah will not envelope them or that the Hour[22] may not come to them suddenly and unknowingly?

---

22. The Last Day.

قُلْ هَـٰذِهِۦ سَبِيلِىٓ أَدْعُوٓاْ إِلَى ٱللَّهِ عَلَىٰ بَصِيرَةٍ أَنَا۠ وَمَنِ ٱتَّبَعَنِى ۖ وَسُبْحَـٰنَ ٱللَّهِ وَمَآ أَنَا۠ مِنَ ٱلْمُشْرِكِينَ ۝

108. Qul hathihi sabeelee adAAoo ila Allahi AAala baseeratin ana wamani ittabaAAanee wasubhana Allahi wama ana mina almushrikeena

---

12:108. Say, "This is my path: I call to Allah. I and my followers are on right guidance. And glory is to Allah! I am not one of those who worship others besides Allah."

وَمَآ أَرْسَلْنَا مِن قَبْلِكَ إِلَّا رِجَالًا نُّوحِىٓ إِلَيْهِم مِّنْ أَهْلِ ٱلْقُرَىٰٓ أَفَلَمْ يَسِيرُواْ فِى ٱلْأَرْضِ فَيَنظُرُواْ كَيْفَ كَانَ عَـٰقِبَةُ ٱلَّذِينَ مِن قَبْلِهِمْ وَلَدَارُ ٱلْآخِرَةِ خَيْرٌ لِّلَّذِينَ ٱتَّقَوْاْ أَفَلَا تَعْقِلُونَ ۝

109. Wama arsalna min qablika illa rijalan noohee ilayhim min ahli alqura afalam yaseeroo fee al-ardi fayanthuroo kayfa kana AAaqibatu allatheena min qablihim waladaru al-akhirati khayrun lillatheena ittaqaw afala taAAqiloona

---

12:109. And We did not send before you any but men, from among the same communities, to whom We sent revelations. Have they not then travelled on land and seen for themselves what end those before them met with? And the abode of the Hereafter is certainly better for those who fear Allah. Do you not understand this?

حَتَّىٰ إِذَا ٱسْتَيْـَٔسَ ٱلرُّسُلُ وَظَنُّوٓاْ أَنَّهُمْ قَدْ كُذِبُواْ جَآءَهُمْ نَصْرُنَا فَنُجِّىَ مَن نَّشَآءُ وَلَا يُرَدُّ بَأْسُنَا عَنِ ٱلْقَوْمِ ٱلْمُجْرِمِينَ ۝

110. *Hatta itha* istay-asa alrrusulu wa*th*annoo annahum qad ku*th*iboo *j*aahum na*s*runa fanujjiya man nash*a*o wal*a* yuraddu ba/sun*a* AAani alqawmi almujrimeen**a**

12:110. The Messengers continued propagating the divine Message to the people until the Messengers despaired and reckoned that the people would not believe them. Then did Our help come to them and every person, whom We pleased, was saved. And Our punishment was not dispensed with for the sinners.

لَقَدْ كَانَ فِى قَصَصِهِمْ عِبْرَةٌ لِّأُوْلِى ٱلْأَلْبَـٰبِ مَا كَانَ حَدِيثًا يُفْتَرَىٰ وَلَـٰكِن تَصْدِيقَ ٱلَّذِى بَيْنَ يَدَيْهِ وَتَفْصِيلَ كُلِّ شَىْءٍ وَهُدًى وَرَحْمَةً لِّقَوْمٍ يُؤْمِنُونَ ۝

111. Laqad k*a*na fee qa*s*a*s*ihim AAibratun li-olee al-alb*a*bi m*a* k*a*na *h*adeethan yuftara wal*a*kin ta*s*deeqa alla*th*ee bayna yadayhi watafseela kulli shay-in wahudan wara*h*matan liqawmin yu/minoon**a**

12:111. In their annals there is certainly a lesson for those endowed with insight.[23] This is not a fabricated *hadeeth*[24], but a confirmation of what has preceded it and a detailed explanation of all things and a guide and a mercy to people who believe.

23. The Qur'aanic narrative in relation to Joseph ends at this point. What follows in the remaining portion of this Verse – as the context therein itself clearly indicates – refers to the Qur'aanic Message as a whole.

24. *Hadeeth* literally means a saying. And in that meaning of the term, the Verse reiterates that nothing mentioned in the Qur'aan is fabricated. But in the context of the later (after the death of the Prophet) development of *ahaadeeth* (collection of sayings attributed to the Prophet and his companions) as a parallel source of Islam along with the Qur'aan, there is a divine forecast here that some of such *ahaadeeth* could be fabricated. There is also a confirmation here that the Qur'aan itself contains all the necessary details, nipping the contention in the bud that the Qur'aan, by itself, is incomplete and therefore needs *ahaadeeth* as a complementary source of Islam.

سُوْرَةُ الرَّعْدِ

Chapter 13: Ar-Ruad (The Thunder)

بِسْمِ اللهِ الرَّحْمٰنِ الرَّحِيْمِ

In the Name of Allah, the Gracious, the Merciful

الٓمٓرۚ تِلْكَ ءَايَٰتُ ٱلْكِتَٰبِۗ وَٱلَّذِىٓ أُنزِلَ إِلَيْكَ مِن رَّبِّكَ ٱلْحَقُّ وَلَٰكِنَّ أَكْثَرَ ٱلنَّاسِ لَا يُؤْمِنُونَ ﴿١﴾

1. Alif-lam-meem-r*a* tilka *a*y*a*tu alkit*a*bi waalla*th*ee onzila ilayka min rabbika al*h*aqqu wal*a*kinna akthara alnn*a*si l*a* yu/minoon**a**

13:1. Alif Lam Meem Ra. Those are Verses of **the Book**. And that which is revealed to you from your Lord is the truth, but most people believe not.

ٱللَّهُ ٱلَّذِى رَفَعَ ٱلسَّمَٰوَٰتِ بِغَيْرِ عَمَدٍ تَرَوْنَهَاۖ ثُمَّ ٱسْتَوَىٰ عَلَى ٱلْعَرْشِۖ وَسَخَّرَ ٱلشَّمْسَ وَٱلْقَمَرَۖ كُلٌّ يَجْرِى لِأَجَلٍ مُّسَمًّىۚ يُدَبِّرُ ٱلْأَمْرَ يُفَصِّلُ ٱلْأَيَٰتِ لَعَلَّكُم بِلِقَآءِ رَبِّكُمْ تُوقِنُونَ ﴿٢﴾

2. All*a*hu alla*th*ee rafaAAa alssam*a*w*a*ti bighayri AAamadin tarawnah*a* thumma istaw*a* AAal*a* alAAarshi wasakhkhara alshshamsa waalqamara kullun yajree li-ajalin musamman yudabbiru al-amra yufa*ss*ilu al-*a*y*a*ti laAAallakum biliq*a*-i rabbikum tooqinoon**a**

157

13:2. Allah is the One Who raised the heavens without any visible support. He then established Himself on the Throne[1]. And He made the sun and the moon subservient. Each pursues its course till an appointed time. He is the Commander and the Governor. He explains the Verses/signs in detail so that you may be certain of meeting your Lord.

---

1. Refer study note 55 under <u>Verse 9:129</u>.

وَهُوَ ٱلَّذِى مَدَّ ٱلْأَرْضَ وَجَعَلَ فِيهَا رَوَٰسِىَ وَأَنْهَٰرًا ۖ وَمِن كُلِّ ٱلثَّمَرَٰتِ جَعَلَ فِيهَا زَوْجَيْنِ ٱثْنَيْنِ ۖ يُغْشِى ٱلَّيْلَ ٱلنَّهَارَ ۚ إِنَّ فِى ذَٰلِكَ لَءَايَٰتٍ لِّقَوْمٍ يَتَفَكَّرُونَ ۝

3. Wahuwa alla*thee* madda al-ar*da* wajaAAala feeh*a* rawa*s*iya waanh*a*ran wamin kulli alththamar*a*ti jaAAala feeh*a* zawjayni ithnayni yughshee allayla alnnah*a*ra inna fee *tha*lika la*a*yatin liqawmin yatafakkaroona

---

13:3. And He is the One Who has stretched the earth to make mountains and rivers therein. And of every kind of fruit He made a pair mate therein.[2] He draws the night as a veil over the day. Indeed, there are signs in that for people who reflect.

---

2. Every fruit-bearing tree/plant has male stamens and female pistils in the flowers that it produces before the fruits appear. Most flowers have both the reproductive organs within themselves. Bees and insects play their parts in transferring the pollen grains from the stamens to the pistils which then get pollinated to form fruits.

وَفِى ٱلْأَرْضِ قِطَعٌ مُّتَجَـٰوِرَٰتٌ وَجَنَّٰتٌ مِّنْ أَعْنَـٰبٍ وَزَرْعٌ وَنَخِيلٌ صِنْوَانٌ وَغَيْرُ صِنْوَانٍ يُسْقَىٰ بِمَآءٍ وَٰحِدٍ وَنُفَضِّلُ بَعْضَهَا عَلَىٰ بَعْضٍ فِى ٱلْأُكُلِ إِنَّ فِى ذَٰلِكَ لَءَايَـٰتٍ لِّقَوْمٍ يَعْقِلُونَ ۝

4. Wafee al-ar*d*i qi*t*aAAun mutaj*a*wir*a*tun wajann*a*tun min aAAn*a*bin wazarAAun wanakheelun *s*inw*a*nun waghayru *s*inw*a*nin yusq*a* bim*a*-in w*ah*idin wanufa*dd*ilu baAAdaha AAal*a* baAA*d*in fee alokuli inna fee *tha*lika la*a*y*a*tin liqawmin yaAAqiloon**a**

13:4. And on the earth there are tracts side by side with gardens of grapes and corn and palm trees – having one common root and others having distinct roots[3] – all irrigated with same water. And yet We make some of them excel others in flavour. There are signs indeed in that for people who understand.

---

3. Bamboo trees grow in clusters with common root and date-palm trees have distinct roots.

۞ وَإِن تَعْجَبْ فَعَجَبٌ قَوْلُهُمْ أَءِذَا كُنَّا تُرَٰبًا أَءِنَّا لَفِى خَلْقٍ جَدِيدٍ أُوْلَـٰٓئِكَ ٱلَّذِينَ كَفَرُواْ بِرَبِّهِمْ وَأُوْلَـٰٓئِكَ ٱلْأَغْلَـٰلُ فِىٓ أَعْنَاقِهِمْ وَأُوْلَـٰٓئِكَ أَصْحَـٰبُ ٱلنَّارِ هُمْ فِيهَا خَـٰلِدُونَ ۝

5. Wa-in taAAjab faAAajabun qawluhum a-i*tha* kunn*a* tur*a*ban a-inn*a* lafee khalqin jadeedin ol*a*-ika alla*thee*na kafaroo birabbihim waol*a*-ika al-aghl*a*lu fee aAAn*a*qihim waol*a*-ika a*s*-*ha*bu alnn*a*ri hum feeh*a* kh*a*lidoona

---

13:5. And if you would consider anything as strange, then strange it is that they say, "When we turn to dust, shall we even then be there in a new creation?" These are they, who suppress the Truth regarding their Lord. And they shall have chains round their necks, and they shall be the inmates of the Fire. In it they shall ever be.

وَيَسْتَعْجِلُونَكَ بِالسَّيِّئَةِ قَبْلَ الْحَسَنَةِ وَقَدْ خَلَتْ مِن قَبْلِهِمُ الْمَثُلَاتُ وَإِنَّ رَبَّكَ لَذُو مَغْفِرَةٍ لِّلنَّاسِ عَلَىٰ ظُلْمِهِمْ وَإِنَّ رَبَّكَ لَشَدِيدُ الْعِقَابِ ﴿٦﴾

6. WayastaAAjiloonaka bialssayyi-ati qabla alhasanati waqad khalat min qablihimu almathulatu wa-inna rabbaka lathoo maghfiratin lilnnasi AAala thulmihim wa-inna rabbaka lashadeedu alAAiqabi

---

13:6. And they ask you to hasten what is not good rather than what is good, and there certainly have been examples of those before them[4]. And indeed, your Lord is full of forgiveness for people, notwithstanding their wrongdoings. And indeed, your Lord is severe in punishment.

---

4. I.e., examples of earlier peoples like AAad, Thamood, Lot's people etc. who had been punished in this world itself for their intransigence.

وَيَقُولُ الَّذِينَ كَفَرُوا لَوْلَا أُنزِلَ عَلَيْهِ ءَايَةٌ مِّن رَّبِّهِ إِنَّمَا أَنتَ مُنذِرٌ وَلِكُلِّ قَوْمٍ هَادٍ ﴿٧﴾

7. Wayaqoolu allatheena kafaroo lawla onzila AAalayhi ayatun min rabbihi innama anta munthirun walikulli qawmin hadin

---

13:7. And those who suppress the Truth say, "Why has not a sign been sent down upon him from his Lord?" You are only a warner and, for every people, a guide.[5]

---

5. The divine guidance, in the form of the Qur'aan, that the last Prophet (peace be on him) brought, was not meant only for the Arabs, but for the entire mankind till the Last Day. The earlier peoples that lived before the Prophet's time, had their own individual Prophets, who had been given the capacity of performing miraculous acts to convince those pre-historic peoples that they really had come with Messages from Allah Almighty. The Last Prophet with the last divine Message had come at the threshold of the modern age with its proliferation of knowledge and the means to preserve and communicate that knowledge universally. There was therefore no need for those miracles. It was Allah's Will that the peoples of this age should believe in Him, under the guidance of His last Message, with the help of the vast knowledge that they now possess.

ٱللَّهُ يَعْلَمُ مَا تَحْمِلُ كُلُّ أُنثَىٰ وَمَا تَغِيضُ ٱلْأَرْحَامُ وَمَا تَزْدَادُ وَكُلُّ شَىْءٍ عِندَهُۥ بِمِقْدَارٍ ۝

8. All*a*hu yaAAlamu m*a* ta*h*milu kullu ontha wam*a* taghee*d*u al-ar*ha*mu wam*a* tazd*a*du wakullu shay-in AAindahu bimiqd*a*rin

---

13:8. Allah knows what any female conceives, and what makes the wombs shrink and what makes them swell. And everything with Him is measured.[6]

---

6. The science of embryology has opened for us the secrets of the womb. A study of this science should give us enough evidence of an Unseen Hand intricately and intelligently fashioning a tiny speck into a fully grown foetus ready to come out in the open world. When the knowledge of such miracles of creation is made available to modern man, he stands in no need of the miracles brought by Prophets in the pre-historic ages. Refer preceding study note 5 in this context.

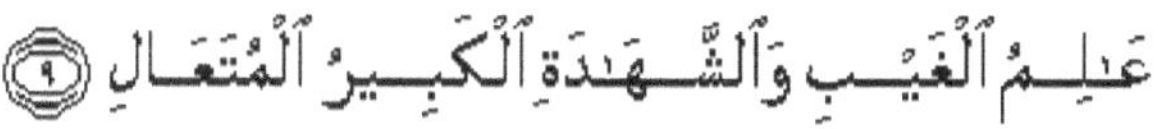

عَٰلِمُ ٱلْغَيْبِ وَٱلشَّهَٰدَةِ ٱلْكَبِيرُ ٱلْمُتَعَالِ ۝

9. AAalimu alghaybi waalshshahadati alkabeeru almutaAAali

13:9. Allah has the knowledge of the unseen and the seen. HE is the One Who is Great, the One Who is High/Exalted.

سَوَآءٌ مِّنكُم مَّنْ أَسَرَّ ٱلْقَوْلَ وَمَن جَهَرَ بِهِۦ وَمَنْ هُوَ مُسْتَخْفٍ بِٱلَّيْلِ وَسَارِبٌ بِٱلنَّهَارِ ﴿١٠﴾

10. Sawaon minkum man asarra alqawla waman jahara bihi waman huwa mustakhfin biallayli wasaribun bialnnahari

---

13:10. The one among you who speaks secretively, the one who speaks openly, the one who hides by night and the one who moves about freely by day – they are all the same for Allah; nothing can escape His notice.

لَهُۥ مُعَقِّبَٰتٌ مِّنْ بَيْنِ يَدَيْهِ وَمِنْ خَلْفِهِۦ يَحْفَظُونَهُۥ مِنْ أَمْرِ ٱللَّهِ إِنَّ ٱللَّهَ لَا يُغَيِّرُ مَا بِقَوْمٍ حَتَّىٰ يُغَيِّرُواْ مَا بِأَنفُسِهِمْ وَإِذَآ أَرَادَ ٱللَّهُ بِقَوْمٍ سُوٓءًا فَلَا مَرَدَّ لَهُۥ وَمَا لَهُم مِّن دُونِهِۦ مِن وَالٍ ﴿١١﴾

11. Lahu muAAaqqibatun min bayni yadayhi wamin khalfihi yahfathoonahu min amri Allahi inna Allaha la yughayyiru ma biqawmin hatta yughayyiroo ma bi-anfusihim wa-itha arada Allahu biqawmin soo-an fala maradda lahu wama lahum min doonihi min walin

---

13:11. For every human being there are angels who take turns, in front of him/her and behind, to guard him/her by Allah's command. Allah does indeed not change the condition of a people until they themselves change it.[7] And when Allah wills adversity on a people, there is no averting it. And besides Him they have no ruling authority to defend and take care of them.

---

7. For centuries after the revelation of the Qur'aan, Muslims enjoyed dominance over others, both politically and culturally. They then, by and large, adhered to Qur'aanic teachings. But, now, the Muslims are down and out among the modern nations of the world. Allah did not change their condition; they changed it themselves. They stopped adhering to Qur'aanic teachings.

هُوَ ٱلَّذِى يُرِيكُمُ ٱلۡبَرۡقَ خَوۡفًا وَطَمَعًا وَيُنشِئُ ٱلسَّحَابَ ٱلثِّقَالَ ﴿١٢﴾

12. Huwa alla*th*ee yureekumu albarqa khawfan wa*r*amaAAan wayunshi-o alssa*h*aba alththiq*a*la

---

13:12. He it is Who shows you the lightning that causes both fear and hope. And He it is Who brings up the heavy cloud.[8]

---

8. The modern world, despite all its technological advances, is still heavily dependent on this divine mercy of rainfall for its sustenance. And yet, mankind, by and large, is thanklessly indifferent to the Provider of this vital need.

وَيُسَبِّحُ ٱلرَّعۡدُ بِحَمۡدِهِۦ وَٱلۡمَلَٰٓئِكَةُ مِنۡ خِيفَتِهِۦ وَيُرۡسِلُ ٱلصَّوَٰعِقَ فَيُصِيبُ بِهَا مَن يَشَآءُ وَهُمۡ يُجَٰدِلُونَ فِى ٱللَّهِ وَهُوَ شَدِيدُ ٱلۡمِحَالِ ﴿١٣﴾

13. Wayusabbi*h*u alrraAAdu bi*h*amdihi waalmal*a*-ikatu min kheefatihi wayursilu al*ss*awaAAiqa fayu*s*eebu bi*h*a man yash*a*o wahum yuj*a*diloona fee All*a*hi wahuwa shadeedu almi*h*ali

13:13. And the thunder proclaims His glory with His praise, and the angels stand in awe of Him. And He sends the thunderbolts and hits with them whom He wills. And they quarrel among themselves about Allah, whereas He is extremely powerful.

14. Lahu daAAwatu al*h*aqqi waalla*th*eena yadAAoona min doonihi l*a* yastajeeboona lahum bishay-in ill*a* kabasi*t*i kaffayhi il*a* alm*a*-i liyablugha f*a*hu wam*a* huwa bib*a*lighihi wam*a* duAA*a*o alk*a*fireena ill*a* fee *d*al*a*lin

13:14. To Him is the true prayer! And those whom they pray to besides Allah give them no response on anything. It is just like one stretching his two hands out for water to reach his mouth, but it reaches not. And the prayer of those who suppress the Truth is nothing but an illusion.

15. Walill*a*hi yasjudu man fee alssam*a*w*a*ti waal-ar*d*i *t*awAAan wakarhan wa*th*ilaluhum bialghuduwwi waal-a*s*ali

13:15. And to Allah does prostrate everything in the heavens and the earth, willingly and unwillingly, as their shadows do morning and evening.[9]

9. All things in the entire universe, in other words, are subservient to Allah.

قُلْ مَن رَّبُّ ٱلسَّمَـٰوَٰتِ وَٱلْأَرْضِ قُلِ ٱللَّهُ قُلْ أَفَٱتَّخَذْتُم مِّن دُونِهِۦٓ أَوْلِيَآءَ لَا يَمْلِكُونَ لِأَنفُسِهِمْ نَفْعًا وَلَا ضَرًّا قُلْ هَلْ يَسْتَوِى ٱلْأَعْمَىٰ وَٱلْبَصِيرُ أَمْ هَلْ تَسْتَوِى ٱلظُّلُمَـٰتُ وَٱلنُّورُ أَمْ جَعَلُوا۟ لِلَّهِ شُرَكَآءَ خَلَقُوا۟ كَخَلْقِهِۦ فَتَشَـٰبَهَ ٱلْخَلْقُ عَلَيْهِمْ قُلِ ٱللَّهُ خَـٰلِقُ كُلِّ شَىْءٍ وَهُوَ ٱلْوَٰحِدُ ٱلْقَهَّـٰرُ ﴿١٦﴾

16. Qul man rabbu alssam*a*wati waal-ar*d*i quli All*a*hu qul afaittakha*th*tum min doonihi awliy*a*a l*a* yamlikoona li-anfusihim nafAAan wal*a* *d*arran qul hal yastawee al-aAAm*a* waalba*s*eeru am hal tastawee al*thth*ulum*a*tu waalnnooru am jaAAaloo lill*a*hi shurak*a*a khalaqoo kakhalqihi fatash*a*baha alkhalqu AAalayhim quli All*a*hu kh*a*liqu kulli shay-in wahuwa alw*a*hidu alqahh*a*ru

13:16. Ask, "Who is the Lord of the heavens and the earth?" Say, "Allah." Ask, "Do you take then, besides Him, *awliya*[10] who have no control over any profit and loss to themselves?" Ask, "Are the blind and those able to see alike? Or can the darknesses and the light be equal? Or have they set up gods besides Allah, who have made creation like He has, and, as a result, the creation creates confusion for them?" Say, "Allah is the Creator of all things. And He is the One and Only, the Almighty!"

10. Refer study note 2:154 **on Chapter 2.**

أَنزَلَ مِنَ ٱلسَّمَآءِ مَآءً فَسَالَتْ أَوْدِيَةٌ بِقَدَرِهَا فَٱحْتَمَلَ ٱلسَّيْلُ زَبَدًا رَّابِيًا وَمِمَّا يُوقِدُونَ عَلَيْهِ فِى ٱلنَّارِ ٱبْتِغَآءَ حِلْيَةٍ أَوْ مَتَٰعٍ زَبَدٌ مِّثْلُهُۥ كَذَٰلِكَ يَضْرِبُ ٱللَّهُ ٱلْحَقَّ وَٱلْبَٰطِلَ فَأَمَّا ٱلزَّبَدُ فَيَذْهَبُ جُفَآءً وَأَمَّا مَا يَنفَعُ ٱلنَّاسَ فَيَمْكُثُ فِى ٱلْأَرْضِ كَذَٰلِكَ يَضْرِبُ ٱللَّهُ ٱلْأَمْثَالَ

17. Anzala mina alssama-i maan fasalat awdiyatun biqadariha faihtamala alssaylu zabadan rabiyan wamimma yooqidoona AAalayhi fee alnnari ibtighaa hilyatin aw mataAAin zabadun mithluhu kathalika yadribu Allahu alhaqqa waalbatila faamma alzzabadu fayathhabu jufaan waamma ma yanfaAAu alnnasa fayamkuthu fee al-ardi kathalika yadribu Allahu al-amthala

---

13:17. He sends down water from the sky. And valleys flow with water as per their given measure. And the stream bears the swelling froth. And from what they melt in the fire for making ornaments or apparatus arises similar froth. Thus, does Allah compare truth with untruth. Then, as for the froth, it just passes away as a worthless thing. And as for that which profits the people, it remains on the earth. Thus, does Allah explain things giving examples.[11]

---

11. Islam, as depicted in the Qur'aan, is the real thing that benefits mankind. All other ways of life, devised and/or manipulated by human hands, is like worthless froth. They are bound, sooner or later, to perish on the surface of this earth, and Islam to prevail.

لِلَّذِينَ ٱسْتَجَابُوا۟ لِرَبِّهِمُ ٱلْحُسْنَىٰ وَٱلَّذِينَ لَمْ يَسْتَجِيبُوا۟ لَهُۥ لَوْ أَنَّ لَهُم مَّا فِى ٱلْأَرْضِ جَمِيعًا وَمِثْلَهُۥ مَعَهُۥ لَٱفْتَدَوْا۟ بِهِۦٓ أُو۟لَٰٓئِكَ لَهُمْ سُوٓءُ ٱلْحِسَابِ وَمَأْوَىٰهُمْ جَهَنَّمُ وَبِئْسَ ٱلْمِهَادُ ۝

18. Lilla*theena* istaj*a*boo lirabbihimu al*h*usn*a* wa**a**lla*theena* lam yastajeeboo lahu law anna lahum m*a* fee al-ar*di* jameeAAan wamithlahu maAAahu laiftadaw bihi ol*a*-ika lahum soo-o al*h*is*a*bi wama/w*a*hum jahannamu wabi/sa almih*a*du

---

13:18. The good is for those who respond to their Lord. And as for those who do not respond to Him, had they all that is in the earth and the like thereof with it, they would certainly offer it for a ransom. An evil reckoning shall await them, and their abode shall be Hell – the worst place to rest in.

۞ أَفَمَن يَعْلَمُ أَنَّمَآ أُنزِلَ إِلَيْكَ مِن رَّبِّكَ ٱلْحَقُّ كَمَنْ هُوَ أَعْمَىٰٓ إِنَّمَا يَتَذَكَّرُ أُو۟لُوا۟ ٱلْأَلْبَٰبِ ﴿١٩﴾

19. Afaman yaAAlamu annam*a* onzila ilayka min rabbika al*h*aqqu kaman huwa aAAm*a* innam*a* yata*th*akkaru oloo al-alb*a*bi

---

13:19. Is he who knows that what has been revealed to you from your Lord is the truth, then, like him who is blind? [12] Only those endowed with insight will ponder on this,

---

12. Every Muslim of today should honestly ponder whether he himself deserves to be included in the first category of people who know. Or is he liable to be included in the second category of those who are blind? The Muslim could deserve inclusion in the first category if, and only if, he believes that everything stated in the Qur'aan is the Truth and nothing but the Truth. But, does he? Let us take one example – one among many. The Qur'aan repeatedly asserts that it explains clearly everything that Allah asks man to follow or abide by. Allah has categorically prohibited *Ar-Riba*. This is an injunction that man has rigorously to follow. Otherwise, the Qur'aan asserts, he is <u>at war</u> with Allah! And, as per the earlier stated Qur'aanic assertion, the term *Ar-Riba* is clearly explained in the Qur'aan itself. But most Muslims, including well-known Islamic scholars, blasphemously believe that *Ar-Riba* is not explained in the Qur'aan!! The scholars are therefore busy giving their own definitions of the Qur'aanic term!!!

ٱلَّذِينَ يُوفُونَ بِعَهْدِ ٱللَّهِ وَلَا يَنقُضُونَ ٱلْمِيثَٰقَ ﴿٢٠﴾

167

20. Alla*th*eena yoofoona biAAahdi All*a*hi wal*a* yanqu*d*oona almeeth*a*q**a**

13:20. Those that fulfill the promise to Allah and break not the covenant, [13]

---

13. The Muslims do, in their daily prayers, make the promise to Allah, "Thee alone we worship; and thee alone we ask for help!" But the moment most of them encounter a problem in this life, they do not hesitate in running to the *mazaar* of a dead saint or bend over backwards to do anything to please any influential human in a position to help them out, by hook or by crook. And, as Muslims, they have entered into a covenant with Allah that they would strictly abide by every Qur'aanic edict. But do they do that?

وَٱلَّذِينَ يَصِلُونَ مَآ أَمَرَ ٱللَّهُ بِهِۦٓ أَن يُوصَلَ وَيَخْشَوْنَ رَبَّهُمْ وَيَخَافُونَ سُوٓءَ ٱلْحِسَابِ ۞

21. Waalla*th*eena ya*s*iloona m*a* amara All*a*hu bihi an yoo*s*ala wayakhshawna rabbahum wayakh*a*foona soo-a al*h*is*a*b**i**

13:21. And those who maintain all the proper relationships that Allah has commanded to be maintained and fear their Lord and dread a bad account of their own deeds.

وَٱلَّذِينَ صَبَرُواْ ٱبْتِغَآءَ وَجْهِ رَبِّهِمْ وَأَقَامُواْ ٱلصَّلَوٰةَ وَأَنفَقُواْ مِمَّا رَزَقْنَـٰهُمْ سِرًّا وَعَلَانِيَةً وَيَدْرَءُونَ بِٱلْحَسَنَةِ ٱلسَّيِّئَةَ أُوْلَـٰٓئِكَ لَهُمْ عُقْبَى ٱلدَّارِ ۞

22. Waalla*th*eena *s*abaroo ibtigh*a*a wajhi rabbihim waaq*a*moo al*s*al*a*ta waanfaqoo mimm*a* razaqn*a*hum sirran waAAal*a*niyatan wayadraoona bial*h*asanati al*s*ayyi-ata ol*a*-ika lahum AAuqb*a* aldd*a*r**i**

13:22. And those who exercise patience seeking the pleasure of their Lord, establish regular prayer, spend out of what We have given them secretly and openly, and repel evil with good. For them is the ultimate/best abode.

جَنَّٰتُ عَدْنٍ يَدْخُلُونَهَا وَمَن صَلَحَ مِنْ ءَابَآئِهِمْ وَأَزْوَٰجِهِمْ وَذُرِّيَّٰتِهِمْ وَٱلْمَلَٰٓئِكَةُ يَدْخُلُونَ عَلَيْهِم مِّن كُلِّ بَابٍ ۝

23. Jannatu AAadnin yadkhuloonaha waman salaha min aba-ihim waazwajihim wathurriyyatihim waalmala-ikatu yadkhuloona AAalayhim min kulli babin

13:23. The gardens of perpetual abode which they will enter along with those who had done good deeds from among their parents and their spouses and their offspring. And the angels will enter in upon them from every gate, saying,

سَلَٰمٌ عَلَيْكُم بِمَا صَبَرْتُمْ فَنِعْمَ عُقْبَى ٱلدَّارِ ۝

24. Salamun AAalaykum bima sabartum faniAAma AAuqba alddari

13:24. "Peace on you because you exercised patience. How excellent, then, is the ultimate/best abode!"

وَٱلَّذِينَ يَنقُضُونَ عَهْدَ ٱللَّهِ مِنْ بَعْدِ مِيثَـٰقِهِۦ وَيَقْطَعُونَ مَآ أَمَرَ ٱللَّهُ بِهِۦٓ أَن يُوصَلَ وَيُفْسِدُونَ فِى ٱلْأَرْضِ أُو۟لَـٰٓئِكَ لَهُمُ ٱللَّعْنَةُ وَلَهُمْ سُوٓءُ ٱلدَّارِ ﴿٢٥﴾

25. Waalla*th*eena yanqu*d*oona AAahda All*a*hi min baAAdi meeth*a*qihi wayaq*t*aAAoona m*a* amara All*a*hu bihi an yoo*s*ala wayufsidoona fee al-ar*d*i ol*a*-ika lahumu allaAAnatu walahum soo-o aldd*a*ri

---

13:25. And those that break the pledge with Allah after affirming it, sever ties that Allah has ordered to be honoured and spread corruption in the land – for them there is the curse and the wicked abode.

ٱللَّهُ يَبْسُطُ ٱلرِّزْقَ لِمَن يَشَآءُ وَيَقْدِرُ وَفَرِحُوا۟ بِٱلْحَيَوٰةِ ٱلدُّنْيَا وَمَا ٱلْحَيَوٰةُ ٱلدُّنْيَا فِى ٱلْأَخِرَةِ إِلَّا مَتَـٰعٌ ﴿٢٦﴾

26. All*a*hu yabsu*t*u alrrizqa liman yash*a*o wayaqdiru wafari*h*oo bial*h*ay*a*ti aldduny*a* wam*a* al*h*ay*a*tu aldduny*a* fee al-*a*khirati ill*a* mata*A*Aun

---

13:26. Allah provides – in abundance or in short measure – for whom He wills. And they rejoice the life of this world, and the life of this world is nothing but a passing provision in the Hereafter.

وَيَقُولُ ٱلَّذِينَ كَفَرُواْ لَوْلَآ أُنزِلَ عَلَيْهِ ءَايَةٌ مِّن رَّبِّهِۦ قُلْ إِنَّ ٱللَّهَ يُضِلُّ مَن يَشَآءُ وَيَهْدِىٓ إِلَيْهِ مَنْ أَنَابَ ﴿٢٧﴾

27. Wayaqoolu alla*theena* kafaroo lawl*a* onzila AAalayhi *a*yatun min rabbihi qul inna All*a*ha yu*d*illu man yash*a*o wayahdee ilayhi man an*a*b**a**

13:27. And those who suppress the Truth say, "Why is not a sign sent down upon him from his Lord?" Say, "Allah does indeed let him go astray whom He wills. And He guides to Himself those who turn to Him."

ٱلَّذِينَ ءَامَنُواْ وَتَطْمَئِنُّ قُلُوبُهُم بِذِكْرِ ٱللَّهِ أَلَا بِذِكْرِ ٱللَّهِ تَطْمَئِنُّ ٱلْقُلُوبُ ﴿٢٨﴾

28. Alla*theena a*manoo wata*t*ma-innu quloobuhum bi*th*ikri All*a*hi al*a* bi*th*ikri All*a*hi ta*t*ma-innu alquloob**u**

13:28. Those who believe and whose hearts find satisfaction in the remembrance of Allah! Surely, in Allah's remembrance hearts do find satisfaction.

ٱلَّذِينَ ءَامَنُواْ وَعَمِلُواْ ٱلصَّٰلِحَٰتِ طُوبَىٰ لَهُمْ وَحُسْنُ مَـَٔابٍ ﴿٢٩﴾

29. Alla*theena a*manoo waAAamiloo al*ss*ali*ha*ti *t*ooba lahum wa*h*usnu ma*a*b**in**

13:29. Those that believe and do good deeds – for them, a state of happiness and a good place to return to.

كَذَٰلِكَ أَرْسَلْنَٰكَ فِىٓ أُمَّةٍ قَدْ خَلَتْ مِن قَبْلِهَآ أُمَمٌ لِّتَتْلُوَاْ عَلَيْهِمُ ٱلَّذِىٓ أَوْحَيْنَآ إِلَيْكَ وَهُمْ يَكْفُرُونَ بِٱلرَّحْمَٰنِ قُلْ هُوَ رَبِّى لَآ إِلَٰهَ إِلَّا هُوَ عَلَيْهِ تَوَكَّلْتُ وَإِلَيْهِ مَتَابِ ﴿٣٠﴾

30. Kathalika arsalnaka fee ommatin qad khalat min qabliha omamun litatluwa AAalayhimu allathee awhayna ilayka wahum yakfuroona bialrrahmani qul huwa rabbee la ilaha illa huwa AAalayhi tawakkaltu wa-ilayhi matabi

13:30. Just as We had sent Messengers to their peoples before, We have sent you to these people now, so that you recite to them what We have revealed to you. And they have been suppressing their belief in the Gracious Being! Say, "He is my Lord. There is no god but Him. In Him do I trust and to Him is my return."

وَلَوْ أَنَّ قُرْءَانًا سُيِّرَتْ بِهِ ٱلْجِبَالُ أَوْ قُطِّعَتْ بِهِ ٱلْأَرْضُ أَوْ كُلِّمَ بِهِ ٱلْمَوْتَىٰ بَل لِّلَّهِ ٱلْأَمْرُ جَمِيعًا أَفَلَمْ يَا۟يْـَٔسِ ٱلَّذِينَ ءَامَنُوٓاْ أَن لَّوْ يَشَآءُ ٱللَّهُ لَهَدَى ٱلنَّاسَ جَمِيعًا وَلَا يَزَالُ ٱلَّذِينَ كَفَرُواْ تُصِيبُهُم بِمَا صَنَعُواْ قَارِعَةٌ أَوْ تَحُلُّ قَرِيبًا مِّن دَارِهِمْ حَتَّىٰ يَأْتِىَ وَعْدُ ٱللَّهِ إِنَّ ٱللَّهَ لَا يُخْلِفُ ٱلْمِيعَادَ ﴿٣١﴾

31. Walaw anna qur-anan suyyirat bihi aljibalu aw quttiAAat bihi al-ardu aw kullima bihi almawta bal lillahi al-amru jameeAAan afalam yay-asi allatheena amanoo an law yashao Allahu lahada alnnasa jameeAAan wala yazalu allatheena kafaroo tuseebuhum bima sanaAAoo qariAAatun aw tahullu qareeban min darihim hatta ya/tiya waAAdu Allahi inna Allaha la yukhlifu almeeAAada

13:31. And the suppressors of the Truth like to think that they would believe if only the mountains were moved by the Qur'aan, or the earth was cut asunder thereby, or the dead were made to speak! But it is Allah Who can do anything and everything. Have the believers then become despaired of the Truth that had Allah so willed, He could have guided all mankind!? And disaster shall not cease to afflict those that suppress the Truth because of what they do, or to strike near their homes, until what Allah has promised comes to pass. And, indeed, Allah fails not to keep the appointment.

وَلَقَدِ ٱسْتُهْزِئَ بِرُسُلٍ مِّن قَبْلِكَ فَأَمْلَيْتُ لِلَّذِينَ كَفَرُواْ ثُمَّ أَخَذْتُهُمْ فَكَيْفَ كَانَ عِقَابِ ﴿٣٢﴾

32. Walaqadi istuhzi-a birusulin min qablika faamlaytu lilla*th*eena kafaroo thumma akha*th*tuhum fakayfa k*a*na AAiq*a*bi

13:32. And Messengers that came before you did get mocked at. And I gave those that suppressed the Truth a long rope, and then seized them. And what a punishment it was!

أَفَمَنْ هُوَ قَآئِمٌ عَلَىٰ كُلِّ نَفْسٍ بِمَا كَسَبَتْ وَجَعَلُواْ لِلَّهِ شُرَكَآءَ قُلْ سَمُّوهُمْ أَمْ تُنَبِّئُونَهُۥ بِمَا لَا يَعْلَمُ فِى ٱلْأَرْضِ أَم بِظَـٰهِرٍ مِّنَ ٱلْقَوْلِ بَلْ زُيِّنَ لِلَّذِينَ كَفَرُواْ مَكْرُهُمْ وَصُدُّواْ عَنِ ٱلسَّبِيلِ وَمَن يُضْلِلِ ٱللَّهُ فَمَا لَهُۥ مِنْ هَادٍ ﴿٣٣﴾

33. Afaman huwa q*a*-imun AAal*a* kulli nafsin bim*a* kasabat wajaAAaloo lill*a*hi shurak*a*a qul sammoohum am tunabbi-oonahu bim*a* l*a* yaAAlamu fee al-ar*d*i am bi*th*ahirin mina alqawli bal zuyyina lilla*th*eena kafaroo makruhum wa*s*uddoo AAani alssabeeli waman yu*d*lili All*a*hu fam*a* lahu min h*a*din

173

13:33. And they worship others besides Allah – the One Who is ever alert over what everybody does and accordingly deserves! Say, "Name them!" Or, do they tell Him something on the earth of which He is not aware? Or, is it just a show that they make with the words they utter? Nay, the intrigue indulged in by the suppressors of the Truth is made to look pleasing to them and they are held back from the Right Path. And him whom Allah has led astray, no one can guide.

لَّهُمْ عَذَابٌ فِى ٱلْحَيَوٰةِ ٱلدُّنْيَا ۖ وَلَعَذَابُ ٱلْأَخِرَةِ أَشَقُّ ۖ وَمَا لَهُم مِّنَ ٱللَّهِ مِن وَاقٍ ۝

34. Lahum AAa*tha*bun fee al*h*ay*a*ti aldduny*a* walaAAa*tha*bu al-*a*khirati ashaqqu wam*a* lahum mina All*a*hi min w*a*q**in**

13:34. For them a punishment in the life of this world. And the punishment of the Hereafter is certainly harder. And, there is none to defend them against Allah.

۞ مَّثَلُ ٱلْجَنَّةِ ٱلَّتِى وُعِدَ ٱلْمُتَّقُونَ ۖ تَجْرِى مِن تَحْتِهَا ٱلْأَنْهَارُ ۖ أُكُلُهَا دَآئِمٌ وَظِلُّهَا ۚ تِلْكَ عُقْبَى ٱلَّذِينَ ٱتَّقَواْ ۖ وَّعُقْبَى ٱلْكَـٰفِرِينَ ٱلنَّارُ ۝

35. Mathalu aljannati allatee wuAAida almuttaqoona tajree min ta*h*tiha al-an*h*aru okuluh*a* da-imun wa*th*illuha tilka AAuqb*a* alla*th*eena ittaqaw waAAuqb*a* alk*a*fireena aln*na*ru

13:35. Some of the things provided in the Garden promised to those who fear Allah: rivers flowing underneath, its fruits and shade everlasting. This is what those who fear Allah shall get in the end. And those who suppress the Truth shall end up in the Fire.

$$\text{وَٱلَّذِينَ ءَاتَيْنَـٰهُمُ ٱلْكِتَـٰبَ يَفْرَحُونَ بِمَآ أُنزِلَ إِلَيْكَ وَمِنَ ٱلْأَحْزَابِ}$$

$$\text{مَن يُنكِرُ بَعْضَهُۥ قُلْ إِنَّمَآ أُمِرْتُ أَنْ أَعْبُدَ ٱللَّهَ وَلَآ أُشْرِكَ بِهِۦ}$$

$$\text{إِلَيْهِ أَدْعُواْ وَإِلَيْهِ مَـَٔابِ ۝}$$

36. Waalla*theena ataynahumu alkitaba yafrahoona bima onzila ilayka wamina al-ahzabi man yunkiru baAAdahu qul innama omirtu an aAAbuda Allaha wala oshrika bihi ilayhi adAAoo wa-ilayhi maabi

---

13:36. And those to whom We have given the Book rejoice in that which has been revealed to you.[14] And among groups of people there are some who deny a part of it. Say, "I am commanded that I should worship only Allah and none else. Him I pray to and to Him I return."

---

14. The divine Book is given to those who believe in it – and not to those who do not believe it to be divine.

$$\text{وَكَذَٰلِكَ أَنزَلْنَـٰهُ حُكْمًا عَرَبِيًّا وَلَئِنِ ٱتَّبَعْتَ أَهْوَآءَهُم بَعْدَمَا جَآءَكَ مِنَ}$$

$$\text{ٱلْعِلْمِ مَا لَكَ مِنَ ٱللَّهِ مِن وَلِيٍّ وَلَا وَاقٍ ۝}$$

37. Waka*thalika anzalnahu hukman AAarabiyyan wala-ini ittabaAAta ahwaahum baAAda ma jaaka mina alAAilmi ma laka mina Allahi min waliyyin wala waqin

---

13:37. And thus have We revealed it as the divine code of conduct for humanity in Arabic[15]. And if you follow their desires after what has come to you of knowledge, you shall have neither any *wali*[16] nor anyone to defend you against Allah.

---

15. It has been clarified in Verses 16:103 and 41:44 that since Allah had chosen an Arab to be His last Messenger for mankind, the Book revealed to this Messenger had necessarily to be in Arabic

16. Refer study note 2:154.

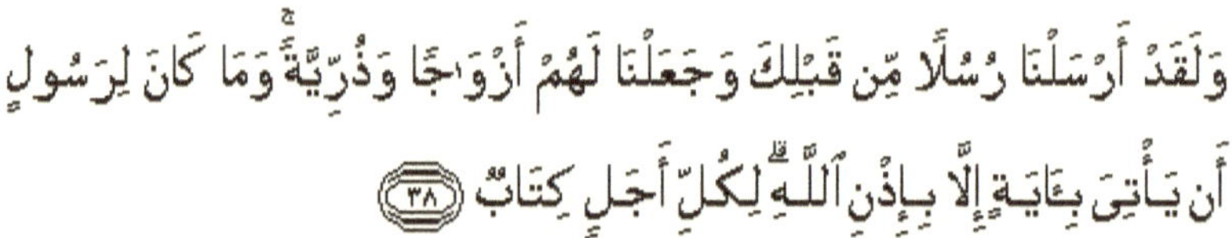

38. Walaqad arsalna rusulan min qablika wajaAAalna lahum azwajan wathurriyyatan wama kana lirasoolin an ya/tiya bi-ayatin illa bi-ithni Allahi likulli ajalin kitabun

13:38. And We had certainly sent Messengers before you and gave them wives and children.[17] And no Messenger could bring a sign save by Allah's leave. [18, 19] For every age there is a Book decreed.

17. This divine statement does indeed give credence to the story among some people that Prphet Jesus (peace on him) did have a wife and children, although most Christians believe that he had not married.

18. There are *ahaadeeth* galore attributing miraculous acts, like those exhibited by earlier Prophets Jesus, Moses etc., to Prophet Muhammad (peace on him) as well. But as Verse 27 above and many other Verses in the Qur'aan clearly indicate, no such miraculous signs were given to the last Prophet. People in the pre-historic times, who had far less knowledge as compared to people now, needed such signs. But with the proliferation of knowledge among the people, Allah wants them to search for His signs in the natural phenomena abounding in nature all around them.

19. But in the context of what follows, in this Verse as well as in the next, the Arabic word *ayah* here could as well mean divine revelation. Most Prophets did not come with divine books individually revealed to them. There were many Prophets between Moses and Jesus, but they all followed the Torah revealed to Moses.

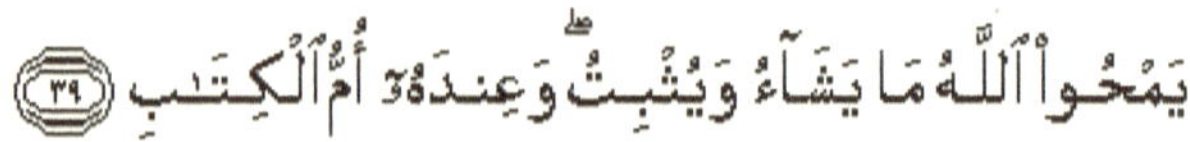

39. Yamhoo Allahu ma yashao wayuthbitu waAAindahu ommu alkitabi

13:39. Allah obliterates or preserves what He wills. And with Him is the Master Copy of the (or the Original) Book.

وَإِن مَّا نُرِيَنَّكَ بَعْضَ ٱلَّذِى نَعِدُهُمْ أَوْ نَتَوَفَّيَنَّكَ فَإِنَّمَا عَلَيْكَ ٱلْبَلَـٰغُ وَعَلَيْنَا ٱلْحِسَابُ ﴿٤٠﴾

40. Wa-in *ma* nuriyannaka baAA*da* alla*thee* naAAiduhum aw natawaffayannaka fa-innam*a* AAalayka albal*a*ghu waAAalayn*a* al*h*is*a*b**u**

13:40. And whether We let you see part of what We promise them, or We cause you to die before that, your responsibility is only the delivery of the divine Message, and it is for Us to call them to account.

أَوَلَمْ يَرَوْاْ أَنَّا نَأْتِى ٱلْأَرْضَ نَنقُصُهَا مِنْ أَطْرَافِهَا وَٱللَّهُ يَحْكُمُ لَا مُعَقِّبَ لِحُكْمِهِۦ وَهُوَ سَرِيعُ ٱلْحِسَابِ ﴿٤١﴾

41. Awa lam yaraw ann*a* na/tee al-ar*d*a nanqu*s*uh*a* min a*t*r*a*fih*a* waAll*a*hu ya*h*kumu l*a* muAAaqqiba li*h*ukmihi wahuwa sareeAAu al*h*is*a*b**i**

13:41. Do they not see that We are closing in on them from all sides? And Allah judges; His judgment is irrevocable. And He is swift to keeping accounts.

وَقَدْ مَكَرَ ٱلَّذِينَ مِن قَبْلِهِمْ فَلِلَّهِ ٱلْمَكْرُ جَمِيعًا يَعْلَمُ مَا تَكْسِبُ كُلُّ نَفْسٍ وَسَيَعْلَمُ ٱلْكُفَّـٰرُ لِمَنْ عُقْبَى ٱلدَّارِ ﴿٤٢﴾

42. Waqad makara alla*theena* min qablihim falill*a*hi almakru jamee*AA*an ya*AA*lamu m*a* taksibu kullu nafsin wasaya*AA*lamu alkuff*a*ru liman *AA*uqb*a* alddari

---

13:42. And those before them did make plans, but all planning is Allah's.[20] He knows what everyone earns, and those who suppress the Truth shall come to know for whom the Ultimate Abode is.

---

20. A man may make a plan for a thing to be done. But that plan will succeed if, and only if, it synchronises with Allah's. In the ultimate analysis, therefore, it is Allah's plan that makes anything happen, and not man's.

وَيَقُولُ ٱلَّذِينَ كَفَرُوٓاْ لَسْتَ مُرْسَلًا قُلْ كَفَىٰ بِٱللَّهِ شَهِيدًا بَيْنِى وَبَيْنَكُمْ وَمَنْ عِندَهُۥ عِلْمُ ٱلْكِتَـٰبِ ﴿٤٣﴾

43. Wayaqoolu alla*theena* kafaroo lasta mursalan qul kaf*a* bi*A*ll*a*hi shaheedan baynee wabaynakum waman *AA*indahu *AA*ilmu alkit*a*bi

---

13:43. And those who suppress the Truth say, "You are not a Messenger of Allah." Say, "Allah – and whoever has knowledge of the Book – is a sufficient witness between me and you."

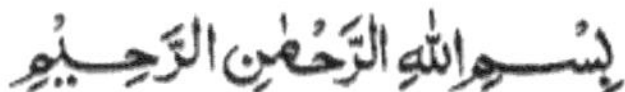

In the Name of Allah, the Gracious, the Merciful

الٓرۚ كِتَـٰبٌ أَنزَلْنَـٰهُ إِلَيْكَ لِتُخْرِجَ ٱلنَّاسَ مِنَ ٱلظُّلُمَـٰتِ إِلَى ٱلنُّورِ بِإِذْنِ رَبِّهِمْ إِلَىٰ صِرَٰطِ ٱلْعَزِيزِ ٱلْحَمِيدِ ①

1. Alif-lam-ra kitabun anzalnahu ilayka litukhrija alnnasa mina alththulumati ila alnnoori bi-ithni rabbihim ila sirati alAAazeezi alhameedi

---

14:1. Alif Lam Ra.[1] A Book that We have revealed to you to bring out mankind, by their Lord's permission, from darknesses towards light – towards the way of the Omnipotent, the Praised One,

---

1. Refer study note 2:1 about such initials appearing at the start of some Qur'aanic Chapters.

ٱللَّهِ ٱلَّذِى لَهُۥ مَا فِى ٱلسَّمَـٰوَٰتِ وَمَا فِى ٱلْأَرْضِ وَوَيْلٌ لِّلْكَـٰفِرِينَ مِنْ عَذَابٍ شَدِيدٍ ②

2. Allahi allathee lahu ma fee alssamawati wama fee al-ardi wawaylun lilkafireena min AAathabin shadeedin

---

14:2. Allah is He to Whom belongs whatever there is in the heavens and the earth. And woe, from severe punishment, unto those who suppress the Truth.

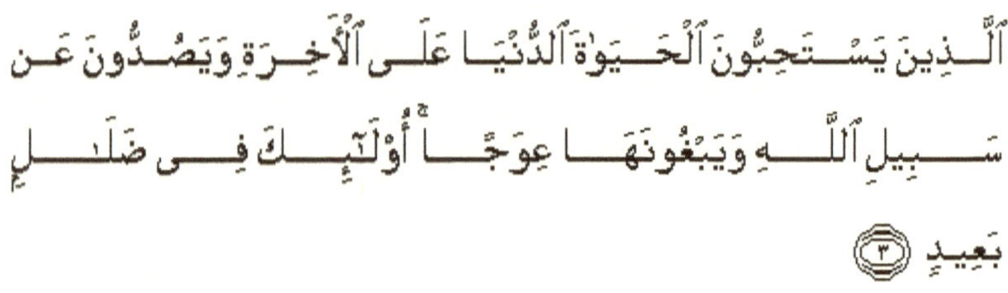

3. Alla*theena* yasta*h*ibboona al*h*ay*a*ta aldduny*a* AAal*a* al-*a*khirati wayas*u*ddoona AAan sabeeli All*a*hi wayabghoonah*a* AAiwajan ol*a*-ika fee *d*al*a*lin baAAeed*i*n

14:3. Those who love the life of this world more than the Hereafter and turn people away from Allah's Path and seek perversity[2] in it. They are in deep delusion.

2. One could understand non-Muslims seeking faults in the Qur'aan, the only authentic source depicting Allah's Path. But there are many of those who call themselves Muslims, and yet find faults in the divine Book. They say, despite repeated assertions therein to the contrary, that the Book does not have all the necessary explanations. [Refer study note 12 on Verse 13:19.] So, the Muslims are busy searching for 'what Allah has missed', in books other than the Qur'aan or are busy concocting their own explanations.

4. Wam*a* arsaln*a* min rasoolin ill*a* bilis*a*ni qawmihi liyubayyina lahum fayu*d*illu All*a*hu man yashao wayahdee man yashao wahuwa alAAazeezu al*h*akeemu

14:4. And We did not send any Messenger with Our Message but in the language of his people, so that he might narrate it to them clearly. Allah then leaves whom He wills to stray away from His Path and He guides whom He wills to His Path. And He is the Omnipotent, the Wise.

وَلَقَدْ أَرْسَلْنَا مُوسَىٰ بِـَٔايَـٰتِنَآ أَنْ أَخْرِجْ قَوْمَكَ مِنَ ٱلظُّلُمَـٰتِ إِلَى ٱلنُّورِ وَذَكِّرْهُم بِأَيَّـٰمِ ٱللَّهِ ۚ إِنَّ فِى ذَٰلِكَ لَـَٔايَـٰتٍ لِّكُلِّ صَبَّارٍ شَكُورٍ ۝

5. Walaqad arsalna moosa bi-ayatina an akhrij qawmaka mina al*th*thulum*a*ti il*a* alnnoori wa*th*akkirhum bi-ayy*a*mi All*a*hi inna fee *th*alika la*a*y*a*tin likulli *s*abb*a*rin shakoor**in**

14:5. And We did certainly send Moses with Our signs, "Bring out your people from the darknesses towards light and remind them of the annals of Allah. Therein indeed are signs for everyone who is patient and grateful."

وَإِذْ قَالَ مُوسَىٰ لِقَوْمِهِ ٱذْكُرُوا۟ نِعْمَةَ ٱللَّهِ عَلَيْكُمْ إِذْ أَنجَىٰكُم مِّنْ ءَالِ فِرْعَوْنَ يَسُومُونَكُمْ سُوٓءَ ٱلْعَذَابِ وَيُذَبِّحُونَ أَبْنَآءَكُمْ وَيَسْتَحْيُونَ نِسَآءَكُمْ ۚ وَفِى ذَٰلِكُم بَلَآءٌ مِّن رَّبِّكُمْ عَظِيمٌ ۝

6. Wa-i*th* qala moosa liqawmihi o*th*kuroo niAAmata All*a*hi AAalaykum i*th* anjakum min *a*li firAAawna yasoomoonakum soo-a alAAa*th*abi wayu*th*abbi*h*oona abn*a*akum wayasta*h*yoona nis*a*akum wafee *th*alikum bal*a*on min rabbikum AAa*th*eem**un**

14:6. And when Moses said to his people, "Remember Allah's favour upon you when He delivered you from Pharaoh's people who had subjected you to severe persecution and killed your sons and spared your women. And in this there was a great test from your Lord."

وَإِذْ تَأَذَّنَ رَبُّكُمْ لَئِن شَكَرْتُمْ لَأَزِيدَنَّكُمْ وَلَئِن كَفَرْتُمْ إِنَّ عَذَابِى لَشَدِيدٌ ۝

7. Wa-*ith* taa*thth*ana rabbukum la-in shakartum laazeedannakum wala-in kafartum inna AAa*tha*bee lashadee**dun**

14:7. And when your Lord declared, "If you are grateful, I will certainly give you more. And if you are ungrateful, My punishment is indeed severe."

وَقَالَ مُوسَىٰ إِن تَكْفُرُوٓا۟ أَنتُمْ وَمَن فِى ٱلْأَرْضِ جَمِيعًا فَإِنَّ ٱللَّهَ لَغَنِىٌّ حَمِيدٌ ۝

8. Waq*a*la moos*a* in takfuroo antum waman fee al-ar*d*i jameeAAan fa-inna All*a*ha laghaniyyun *h*ameed**un**

14:8. And Moses said, "Even if you are ungrateful – you and those on earth all together – Allah certainly indeed can do without you being grateful to Him. HE is Self-sufficient, Praiseworthy."

أَلَمْ يَأْتِكُمْ نَبَؤُاْ ٱلَّذِينَ مِن قَبْلِكُمْ قَوْمِ نُوحٍ وَعَادٍ وَثَمُودَ وَٱلَّذِينَ مِنْ

بَعْدِهِمْ لَا يَعْلَمُهُمْ إِلَّا ٱللَّهُ جَآءَتْهُمْ رُسُلُهُم بِٱلْبَيِّنَـٰتِ فَرَدُّوٓاْ أَيْدِيَهُمْ فِىٓ

أَفْوَٰهِهِمْ وَقَالُوٓاْ إِنَّا كَفَرْنَا بِمَآ أُرْسِلْتُم بِهِۦ وَإِنَّا لَفِى شَكٍّ مِّمَّا تَدْعُونَنَآ

إِلَيْهِ مُرِيبٍ ۝

9. Alam ya/tikum nabao alla*theena* min qablikum qawmi noo*h*in waAA*a*din wathamooda waalla*theena* min baAAdihim l*a* yaAAlamuhum ill*a* All*a*hu j*a*at-hum rusuluhum bialbayyin*a*ti faraddoo aydiyahum fee afw*a*hihim waq*a*loo inn*a* kafarn*a* bim*a* orsiltum bihi wa-inn*a* lafee shakkin mimm*a* tadAAoonan*a* ilayhi mureeb**un**

14:9. Have you not heard of those before you – of the people of Noah and AA<u>a</u>d and Thamood, and those after them? None knows them but Allah. Their Messengers came to them with clear signs. And they thrust their hands into their mouths in astonishment while witnessing those signs, but said, "We do not believe in the Message that you are sent with, and we are indeed utterly in doubt about what you invite us to."[3]

---

3. Those ancient peoples were astonished to see the miraculous signs Allah's Messengers had brought to them, and yet they did not believe in the divine Message they had brought! And today's modern peoples are no better. They too refuse to believe in the divine Message given to them through Allah's last Prophet, even when He has opened to them a vast reservoir of His infinite knowledge of innumerable miraculous happenings, day in and day out, throughout the universe. Glimpses of these miraculous happenings are shown, inter alia, in TV channels like Discovery Channel, National Geographic, Animal Planet etc. They dismiss these discoveries as just wonderful nature but refuse to believe in any Intelligent Creator behind their creation.

قَالَتْ رُسُلُهُمْ أَفِى ٱللَّهِ شَكٌّ فَاطِرِ ٱلسَّمَوَٰتِ وَٱلْأَرْضِ يَدْعُوكُمْ لِيَغْفِرَ لَكُم مِّن ذُنُوبِكُمْ وَيُؤَخِّرَكُمْ إِلَىٰ أَجَلٍ مُّسَمًّى قَالُوٓاْ إِنْ أَنتُمْ إِلَّا بَشَرٌ مِّثْلُنَا تُرِيدُونَ أَن تَصُدُّونَا عَمَّا كَانَ يَعْبُدُ ءَابَآؤُنَا فَأْتُونَا بِسُلْطَٰنٍ مُّبِينٍ

10. Qalat rusuluhum afee Allahi shakkun fatiri alssamawati waal-ardi yadAAookum liyaghfira lakum min thunoobikum wayu-akhkhirakum ila ajalin musamman qaloo in antum illa basharun mithluna tureedoona an tasuddoona AAamma kana yaAAbudu abaona fa/toona bisultanin mubeenin

---

14:10. Their Messengers said, "Is there any doubt about Allah, the Maker of the heavens and the earth? He invites you to Him so that He may forgive you your sins and give you time till an appointed term to redeem yourselves." They said, "You are but mortals like us. You wish to turn us away from what our fathers worshipped. Bring to us then some clear evidence for this."

قَالَتْ لَهُمْ رُسُلُهُمْ إِن نَّحْنُ إِلَّا بَشَرٌ مِّثْلُكُمْ وَلَٰكِنَّ ٱللَّهَ يَمُنُّ عَلَىٰ مَن يَشَآءُ مِنْ عِبَادِهِۦ وَمَا كَانَ لَنَآ أَن نَّأْتِيَكُم بِسُلْطَٰنٍ إِلَّا بِإِذْنِ ٱللَّهِ وَعَلَى ٱللَّهِ فَلْيَتَوَكَّلِ ٱلْمُؤْمِنُونَ

11. Qalat lahum rusuluhum in nahnu illa basharun mithlukum walakinna Allaha yamunnu AAala man yashao min AAibadihi wama kana lana an na/tiyakum bisultanin illa bi-ithni Allahi waAAala Allahi falyatawakkali almu/minoona

---

14:11. Their Messengers said to them, "We are but mortals like you, but Allah bestows His favours upon whom He wills of His worshippers. And we cannot bring you any evidence except by Allah's permission. And in Allah then the believers should have trust."

وَمَا لَنَا أَلَّا نَتَوَكَّلَ عَلَى ٱللَّهِ وَقَدْ هَدَىٰنَا سُبُلَنَا وَلَنَصْبِرَنَّ عَلَىٰ مَآ ءَاذَيْتُمُونَا وَعَلَى ٱللَّهِ فَلْيَتَوَكَّلِ ٱلْمُتَوَكِّلُونَ ﴿١٢﴾

12. Wama lana alla natawakkala AAala Allahi waqad hadana subulana walanasbiranna AAala ma athaytumoona waAAala Allahi falyatawakkali almutawakkiloona

14:12. "And what reason have we that we should have no trust in Allah, when, surely, He has guided us to our paths? And we shall certainly bear your persecution with patience. And those that trust do trust in Allah."

وَقَالَ ٱلَّذِينَ كَفَرُواْ لِرُسُلِهِمْ لَنُخْرِجَنَّكُم مِّنْ أَرْضِنَآ أَوْ لَتَعُودُنَّ فِى مِلَّتِنَا فَأَوْحَىٰ إِلَيْهِمْ رَبُّهُمْ لَنُهْلِكَنَّ ٱلظَّٰلِمِينَ ﴿١٣﴾

13. Waqala allatheena kafaroo lirusulihim lanukhrijannakum min ardina aw lataAAoodunna fee millatina faawha ilayhim rabbuhum lanuhlikanna alththalimeena

14:13. And those who suppressed the Truth told their Messengers, "We shall drive you out of our land, or you shall come back into our lifestyle." Their Lord then revealed to them, "We will destroy the wicked people."

14. Walanuskinannakumu al-ar*d*a min baAAdihim *tha*lika liman kh*a*fa maq*a*mee wakh*a*fa waAAeedi

---

14:14. "And We shall certainly settle you in the land after them. That is for him who fears standing in My presence and who fears My warnings."

15. Waistafta*h*oo wakh*a*ba kullu jabb*a*rin AAaneedin

14:15. And they sought victory and every obstinate tyrant was frustrated.

---

16. Min war*a*-ihi jahannamu wayusq*a* min m*a*-in *s*adeedin

---

14:16. Behind him [every obstinate tyrant] is Hell waiting to quench his thirst with fetid water.

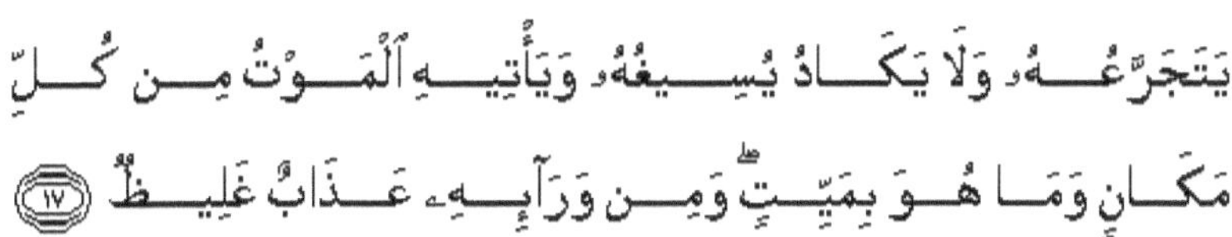

17. Yatajarra*AA*uhu wal*a* yak*a*du yuseeghuhu waya/teehi almawtu min kulli mak*a*nin wam*a* huwa bimayyitin wamin war*a*-ihi *AA*a*th*abun ghalee*th***un

14:17. He will sip at it and it will not be easy for him to swallow it. And death will come to him from every quarter, but he shall not die. And further severe punishment shall await just behind him.

18. Mathalu alla*th*eena kafaroo birabbihim a*AA*m*a*luhum karam*a*din ishtaddat bihi alrree*h*u fee yawmin *AA*asifin l*a* yaqdiroona mimm*a* kasaboo *AA*al*a* shay-in *th*alika huwa al*dd*alalu albaAAeed**u**

14:18. Deeds of those who suppress the Truth about their Lord are like ashes on which the wind blows hard on a stormy day. They shall have no power over any thing they earn. That is far too grievous a loss of way.

19. Alam tara anna All*a*ha khalaqa alssam*a*w*a*ti waal-ar*d*a bial*h*aqqi in yasha/ yu*th*hibkum waya/ti bikhalqin jadee**din**

14:19. Do you not see that Allah created the heavens and the earth in Truth? If He wills He will take you off and bring a new creation.[4]

---

4. The creation of the heavens and the earth could, by no stretch of imagination, be considered purposeless. The purpose, as clarified in <u>Verse 11:7</u>**, is to test humans by making its members His vicegerents on earth. All His creation is, apparently and essentially, to serve that purpose. If any section of humans proves itself to be incapable of holding on to that high office, it is liable to be replaced by the Almighty Creator with a new generation.**

20. Wam*a thalika AAala Allahi biAAazeez**in**

14:20. And that is not at all difficult for Allah!

---

21. Wabarazoo lill*a*hi jameeAAan faq*a*la al*ddu*AAaf*a*o lilla*theena istakbaroo inna kunna lakum tabaAAan fahal antum mughnoona AAanna min AAa*th*abi Allahi min shay-in q*a*loo law had*a*na Allahu lahadaynakum saw*a*on AAalayna ajaziAAna am s*a*barna ma lana min ma*h*ee*s*in

14:21. And they shall all present themselves before Allah. Then the weak shall say to those who were proud, "We had indeed been your followers. Would you then withstand anything of Allah's punishment from us?" They would say, "If Allah had guided us, we too would have guided you. It is immaterial to us now whether we bewail or be patient. There is no place for us to escape to."

وَقَالَ ٱلشَّيْطَٰنُ لَمَّا قُضِىَ ٱلْأَمْرُ إِنَّ ٱللَّهَ وَعَدَكُمْ وَعْدَ ٱلْحَقِّ وَوَعَدتُّكُمْ فَأَخْلَفْتُكُمْ وَمَا كَانَ لِىَ عَلَيْكُم مِّن سُلْطَٰنٍ إِلَّا أَن دَعَوْتُكُمْ فَٱسْتَجَبْتُمْ لِى فَلَا تَلُومُونِى وَلُومُوٓا۟ أَنفُسَكُم مَّآ أَنَا۠ بِمُصْرِخِكُمْ وَمَآ أَنتُم بِمُصْرِخِىَّ إِنِّى كَفَرْتُ بِمَآ أَشْرَكْتُمُونِ مِن قَبْلُ إِنَّ ٱلظَّٰلِمِينَ لَهُمْ عَذَابٌ أَلِيمٌ ﴿٢٢﴾

22. Waq*a*la alshshay*ta*nu lamm*a* qu*d*iya al-amru inna All*a*ha waAAadakum waAAda al*h*aqqi wawaAAadtukum faakhlaftukum wam*a* k*a*na liya AAalaykum min sul*ta*nin ill*a* an daAAawtukum faistajabtum lee fal*a* taloomoonee waloomoo anfusakum m*a* an*a* bimu*s*rikhikum wam*a* antum bimu*s*rikhiyya innee kafartu bim*a* ash*r*aktumooni min qablu inna al*ththa*limeena lahum AAa*tha*bun aleemun

14:22. And the Satan shall say after the Judgment is pronounced, "Allah did indeed give you the true promise. And I gave you promises but failed to keep them. And I had no authority over you except to call you to me, and you obeyed me! So, blame me not, but blame yourselves. I cannot be of any help to you now, nor can you be of any help to me. I do indeed deny that you had worshipped me, besides Allah, before." For the wicked people there shall indeed be a painful punishment.

وَأُدْخِلَ ٱلَّذِينَ ءَامَنُوا۟ وَعَمِلُوا۟ ٱلصَّلِحَتِ جَنَّتٍ تَجْرِى مِن
تَحْتِهَا ٱلْأَنْهَـٰرُ خَـٰلِدِينَ فِيهَا بِإِذْنِ رَبِّهِمْ تَحِيَّتُهُمْ فِيهَا سَلَـٰمٌ ﴿٢٣﴾

23. Waodkhila alla*th*eena *a*manoo waAAamiloo al*ss*ali*h*ati jann*a*tin tajree min ta*h*ti*h*a al-anh*a*ru khalideena
feeh*a* bi-i*th*ni rabbihim ta*h*iyyatuhum feeh*a* sal*a*m**un**

14:23. And those who believe and do good deeds shall be admitted to gardens beneath which rivers flow. They shall stay eternally therein by their Lord's leave. Their greeting therein shall be, "Peace."

أَلَمْ تَرَ كَيْفَ ضَرَبَ ٱللَّهُ مَثَلًا كَلِمَةً طَيِّبَةً
كَشَجَرَةٍ طَيِّبَةٍ أَصْلُهَا ثَابِتٌ وَفَرْعُهَا فِى ٱلسَّمَآءِ ﴿٢٤﴾

24. Alam tara kayfa *d*araba All*a*hu mathalan kalimatan *t*ayyibatan kashajaratin *t*ayyibatin a*s*lu*ha* th*a*bitun
wafarAAuh*a* fee alssam*a*/-**i**

14:24. Don't you see how Allah exemplifies a good word as a good tree with firm roots and with its branches spread out in the sky.

تُؤْتِى أُكُلَهَا كُلَّ حِينٍ بِإِذْنِ رَبِّهَا وَيَضْرِبُ ٱللَّهُ ٱلْأَمْثَالَ لِلنَّاسِ لَعَلَّهُمْ
يَتَذَكَّرُونَ ﴿٢٥﴾

25. Tu/tee okulah*a* kulla *h*eenin bi-i*th*ni rabbih*a* wayad*r*ibu All*a*hu al-amth*a*la lilnn*a*si laAAallahum
yata*th*akkaroon**a**

14:25. Yielding its fruits every season by its Lord's leave? [5] And Allah gives examples for the benefit of mankind so that they may ponder and remember.

5. Through this example, we understand that a good word is anything written or spoken that is firmly based on truth and reality. It gives solace to those who hear or read it and benefits them repeatedly as well. A good example of a good word is the Qur'aan itself. It is firmly based on Truth. It gives solace to those who read and ponder over it. And history is witness to the fact that it has benefited nondescript communities to become the most potent forces on earth – culturally, economically and militarily. This good word has not been seen yielding fruits nowadays as most people listen to it not to understand and implement its teachings. They have relegated it to just ritualistic reading.

وَمَثَلُ كَلِمَةٍ خَبِيثَةٍ كَشَجَرَةٍ خَبِيثَةٍ ٱجْتُثَّتْ مِن فَوْقِ ٱلْأَرْضِ مَا لَهَا مِن قَرَارٍ ۝

26. Wamathalu kalimatin khabeethatin kashajaratin khabeethatin ijtuththat min fawqi al-ar*d*i m*a* lah*a* min qar*a***rin**

14:26. And the example of a bad word is a bad tree which can easily be uprooted from the earth's surface; it has no stability.

يُثَبِّتُ ٱللَّهُ ٱلَّذِينَ ءَامَنُواْ بِٱلْقَوْلِ ٱلثَّابِتِ فِى ٱلْحَيَوٰةِ ٱلدُّنْيَا وَفِى ٱلْأَخِرَةِ وَيُضِلُّ ٱللَّهُ ٱلظَّلِمِينَ وَيَفْعَلُ ٱللَّهُ مَا يَشَآءُ ۝

27. Yuthabbitu All*a*hu alla*th*eena *a*manoo bialqawli al*th*th*a*biti fee al*h*ay*a*ti aldduny*a* wafee al-*a*khirati wayu*d*illu All*a*hu al*th*th*a*limeena wayaf*AA*alu All*a*hu m*a* yasha/o

14:27. Allah establishes, in the life of this world and in the Hereafter, those who believe in the firm Testament[6]. And Allah leads the wicked persons astray, and Allah does what He wills.

6. The Qur'aan.

۞ أَلَمْ تَرَ إِلَى ٱلَّذِينَ بَدَّلُواْ نِعْمَتَ ٱللَّهِ كُفْرًا وَأَحَلُّواْ قَوْمَهُمْ دَارَ ٱلْبَوَارِ ﴿٢٨﴾

28. Alam tara il*a* alla*th*eena baddaloo ni*AA*mata All*a*hi kufran waa*h*alloo qawmahum d*a*ra albawa*r*i

14:28. Have you not seen those who have changed Allah's favour by being ungrateful, and made their people eligible for the abode of ruin?

جَهَنَّمَ يَصْلَوْنَهَا وَبِئْسَ ٱلْقَرَارُ ﴿٢٩﴾

29. Jahannama ya*s*lawnah*a* wabi/sa alqar*a*ru

14:29. Hell – they shall burn therein. And a very bad place it is to settle in!

وَجَعَلُواْ لِلَّهِ أَندَادًا لِّيُضِلُّواْ عَن سَبِيلِهِۦ قُلْ تَمَتَّعُواْ فَإِنَّ مَصِيرَكُمْ إِلَى ٱلنَّارِ ﴿٣٠﴾

30. WajaAAaloo lillahi andadan liyudilloo AAan sabeelihi qul tamattaAAoo fa-inna maseerakum ila alnnari

---

14:30. And they set up rivals to Allah that they may lead people away from His Path. Say, "Enjoy for now! Your destination then shall indeed be to the Fire."

قُل لِّعِبَادِىَ ٱلَّذِينَ ءَامَنُواْ يُقِيمُواْ ٱلصَّلَوٰةَ وَيُنفِقُواْ مِمَّا رَزَقْنَـٰهُمْ سِرًّا وَعَلَانِيَةً مِّن قَبْلِ أَن يَأْتِىَ يَوْمٌ لَّا بَيْعٌ فِيهِ وَلَا خِلَـٰلٌ ﴿٣١﴾

31. Qul liAAibadiya allatheena amanoo yuqeemoo alssalata wayunfiqoo mimma razaqnahum sirran waAAalaniyatan min qabli an ya/tiya yawmun la bayAAun feehi wala khilalun

---

14:31. Tell My subjects who believe that they should establish regular prayer[7] and spend[8] out of what We have given them, secretly and openly, before the coming of the Day in which there shall be no trading nor any friendly give-and-take.

---

7. For the Qur'aanic explanation of the corresponding Arabic term, *aqeemoo alssalata,* **refer study notes** 2:4 **&** 2:108.

8. Refer study note 2:5.

اللَّهُ الَّذِى خَلَقَ السَّمَـٰوَٰتِ وَالْأَرْضَ وَأَنزَلَ مِنَ السَّمَآءِ مَآءً فَأَخْرَجَ بِهِۦ مِنَ الثَّمَرَٰتِ رِزْقًا لَّكُمْ وَسَخَّرَ لَكُمُ الْفُلْكَ لِتَجْرِىَ فِى الْبَحْرِ بِأَمْرِهِۦ وَسَخَّرَ لَكُمُ الْأَنْهَـٰرَ ﴿٣٢﴾

32. Allahu allathee khalaqa alssamawati waal-arda waanzala mina alssama-i maan faakhraja bihi mina alththamarati rizqan lakum wasakhkhara lakumu alfulka litajriya fee albahri bi-amrihi wasakhkhara lakumu al-anhara

14:32. Allah is He Who created the heavens and the earth and sent down water from the sky. Then, with it, He brought forth fruits as sustenance for you. And He made the ship subservient to you, so that it sails on the sea by His command. And He made the rivers serve your needs.

وَسَخَّرَ لَكُمُ الشَّمْسَ وَالْقَمَرَ دَآئِبَيْنِ وَسَخَّرَ لَكُمُ الَّيْلَ وَالنَّهَارَ ﴿٣٣﴾

33. Wasakhkhara lakumu alshshamsa waalqamara da-ibayni wasakhkhara lakumu allayla waalnnahara

14:33. And He made the sun and the moon – both pursuing their respective courses – serve your needs. And He made the night and the day serve you.

وَءَاتَىٰكُم مِّن كُلِّ مَا سَأَلْتُمُوهُ وَإِن تَعُدُّوا نِعْمَتَ اللَّهِ لَا تُحْصُوهَآ إِنَّ الْإِنسَـٰنَ لَظَلُومٌ كَفَّارٌ ﴿٣٤﴾

34. Waatakum min kulli ma saaltumoohu wa-in taAAuddoo niAAmata Allahi la tuhsooha inna al-insana lathaloomun kaffarun

14:34. And He gives you of all that you ask Him. And if you would like to know the number of times Allah favours you, you will not be able to count. Man is indeed very wicked, thankless.

$$\text{وَإِذْ قَالَ إِبْرَٰهِيمُ رَبِّ ٱجْعَلْ هَٰذَا ٱلْبَلَدَ ءَامِنًا وَٱجْنُبْنِى وَبَنِىَّ}$$
$$\text{أَن نَّعْبُدَ ٱلْأَصْنَامَ ﴿٣٥﴾}$$

35. Wa-ith qala ibraheemu rabbi ijAAal hatha albalada aminan waojnubnee wabaniyya an naAAbuda al-asnama

14:35. And when Abraham said, "My Lord! Make this a city[9] of peace. And save me and my sons from worshipping idols."

9. Makkah.

$$\text{رَبِّ إِنَّهُنَّ أَضْلَلْنَ كَثِيرًا مِّنَ ٱلنَّاسِ فَمَن تَبِعَنِى فَإِنَّهُۥ مِنِّى وَمَنْ عَصَانِى}$$
$$\text{فَإِنَّكَ غَفُورٌ رَّحِيمٌ ﴿٣٦﴾}$$

36. Rabbi innahunna adlalna katheeran mina alnnasi faman tabiAAanee fa-innahu minnee waman AAasanee fa-innaka ghafoorun raheemun

14:36. "My Lord! They have indeed led many of mankind astray. The one, then, that follows me, is indeed of me. And as for the one that disobeys me, You indeed arc Forgiving, Merciful."

رَّبَّنَا إِنِّى أَسْكَنتُ مِن ذُرِّيَّتِى بِوَادٍ غَيْرِ ذِى زَرْعٍ عِندَ بَيْتِكَ ٱلْمُحَرَّمِ رَبَّنَا لِيُقِيمُواْ ٱلصَّلَوٰةَ فَٱجْعَلْ أَفْئِدَةً مِّنَ ٱلنَّاسِ تَهْوِىٓ إِلَيْهِمْ وَٱرْزُقْهُم مِّنَ ٱلثَّمَرَٰتِ لَعَلَّهُمْ يَشْكُرُونَ ﴿٣٧﴾

37. Rabbana innee askantu min *th*urriyyatee biwadin ghayri *th*ee zarAAin AAinda baytika almu*h*arrami rabbana liyuqeemoo al*s*salata faijAAal af-idatan mina alnn*a*si tahwee ilayhim waorzuqhum mina alththamar*a*ti laAAallahum yashkuroon*a*

14:37. "O our Lord! I have indeed inhabited some of my offspring in an uncultivable valley near Your Sacred House, our Lord, that they may establish regular prayer there. Hence make some people come and settle near them and provide them with fruits that they may be grateful."[10]

10. Allah Almighty thus informs us that some members of Abraham's family were the first settlers of Makkah.

رَبَّنَا إِنَّكَ تَعْلَمُ مَا نُخْفِى وَمَا نُعْلِنُ وَمَا يَخْفَىٰ عَلَى ٱللَّهِ مِن شَىْءٍ فِى ٱلْأَرْضِ وَلَا فِى ٱلسَّمَآءِ ﴿٣٨﴾

38. Rabban*a* innaka taAAlamu m*a* nukhfee wam*a* nuAAlinu wam*a* yakhf*a* AAal*a* All*a*hi min shay-in fee al-ar*di* wal*a* fee alssam*a*/-i

14:38. "O our Lord! You do indeed know what we hide and what we do not. And nothing in the earth or in the heaven above is hidden from Allah."

ٱلْحَمْدُ لِلَّهِ ٱلَّذِى وَهَبَ لِى عَلَى ٱلْكِبَرِ إِسْمَٰعِيلَ وَإِسْحَٰقَ إِنَّ رَبِّى لَسَمِيعُ ٱلدُّعَآءِ ۝

39. Alhamdu lillahi allathee wahaba lee AAala alkibari ismaAAeela wa-ishaqa inna rabbee lasameeAAu aldduAAa/-i

14:39. "Praise to Allah, Who has given me, in old age, Ishmael and Isaac. My Lord does indeed hear the prayer."

رَبِّ ٱجْعَلْنِى مُقِيمَ ٱلصَّلَوٰةِ وَمِن ذُرِّيَّتِى رَبَّنَا وَتَقَبَّلْ دُعَآءِ ۝

40. Rabbi ijAAalnee muqeema alssalati wamin thurriyyatee rabbana wtaqabbal duAAa/-i

14:40. "My Lord! Inspire me to establish regular prayer and inspire those from my offspring too. And, O our Lord, accept my prayer!"

رَبَّنَا ٱغْفِرْ لِى وَلِوَٰلِدَىَّ وَلِلْمُؤْمِنِينَ يَوْمَ يَقُومُ ٱلْحِسَابُ ۝

41. Rabbana ighfir lee waliwalidayya walilmu/mineena yawma yaqoomu alhisabu

14:41. "O our Lord! Pardon me, my parents and the believers on the Day of Accounting!"

وَلَا تَحْسَبَنَّ ٱللَّهَ غَـٰفِلًا عَمَّا يَعْمَلُ ٱلظَّـٰلِمُونَ إِنَّمَا يُؤَخِّرُهُمْ لِيَوْمٍ تَشْخَصُ فِيهِ ٱلْأَبْصَـٰرُ ﴿٤٢﴾

42. Wala tahsabanna Allaha ghafilan AAamma yaAAmalu alththalimoona innama yu-akhkhiruhum liyawmin tashkhasu feehi al-absaru

---

14:42. And do not think that Allah is unaware of what the wicked people do. He does but give them respite till the day when the eyes shall get transfixed,

---

مُهْطِعِينَ مُقْنِعِى رُءُوسِهِمْ لَا يَرْتَدُّ إِلَيْهِمْ طَرْفُهُمْ وَأَفْئِدَتُهُمْ هَوَآءٌ ﴿٤٣﴾

43. MuhtiAAeena muqniAAee ruoosihim la yartaddu ilayhim tarfuhum waaf-idatuhum hawa/on

---

14:43. Hurrying on in fear, their heads upraised – not glancing at themselves – and their hearts vacant.

وَأَنذِرِ ٱلنَّاسَ يَوْمَ يَأْتِيهِمُ ٱلْعَذَابُ فَيَقُولُ ٱلَّذِينَ ظَلَمُوا۟ رَبَّنَا أَخِّرْنَا إِلَىٰٓ أَجَلٍ قَرِيبٍ نُّجِبْ دَعْوَتَكَ وَنَتَّبِعِ ٱلرُّسُلَ أَوَلَمْ تَكُونُوا۟ أَقْسَمْتُم مِّن قَبْلُ مَا لَكُم مِّن زَوَالٍ ﴿٤٤﴾

44. Waan*th*iri alnn*a*sa yawma ya/teehimu alAAa*th*abu fayaqoolu alla*th*eena *th*alamoo rabban*a* akhkhirn*a* il*a* ajalin qareebin nujib daAAwataka wanattabiAAi alrrusula awa lam takoonoo aqsamtum min qablu m*a* lakum min zaw*a*l**in**

14:44. And warn people of the Day when the punishment shall come to them. Then those who were wicked will say, "O our Lord! Give us respite for a short term to enable us to respond to Your call and follow the Messengers." Did you not swear before that you shall have no downfall?

وَسَكَنتُمْ فِــى مَسَــٰكِنِ ٱلَّـذِينَ ظَلَمُــوٓاْ أَنفُسَـهُمْ وَتَبَيَّــنَ لَكُــمْ كَيْفَ فَعَلْنَا بِهِــمْ وَضَرَبْنَــا لَكُــمُ ٱلْأَمْثَــالَ ﴿٤٥﴾

45. Wasakantum fee mas*a*kini alla*th*eena *th*alamoo anfusahum watabayyana lakum kayfa faAAaln*a* bihim wa*d*arabn*a* lakumu al-amth*a*l**a**

14:45. And you had lived where those, who had transgressed against themselves, lived. And it was clear to you how We had dealt with them. And We had given you examples.

وَقَـدْ مَكَـرُواْ مَكْـرَهُمْ وَعِنـدَ ٱللَّـهِ مَكْـرُهُمْ وَإِن كَانَ مَكْـرُهُمْ لِتَزُولَ مِنْـهُ ٱلْجِبَــالُ ﴿٤٦﴾

46. Waqad makaroo makrahum waAAinda All*a*hi makruhum wa-in k*a*na makruhum litazoola minhu aljib*a*l**u**

14:46. And they did plan their plan. But their plan is with Allah, though their plan was such that the mountains could come down thereby.

فَلَا تَحْسَبَنَّ ٱللَّهَ مُخْلِفَ وَعْدِهِ رُسُلَهُۥ إِنَّ ٱللَّهَ عَزِيزٌ ذُو ٱنتِقَامٍ ﴿٤٧﴾

47. Fala tahsabanna Allaha mukhlifa waAAdihi rusulahu inna Allaha AAazeezun thoo intiqamin

---

14:47. Think not then that Allah is one to fail in His promise to His Messengers. Allah is indeed Omnipotent and has the power to give a fitting retribution.

يَوْمَ تُبَدَّلُ ٱلْأَرْضُ غَيْرَ ٱلْأَرْضِ وَٱلسَّمَٰوَٰتُ وَبَرَزُوا۟ لِلَّهِ ٱلْوَٰحِدِ ٱلْقَهَّارِ ﴿٤٨﴾

48. Yawma tubaddalu al-ardu ghayra al-ardi waalssamawatu wabarazoo lillahi alwahidi alqahhari

---

14:48. On the Day when the earth shall be changed into a different earth – and the heavens too! And they shall present themselves before Allah, the One, the Almighty.

وَتَرَى ٱلْمُجْرِمِينَ يَوْمَئِذٍ مُّقَرَّنِينَ فِى ٱلْأَصْفَادِ ﴿٤٩﴾

49. Watara almujrimeena yawma-ithin muqarraneena fee al-asfadi

---

14:49. And you will see the sinners on that day bound together in chains.

$$\text{سَرَابِيلُهُم مِّن قَطِرَانٍ وَتَغْشَىٰ وُجُوهَهُمُ ٱلنَّارُ} \quad ⑤⓪$$

50. Sarabeeluhum min qatranin wataghsha wujoohahumu alnnaru

14:50. Their dresses made of tar and the fire covering their faces.

$$\text{لِيَجْزِيَ ٱللَّهُ كُلَّ نَفْسٍ مَّا كَسَبَتْ إِنَّ ٱللَّهَ سَرِيعُ ٱلْحِسَابِ} \quad ⑤①$$

51. Liyajziya Allahu kulla nafsin ma kasabat inna Allaha sareeAAu alhisabi

---

14:51. That Allah may repay everyone for what it earned. Allah is indeed quick in keeping accounts.

$$\text{هَٰذَا بَلَٰغٌ لِّلنَّاسِ وَلِيُنذَرُوا۟ بِهِۦ وَلِيَعْلَمُوٓا۟ أَنَّمَا هُوَ إِلَٰهٌ وَٰحِدٌ وَلِيَذَّكَّرَ}$$
$$\text{أُو۟لُوا۟ ٱلْأَلْبَٰبِ} \quad ⑤②$$

52. Hatha balaghun lilnnasi waliyuntharoo bihi waliyaAAlamoo annama huwa ilahun wahidun waliyaththakkara oloo al-albabi

---

14:52. This (Qur'aan) is enough and eloquent exposition of the divine Message for the people that they may be warned thereby, that they may know that He is the One and Only Being worthy of being worshipped, and those endowed with insight may remember it and remind other people about it.

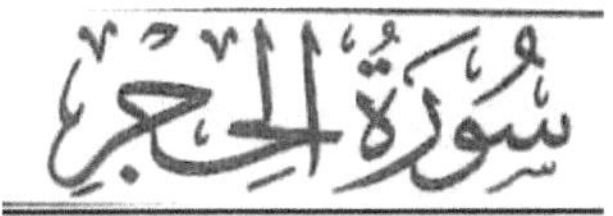

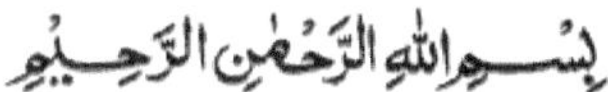

In the Name of Allah, the Gracious, the Merciful

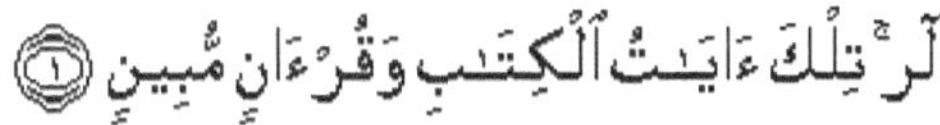

1. Alif-lam-ra tilka *aya*tu alkit*a*bi waqur-*a*nin mubeen**in**

15:1. Alif Lam Ra.[1] Those are Verses of the Book and it is a clear Qur'aan (Reader).

---

1. Refer study note 2:1 **(Chapter 2) regarding such initial letters at the beginning of some Qur'aanic Chapters.**

رُّبَمَا يَوَدُّ ٱلَّذِينَ كَفَرُوا۟ لَوْ كَانُوا۟ مُسْلِمِينَ ۝

2. Rubam*a* yawaddu alla*th*eena kafaroo law k*a*noo muslimeen**a**

15:2. Those who suppress the Truth shall frequently wish that they had been Muslims (submitters to divine Will).[2]

---

2. The suppressors of Truth shall so wish while suffering in Hell.

ذَرْهُمْ يَأْكُلُواْ وَيَتَمَتَّعُواْ وَيُلْهِهِمُ ٱلْأَمَلُ فَسَوْفَ يَعْلَمُونَ ﴿٣﴾

3. *Th*arhum ya/kuloo wayatamattaAAoo wayulhihimu al-amalu fasawfa yaAAlamoona

15:3. Leave them free to eat and enjoy, and let desire distract them. They will soon know.

وَمَآ أَهْلَكْنَا مِن قَرْيَةٍ إِلَّا وَلَهَا كِتَابٌ مَّعْلُومٌ ﴿٤﴾

4. Wam*a* ahlakn*a* min qaryatin ill*a* walah*a* kit*a*bun maAAloom**un**

15:4. And never did We destroy any population, but only when it had reached its known destiny.

مَّا تَسْبِقُ مِنْ أُمَّةٍ أَجَلَهَا وَمَا يَسْتَـْٔخِرُونَ ﴿٥﴾

5. M*a* tasbiqu min ommatin ajalah*a* wam*a* yasta/khiroona

15:5. No people can prepone their end nor can they postpone it.

وَقَالُواْ يَـٰٓأَيُّهَا ٱلَّذِى نُزِّلَ عَلَيْهِ ٱلذِّكْرُ إِنَّكَ لَمَجْنُونٌ ۝

6. Waqaloo ya ayyuha alla*th*ee nuzzila AAalayhi al*thth*ikru innaka lamajnoon**un**

15:6. And they say, "O you to whom the Reminder (Qur'aan) has been revealed! You are indeed mad."

لَّوْ مَا تَأْتِينَا بِٱلْمَلَـٰٓئِكَةِ إِن كُنتَ مِنَ ٱلصَّـٰدِقِينَ ۝

7. Law m*a* ta/teen*a* bi*a*lmal*a*-ikati in kunta mina al*ss*adiqeen*a*

15:7. "Why do you not bring to us the angels if what you claim is true?"

مَا نُنَزِّلُ ٱلْمَلَـٰٓئِكَةَ إِلَّا بِٱلْحَقِّ وَمَا كَانُوٓاْ إِذًا مُّنظَرِينَ ۝

8. M*a* nunazzilu almal*a*-ikata ill*a* bi*a*l*h*aqqi wam*a* k*a*noo i*th*an mun*th*areen*a*

15:8. We do not send the angels but only when necessary (to destroy wicked persons, for instance), and then they would not be given any respite.

إِنَّا نَحْنُ نَزَّلْنَا ٱلذِّكْرَ وَإِنَّا لَهُۥ لَحَـٰفِظُونَ ۝

9. Inna nahnu nazzalna alththikra wa-inna lahu lahafithoona

15:9. Indeed, We have sent down the Reminder (Qur'aan) and indeed We are most certainly guardians to it.

وَلَقَدْ أَرْسَلْنَا مِن قَبْلِكَ فِى شِيَعِ ٱلْأَوَّلِينَ ۝

10. Walaqad arsalna min qablika fee shiyaAAi al-awwaleena

15:10. And We did certainly send Messengers, before you, among the earlier generations.

وَمَا يَأْتِيهِم مِّن رَّسُولٍ إِلَّا كَانُوا۟ بِهِۦ يَسْتَهْزِءُونَ ۝

11. Wama ya/teehim min rasoolin illa kanoo bihi yastahzi-oona

---

15:11. And never did a Messenger come to them but they mocked him.

كَذَٰلِكَ نَسْلُكُهُۥ فِى قُلُوبِ ٱلْمُجْرِمِينَ ﴿١٢﴾

12. Ka*tha*lika naslukuhu fee quloobi almujrimeen**a**

15:12. Thus do We make it (making a mockery of a Messenger) enter the hearts of the sinners.

لَا يُؤْمِنُونَ بِهِۦ ۖ وَقَدْ خَلَتْ سُنَّةُ ٱلْأَوَّلِينَ ﴿١٣﴾

13. *La* yu/minoona bihi waqad khalat sunnatu al-awwaleen**a**

15:13. They believe not in it (the divine Message brought by the Messenger), just as the earlier peoples, that passed away, did not believe (in the divine Messages brought to them by Messengers sent to them).

وَلَوْ فَتَحْنَا عَلَيْهِم بَابًا مِّنَ ٱلسَّمَآءِ فَظَلُّوا۟ فِيهِ يَعْرُجُونَ ﴿١٤﴾

14. Walaw fata*hna* AAalayhim b*a*ban mina alssam*a*-i fa*th*alloo feehi yaAArujoon**a**

15:14. And they won't believe, even if We open to them a gateway into the sky above, and they keep on ascending thereinto.

لَقَالُوٓاْ إِنَّمَا سُكِّرَتْ أَبْصَـٰرُنَا بَلْ نَحْنُ قَوْمٌ مَّسْحُورُونَ ۝

15. Laqaloo innama sukkirat absaruna bal nahnu qawmun mashooroona

---

15:15. They would still only say, "Our sights.are dazed. Nay, we are a people bewitched!"

وَلَقَدْ جَعَلْنَا فِى ٱلسَّمَآءِ بُرُوجًا وَزَيَّنَّـٰهَا لِلنَّـٰظِرِينَ ۝

16. Walaqad jaAAalna fee alssama-i buroojan wazayyannaha lilnnathireena

---

15:16. And certainly We have made constellations in the skies above and We have made it look beautiful for the beholders.

وَحَفِظْنَـٰهَا مِن كُلِّ شَيْطَـٰنٍ رَّجِيمٍ ۝

17. Wahafithnaha min kulli shaytanin rajeemin

15:17. And We have guarded it against every accursed Satan.

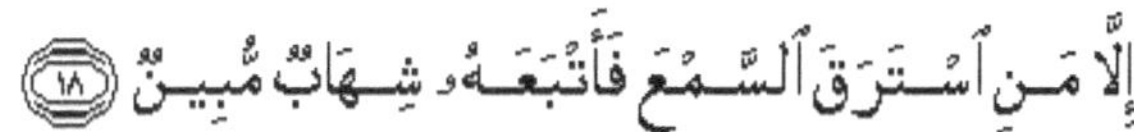

18. Ill*a* mani istaraqa alssamAAa faatbaAAahu shih*a*bun mubee**nun**

15:18. Except that a visible flame follows the one that manages to steal a celestial secret.[3]

---

3. Verses 14 to 18 herein above seem to foretell modern man's forays into outer space and powerful telescopes like the Hubble space telescope, which is taking breathtaking pictures of star constellations and other innumerable wonders of the Universe. These Verses point out to the sad fact that despite Allah facilitating mankind to have this knowledge about the mind-boggling workmanship of His, most men still have no belief in the Creator as He is depicted in the Qur'aan. About a visible flame following a satanic person stealing a secret, we are aware of some ventures into space meeting fiery ends. Maybe, those were examples of astronauts persisting in their atheistic ways despite being witnesses to divine wonders.

19. Wa*a*l-ar*d*a madadn*a*h*a* waalqayn*a* fee*h*a raw*a*siya waanbatn*a* fee*h*a min kulli shay-in mawzoo**nin**

15:19. And We have spread out the earth and cast[4] mountains into it. And We have caused every appropriate thing to grow in it.

---

4. Science does not yet seem to have come to definite conclusions about the formation of mountains. And this word used here appears to suggest that mountains were thrown or bombarded on to the surface of the earth from outer space. Maybe, eons ago, during the formation of the earth, parts from an exploding

star impounded the earth and the mountains were formed. Remember that mountains have deep roots inside the earth. Otherwise they should be flattened out because of the tremendous speed at which the earth rotates.

20. WajaAAalna lakum feeha maAAayisha waman lastum lahu biraziqeena

15:20. And We have created in it means of subsistence for you, and for him whom you do not provide for.

21. Wa-in min shay-in illa AAindana khaza-inuhu wama nunazziluhu illa biqadarin maAAloomin

15:21. And there is nothing of which We do not have treasures with us. And We do not send it down but in a measured quantity.

22. Waarsaln*a* alrriy*a*ha law*a*qi*h*a faanzaln*a* mina alssam*a*-i m*a*an faasqayn*a*kumoohu wam*a* antum lahu bikh*a*zineen**a**

15:22. And We send the winds that facilitate pollination[5], and then send down water from the sky for you to drink. And it is not in your power to store it up.

---

5. The light pollen grains from a flower get carried by the wind and then get deposited on the stigma, resulting in fertilization.

$$\text{وَإِنَّا لَنَحْنُ نُحْيِـۦ وَنُمِيتُ وَنَحْنُ ٱلْوَارِثُونَ}$$

23. Wa-inn*a* lana*h*nu nu*h*yee wanumeetu wana*h*nu alw*a*rithoon**a**

15:23. And indeed it is We Who give life and cause death. And We are the heirs[6].

---

6. Mankind is given just temporary (and only apparent) sway and material possessions on earth. Everything then gets returned to divine Dominion.

$$\text{وَلَقَدْ عَلِمْنَا ٱلْمُسْتَقْدِمِينَ مِنكُمْ وَلَقَدْ عَلِمْنَا ٱلْمُسْتَأْخِرِينَ}$$

24. Walaqad AAalimn*a* almustaqdimeena minkum walaqad AAalimn*a* almusta/khireen**a**

15:24. And We do certainly know those of you who have preceded, and We do certainly know those who would follow.

وَإِنَّ رَبَّكَ هُوَ يَحْشُرُهُمْ إِنَّهُۥ حَكِيمٌ عَلِيمٌ ۝

25. Wa-inna rabbaka huwa ya*h*shuruhum innahu *h*akeemun AAaleem**un**

15:25. And your Lord will indeed gather them together. He is indeed Wise, Knowledgeable.

وَلَقَدْ خَلَقْنَا ٱلْإِنسَـٰنَ مِن صَلْصَـٰلٍ مِّنْ حَمَإٍ مَّسْنُونٍ ۝

26. Walaqad khalaqn*a* al-ins*a*na min *salsa*lin min *h*ama-in masnoon**in**

15:26. And certainly We created man of clay, of moulded mud.

وَٱلْجَآنَّ خَلَقْنَـٰهُ مِن قَبْلُ مِن نَّارِ ٱلسَّمُومِ ۝

27. Waalj*a*nna khalaqn*a*hu min qablu min n*a*ri alssamoom**i**

15:27. And the jinn We created before, of radiating fire.[7]

7. From Verses 26 and 27 above, we learn, in the light of modern-day knowledge:

- Human beings are made of matter.
- Jinn are made of energy radiating from fire. They cannot therefore normally be seen by human beings.
- Jinn were created before humans.

وَإِذْ قَالَ رَبُّكَ لِلْمَلَٰئِكَةِ إِنِّى خَٰلِقٌ بَشَرًا مِّن صَلْصَٰلٍ مِّنْ حَمَإٍ مَّسْنُونٍ 

28. Wa-*ith* qala rabbuka lilmal*a*-ikati innee kh*a*liqun basharan min *sals*alin min *h*ama-in masnoon**in**

15:28. And your Lord said to the angels, "I am going to create a man of clay, of moulded mud."

فَإِذَا سَوَّيْتُهُۥ وَنَفَخْتُ فِيهِ مِن رُّوحِى فَقَعُوا۟ لَهُۥ سَٰجِدِينَ

29. Fa-i*tha* sawwaytuhu wanafakhtu feehi min roo*hee* faqaAAoo lahu *s*ajideena

15:29. "So when I give him a proper form and breathe into him of My *Rooh*[8], get down to your knees prostrating[9]."

8. Verse 17:85 informs us that the *Rooh* is a command of the Lord. The Verse also informs that Man has been given but little knowledge.

9. Refer <u>study notes 2:27 and 2:28</u> **(Chapter 2) in this context.**

فَسَجَدَ ٱلْمَلَٰٓئِكَةُ كُلُّهُمْ أَجْمَعُونَ ٣٠

30. Fasajada almal*a*-ikatu kulluhum ajmaAAoon*a*

15:30. So the angels prostrated – all of them together.

إِلَّآ إِبْلِيسَ أَبَىٰٓ أَن يَكُونَ مَعَ ٱلسَّٰجِدِينَ ٣١

31. Ill*a* ibleesa ab*a* an yakoona maAAa alss*a*jideen*a*

15:31. Except Iblees[10] – he refused to be with those who prostrated.

10. In verse 18:50, Iblees has been described as a Jinni.

قَالَ يَٰٓإِبْلِيسُ مَا لَكَ أَلَّا تَكُونَ مَعَ ٱلسَّٰجِدِينَ ٣٢

32. Q*a*la y*a* ibleesu m*a* laka all*a* takoona maAAa alss*a*jideen*a*

15:32. Allah asked, "O Iblees! What excuses have you that you are not with those who prostrated?"

قَــالَ لَــمْ أَكُــن لِّأَسْــجُدَ لِبَشَــرٍ خَلَقْتَـهُ مِــن صَلْصَــلٍ مِّــنْ حَمَــإٍ مَّسْنُونٍ ۝ ٣٣

33. Qala lam akun li-asjuda libasharin khalaqtahu min *sals*alin min *h*ama-in masnoon**in**

15:33. Iblees said, "I am not the one to prostrate to a man whom You have created of clay, of moulded mud."

قَالَ فَاخْرُجْ مِنْهَا فَإِنَّكَ رَجِيمٌ ۝ ٣٤

34. Qala faokhruj min*h*a fa-innaka rajeem**un**

15:34. Allah said, "Then get out of here! You are indeed damned."

وَإِنَّ عَلَيْــكَ ٱللَّعْنَــةَ إِلَــىٰ يَــوْمِ ٱلـدِّينِ ۝ ٣٥

35. Wa-inna AAalayka allaAAnata il*a* yawmi alddeeni

15:35. "And indeed the curse is on you till the Judgment Day."

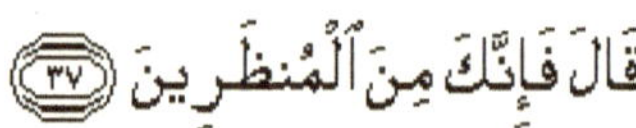

36. Q*a*la rabbi faan*th*irnee il*a* yawmi yubAAathoona

15:36. He said, "My Lord! Then give me respite till the time when they are raised."

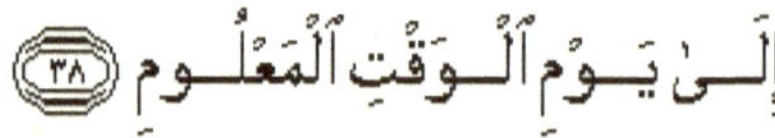

37. Q*a*la fa-innaka mina almun*th*areena

15:37. Allah said, "You are granted the respite"

إِلَـىٰ يَـوُمِ ٱلۡـوَقۡتِ ٱلۡمَعۡلُـومِ ﴿٣٨﴾

38. Il*a* yawmi alwaqti almaAAloomi

15:38. "For the appointed period."

قَالَ رَبِّ بِمَاۤ أَغْوَيْتَنِى لَأُزَيِّنَنَّ لَهُمْ فِى ٱلْأَرْضِ وَلَأُغْوِيَنَّهُمْ أَجْمَعِينَ ۩

39. Qala rabbi bima aghwaytanee laozayyinanna lahum fee al-ardi walaoghwiyannahum ajmaAAeena

---

15:39. He said, "My Lord! As You have made me deviate from the right way, I will certainly keep them enthralled in the earth, and I will certainly cause them all to deviate"

إِلَّا عِبَادَكَ مِنْهُمُ ٱلْمُخْلَصِينَ ۝

40. Illa AAibadaka minhumu almukhlaseena

15:40. "Except for those among them who worship you devotedly and exclusively."

قَالَ هَـٰذَا صِرَاطٌ عَلَىَّ مُسْتَقِيمٌ ۝

41. Qala hatha siratun AAalayya mustaqeemun

15:41. Allah said, "This is the Path that leads straight to Me."

إِنَّ عِبَادِى لَيْسَ لَكَ عَلَيْهِمْ سُلْطَـٰنٌ إِلَّا مَنِ ٱتَّبَعَكَ مِنَ ٱلْغَاوِينَ ﴿٤٢﴾

42. Inna AAibadee laysa laka AAalayhim sultanun illa mani ittabaAAaka mina alghaweena

15:42. "Indeed, you shall have no power over My subjects, except those who follow you in deviating from the right way."

وَإِنَّ جَهَنَّمَ لَمَوْعِدُهُمْ أَجْمَعِينَ ﴿٤٣﴾

43. Wa-inna jahannama lamawAAiduhum ajmaAAeena

15:43. And indeed Hell is the place promised to them all.

لَهَا سَبْعَةُ أَبْوَابٍ لِّكُلِّ بَابٍ مِّنْهُمْ جُزْءٌ مَّقْسُومٌ ﴿٤٤﴾

44. Laha sabAAatu abwabin likulli babin minhum juz-on maqsoomun

15:44. It has seven gates assigned separately to separate sections of them.

إِنَّ ٱلْمُتَّقِينَ فِى جَنَّٰتٍ وَعُيُونٍ ۝

45. Inna almuttaqeena fee jannatin waAAuyoonin

15:45. And those who fear Allah shall indeed be in gardens and fountains.

ٱدْخُلُوهَا بِسَلَٰمٍ ءَامِنِينَ ۝

46. Odkhulooha bisalamin amineena

15:46. They shall enter there in peace and security.

وَنَزَعْنَا مَا فِى صُدُورِهِم مِّنْ غِلٍّ إِخْوَٰنًا عَلَىٰ سُرُرٍ مُّتَقَٰبِلِينَ ۝

47. WanazaAAna ma fee sudoorihim min ghillin ikhwanan AAala sururin mutaqabileena

---

15:47. And We will clean their hearts of any rancour. They shall be on couches face to face as brethren.

لَا يَمَسُّهُمْ فِيهَا نَصَبٌ وَمَا هُم مِّنْهَا بِمُخْرَجِينَ ﴿٤٨﴾

48. *La* yamassuhum feeh*a* na*s*abun wam*a* hum minh*a* bimukhrajeena

---

15:48 They shall not have to suffer any fatigue therein, nor shall they be ever ejected from it.

۞ نَبِّئْ عِبَادِى أَنِّى أَنَا ٱلْغَفُورُ ٱلرَّحِيمُ ﴿٤٩﴾

49. Nabbi/ AAib*a*dee annee an*a* alghafooru alrra*h*eem**u**

15:49. Inform my subjects that I am the Forgiver, the Merciful.

وَأَنَّ عَذَابِى هُوَ ٱلْعَذَابُ ٱلْأَلِيمُ ﴿٥٠﴾

50. Waanna AAa*tha*bee huwa alAAa*tha*bu al-aleem**u**

15:50 And that My punishment is the painful one.

وَنَبِّئْهُمْ عَن ضَيْفِ إِبْرَاهِيمَ ۝

51. Wanabbi/hum AAan *d*ayfi ibr*a*heem*a*

15:51. And tell them about Abraham's guests.

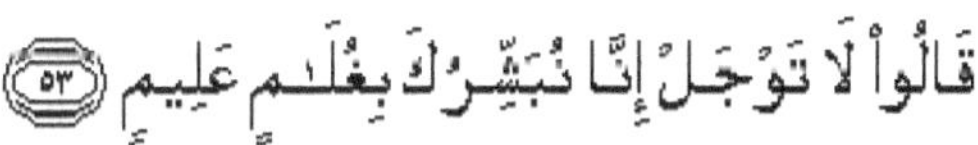

إِذْ دَخَلُواْ عَلَيْهِ فَقَالُواْ سَلَـٰمًا قَالَ إِنَّا مِنكُمْ وَجِلُونَ ۝

52. I*th* dakhaloo AAalayhi faq*a*loo sal*a*man q*a*la inn*a* minkum wajiloon*a*

15:52. When they came to him and greeted, "Peace!" He said, "We are indeed apprehensive of you."

قَالُواْ لَا تَوْجَلْ إِنَّا نُبَشِّرُكَ بِغُلَـٰمٍ عَلِيمٍ ۝

53. Q*a*loo l*a* tawjal inn*a* nubashshiruka bighul*a*min AAaleem*in*

15:53. They said, "Be not afraid! We do indeed give you the good news of a learned son."

قَالَ أَبَشَّرْتُمُونِى عَلَىٰ أَن مَّسَّنِىَ ٱلْكِبَرُ فَبِمَ تُبَشِّرُونَ ﴿٥٤﴾

54. Q*a*la abashshartumoonee AAal*a* an massaniya alkibaru fabima tubashshirooni

---

15:54. He said, "Do you give me the good news when old age has come upon me? What kind of good news is this that you give me?"

قَالُوا بَشَّرْنَٰكَ بِٱلْحَقِّ فَلَا تَكُن مِّنَ ٱلْقَٰنِطِينَ ﴿٥٥﴾

55. Q*a*loo bashsharn*a*ka bial*h*aqqi fal*a* takun mina alq*a*ni*t*eena

---

15:55. They said, "There is truth in the good news We give you! So be not of those who despair.

قَـــالَ وَمَـــن يَقْنَـــطُ مِـــن رَّحْمَـــةِ رَبِّــهِۦٓ إِلَّا ٱلضَّـــٰٓلُّونَ

﴿٥٦﴾

56. Q*a*la waman yaqna*t*u min ra*h*mati rabbihi ill*a* al*dda*lloona

---

15:56. He said, "And who would despair of the Mercy of his Lord but those who have gone astray?"

قَالَ فَمَا خَطْبُكُمْ أَيُّهَا ٱلْمُرْسَلُونَ ۝

57. Qala fama khatbukum ayyuha almursaloona

15:57. He said, "What is your mission then, O Messengers?"

قَالُوٓا۟ إِنَّآ أُرْسِلْنَآ إِلَىٰ قَوْمٍ مُّجْرِمِينَ ۝

58. Qaloo inna orsilna ila qawmin mujrimeena

15:58. They said, "We have indeed been sent towards a sinning people."

إِلَّآ ءَالَ لُوطٍ إِنَّا لَمُنَجُّوهُمْ أَجْمَعِينَ ۝

59. Illa ala lootin inna lamunajjoohum ajmaAAeena

15:59. "Excepting Lot's family, all of whom We certainly will save."

إِلَّا ٱمْرَأَتَهُۥ قَدَّرْنَآ إِنَّهَا لَمِنَ ٱلْغَـٰبِرِينَ ۝

60. Ill*a* imraatahu qaddarn*a* innah*a* lamina algh*a*bireen*a*

15:60. "But not his wife. We ordained that she shall indeed be of those who remain behind."

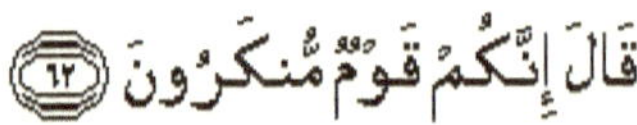

61. Falamm*a* j*aa a*la loo*t*in almursaloon*a*

15:61. So when the Messengers came to Lot's family,

62. Q*a*la innakum qawmun munkaroon*a*

15:62. He said, "You indeed are strangers."

63. Qaloo bal ji/n*a*ka bim*a* k*a*noo feehi yamtaroon*a*

15:63. They said, "But we have come to you with that about which they had doubts."

وَأَتَيْنَاكَ بِالْحَقِّ وَإِنَّا لَصَادِقُونَ ﴿٦٤﴾

64. Wa-ataynaka bialhaqqi wa-inna lasadiqoona

15:64 "And we have come to you with the authority, and what we say is most certainly the truth."

فَأَسْرِ بِأَهْلِكَ بِقِطْعٍ مِّنَ ٱلَّيْلِ وَٱتَّبِعْ أَدْبَـٰرَهُمْ وَلَا يَلْتَفِتْ مِنكُمْ أَحَدٌ وَٱمْضُواْ حَيْثُ تُؤْمَرُونَ ﴿٦٥﴾

65. Faasri bi-ahlika biqitAAin mina allayli waittabiAA adbarahum wala yaltafit minkum ahadun waimdoo haythu tu/maroona

15:65. "So leave this place with members of your family in a part of the night and you yourself follow their rear. And let not any one of you turn around. And proceed whither you are commanded."

وَقَضَيْنَآ إِلَيْهِ ذَٰلِكَ ٱلْأَمْرَ أَنَّ دَابِرَ هَـٰٓؤُلَآءِ مَقْطُوعٌ مُّصْبِحِينَ

66. Waqadayna ilayhi *tha*lika al-amra anna d*a*bira h*a*ola-i maq*t*ooAAun mu*s*bi*h*eena

15:66. And We declared to him that decree, that the roots of these (people left behind) shall be cut off by the morning.

وَجَآءَ أَهْلُ ٱلْمَدِينَةِ يَسْتَبْشِرُونَ ﴿٦٧﴾

67. Waj*a*a ahlu almadeenati yastabshiroon**a**

15:67. And the people of the town came to him rejoicing.

قَالَ إِنَّ هَـٰٓؤُلَآءِ ضَيْفِى فَلَا تَفْضَحُونِ ﴿٦٨﴾

68. Q*a*la inna h*a*ola-i *d*ayfee fal*a* taf*da*hooni

15:68. He said, "These are my guests! Disgrace me not."

وَٱتَّقُوا۟ ٱللَّهَ وَلَا تُخْزُونِ ﴿٦٩﴾

69. Waittaqoo All*a*ha wal*a* tukhzooni

15:69. "And fear Allah and do not put me to shame."

قَالُوٓاْ أَوَلَمۡ نَنۡهَكَ عَنِ ٱلۡعَٰلَمِينَ ۝

70. Qaloo awa lam nanhaka AAani alAAalameena

15:70 They said, "Have we not prohibited you from meddling with other people's matters?"

قَالَ هَٰٓؤُلَآءِ بَنَاتِىٓ إِن كُنتُمۡ فَٰعِلِينَ ۝

71. Qala haola-i banatee in kuntum faAAileena

15:71. He said, "Here are my daughters, if you have to do it.[11]"

11. What Lot tried to tell his people is that Allah Almighty has designed mankind to be heterosexual in nature. Their homosexuality was a wicked perversity that Satan induced in them as a futile attempt to defeat the divine plan. Lot's offer of his daughters here must be read in that context. His people were so steeped in the vice of homosexuality that Lot's offer served the purpose only of highlighting the perverse behaviour of his people. They were not inclined even to look at the daughters. This perverse tendency in some people is sought to be accepted and legalized by modern societies now! Such modern people may not get annihilated now as Lot's people were for their sin as they live in mixed societies, but they may not escape the intensely more painful punishment in the Hereafter.

لَعَمْرُكَ إِنَّهُمْ لَفِى سَكْرَتِهِمْ يَعْمَهُونَ ﴿٧٢﴾

72. LaAAamruka innahum lafee sakratihim yaAAmahoona

15:72. By your life! They were wandering blindly in their intoxication.

فَأَخَذَتْهُمُ ٱلصَّيْحَةُ مُشْرِقِينَ ﴿٧٣﴾

73. Faakha*th*at-humu al*ss*ay*h*atu mushriqeen**a**

15:73. Then, at sunrise, the terribly rumbling sound struck them.

فَجَعَلْنَا عَلِيَهَا سَافِلَهَا وَأَمْطَرْنَا عَلَيْهِمْ حِجَارَةً مِّن سِجِّيلٍ ﴿٧٤﴾

74. FajaAAaln*a* AA*a*liyah*a* *s*afilah*a* waam*t*arn*a* AAalayhim *h*ij*a*ratan min sijjeel**in**

15:74. We turned the place upside down, and rained stones of baked clay upon the people.

إِنَّ فِى ذَٰلِكَ لَآيَٰتٍ لِّلْمُتَوَسِّمِينَ ۝

75. Inna fee *tha*lika la*aya*tin lilmutawassimeen**a**

15:75. In that indeed are signs for those with insight.

وَإِنَّهَا لَبِسَبِيلٍ مُّقِيمٍ ۝

76. Wa-innah*a* labisabeelin muqeem**in**

15:76. And indeed it is located on an established road.[12]

---

12. Watch the YouTube video.

إِنَّ فِى ذَٰلِكَ لَآيَةً لِّلْمُؤْمِنِينَ ۝

77. Inna fee *tha*lika la*aya*tan lilmu/mineen**a**

15:77. Indeed there is a sign in that for the believers.

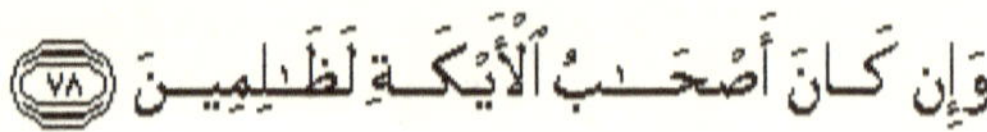

78. Wa-in k*a*na a*s-h*abu al-aykati l*ath*alimeen**a**

15:78. And the dwellers of the wood[13] too were most wicked.

---

13. One of the pre-historic peoples about whom some more details are given in Verses 26:176 to 26:191. Shu'aib was the Prophet sent to them.

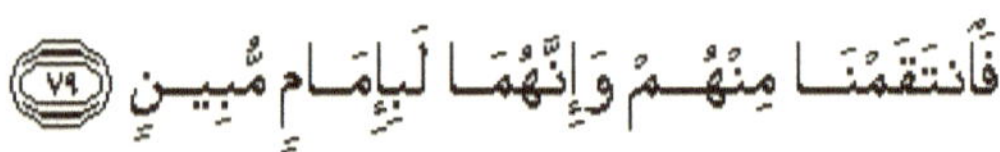

79. Faintaqamn*a* minhum wa-innahum*a* labi-im*a*min mubeen**in**

15:79. So We avenged them, and they are both[14], indeed, on an open road.

---

14. I.e., the remains of the dwellings of the people of Lot and of the people of the wood. Refer note 12 above.

80. Walaqad k*athth*aba a*s-h*abu al*h*ijri almursaleen**a**

15:80. And the dwellers of the Rock[15] did certainly reject the Messengers.

---

15. From Verse 82 below we learn that these people built their houses in the mountains. Verse 7:74 **(Manzil II) informs us that the people of AA<u>a</u>d had built their houses in the mountains. It's likely therefore that the AA<u>a</u>d and the dwellers of the Rock were the same pople.**

وَءَاتَيْنَـٰهُـمْ ءَايَـٰتِنَا فَكَانُواْ عَنْهَا مُعْرِضِينَ ﴿٨١﴾

81. Wa*a*tayn*a*hum *a*yatin*a* fak*a*noo AAanh*a* muAA*a*rid*e*ena

---

15:81. And We gave them Our Verses/signs, but they turned away from them.[16]

---

16. Just as the modern-day Muslims have turned away from the Qur'aan.

وَكَانُواْ يَنْحِتُونَ مِنَ ٱلْجِبَالِ بُيُوتًا ءَامِنِينَ ﴿٨٢﴾

82. Wak*a*noo yan*h*itoona mina aljib*a*li buyootan *a*mineena

---

15:82. And they were wont to hew houses in the mountains for security.

فَأَخَذَتْهُمُ ٱلصَّيْحَةُ مُصْبِحِينَ ۝

83. Faakha*th*at-humu al*s*say*h*atu mu*s*bi*h*eena

15:83. So the terribly rumbling sound[17] seized them in the morning.

---

17. Refer study note 15 under <u>Verse 11.67</u> **(Manzil II).**

فَمَآ أَغْنَىٰ عَنْهُم مَّا كَانُوا۟ يَكْسِبُونَ ۝

84. Fam*a* aghn*a* AAanhum m*a* k*a*noo yaksiboona

15:84. And what they earned availed them not.

وَمَا خَلَقْنَا ٱلسَّمَـٰوَٰتِ وَٱلْأَرْضَ وَمَا بَيْنَهُمَآ إِلَّا بِٱلْحَقِّ وَإِنَّ ٱلسَّاعَةَ لَآتِيَةٌ فَٱصْفَحِ ٱلصَّفْحَ ٱلْجَمِيلَ ۝

85. Wam*a* khalaqn*a* al*s*sam*a*w*a*ti w*a*al-ar*d*a wam*a* baynahum*a* ill*a* bial*h*aqqi wa-inna al*s*saAAata la*a*tiyatun fai*s*fa*h*i al*s*safa aljameela

---

232

15:85. And We did not create the heavens and the earth and what is between them, but by due authority. And the Hour is most surely going to come. So fogive things – those that are forgivable.[18]

---

18. Human beings are Allah's representatives on earth. And Allah is Gracious and Merciful. They should therefoe reflect those divine attributes in their deeds here. A human being is not entitled to punish another, just because the latter would not believe in Islam. Allah will deal with such people on the Judgment Day, which is bound to come. Those who are given authority over other people on this earth ought to exercise their authority only in such cases where any inaction on their part could raise law and order problems here.

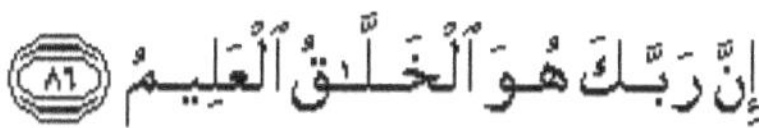

86. Inna rabbaka huwa alkhall*a*qu alAAaleem**u**

15:86. Your Lord is indeed the Knowledgeable Creator of all things.

---

87. Walaqad *a*tayn*a*ka sabAAan mina almath*a*nee waalqur-*a*na alAAa*th*eem**a**

15:87. And certainly We have given you seven of the repeated Verses[19] and the Glorious Qur'aan.

---

19. The word 'Verses' is not specifically mentioned in the Arabic text. It is the general interpretation of what 'seven of the repeated' means. And the seven Verses that are often recited are obviously those of

the opening chapter Al-Fatiha of the Qur'aan. The Shia sect interprets the 'seven' to be seven of their Imams. But their claim has no merit (refer Interpretation of Verse 15:87**).**

لَا تَمُدَّنَّ عَيْنَيْكَ إِلَىٰ مَا مَتَّعْنَا بِهِ أَزْوَٰجًا مِّنْهُمْ وَلَا تَحْزَنْ عَلَيْهِمْ وَٱخْفِضْ جَنَاحَكَ لِلْمُؤْمِنِينَ ۝

88. La tamuddanna AAaynayka ila ma mattaAAna bihi azwajan minhum wala tahzan AAalayhim waikhfid janahaka lilmu/mineena

15:88. Pine not for that which We have given some of them to enjoy, nor grieve for them. And be kind to the believers.

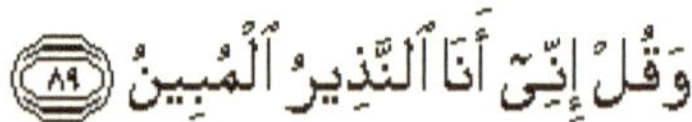

89. Waqul innee ana alnnatheeru almubeenu

15:89. And say, "I am indeed the plain warner."

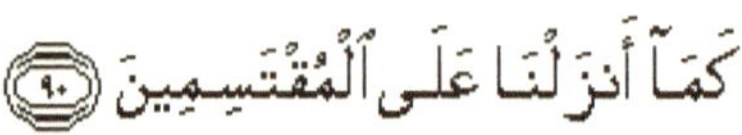

90. Kama anzalna AAala almuqtasimeena

15:90. It is as though what We have sent down is on those who make divisions therein.

91. Alla*thee*na jaAAaloo alqur-*a*na AAi*dee*na

15:91. Those that tear the Qur'aan into shreds.[20]

20. The Qur'aan speaks here about most of mankind in today's world. Most of the world population today is non-Muslim. They have little regard for the Qur'aan. But the tragic fact is that most of the Muslims too treat the Qur'aan as a thing of no consequence in their lives. They have fallen into the habit of reading it just ritualistically, without trying to understand what they read. And even those who read it with some understanding allow themselves to be led astray by extraneous human-influenced sources and deviate from the plain meanings of the Qur'aanic words. These 'learned' people are wont to give the words meanings that suit them, and thus divisions have occurred within those who 'understand' the Qur'aan. Then there are those who abide by what a part of the Qur'aan says, but do not abide by another part of it. Some may offer the ritual prayers but may consider fasting for a month too difficult for them.

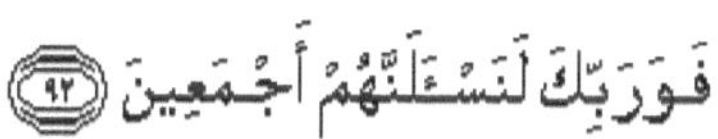

92. Fawarabbika lanas-alannahum ajmaAAeena

15:92. And, by your Lord, We shall certainly question them all

عَمَّا كَانُواْ يَعْمَلُونَ ﴿٩٣﴾

93. AAamma kanoo yaAAamaloona

15:93. As to what they did!

فَٱصْدَعْ بِمَا تُؤْمَرُ وَأَعْرِضْ عَنِ ٱلْمُشْرِكِينَ ﴿٩٤﴾

94. FaisdaAA bima tu/maru waaAArid AAani almushrikeena

15:94. Declare then openly what you are commanded with and turn away from the polytheists.

إِنَّا كَفَيْنَـٰكَ ٱلْمُسْتَهْزِءِينَ ﴿٩٥﴾

95. Inna kafaynaka almustahzi-eena

15:95. We shall certainly provide you enough protection against those who scoff.

اَلَّذِينَ يَجْعَلُونَ مَعَ ٱللَّهِ إِلَـٰهًا ءَاخَرَ فَسَوْفَ يَعْلَمُونَ ﴿٩٦﴾

96. Alla*th*eena yajAAaloona maAAa All*a*hi il*a*han *a*khara fasawfa yaAAlamoon**a**

15:96. Those who worship others besides Allah. They shall soon know their folly!

وَلَقَدْ نَعْلَمُ أَنَّكَ يَضِيقُ صَدْرُكَ بِمَا يَقُولُونَ ﴿٩٧﴾

97. Walaqad naAAlamu annaka ya*d*eequ *s*adruka bim*a* yaqooloon**a**

15:97. And We do know that your (Prophet's) heart is distressed at what they say.

فَسَبِّحْ بِحَمْدِ رَبِّكَ وَكُن مِّنَ ٱلسَّـٰجِدِينَ ﴿٩٨﴾

98. Fasabbi*h* bi*h*amdi rabbika wakun mina alss*a*jideen**a**

15:98. Hymn then the praise of your Lord and be of those who prostrate to Him.

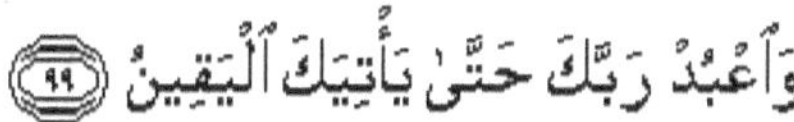

وَٱعْبُدْ رَبَّكَ حَتَّىٰ يَأْتِيَكَ ٱلْيَقِينُ ﴿٩٩﴾

99. WaoAAbud rabbaka *hatta* ya/tiyaka alyaqeen**u**

15:99. And worship your Lord until there comes to you that certain composure.[21]

---

21. Refer in this context to the Prophet's distress mentioned in Verse 97 above.

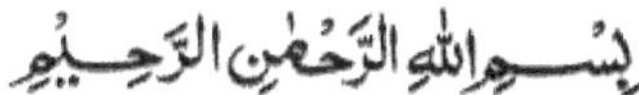

In the Name of Allah, the Gracious, the Merciful

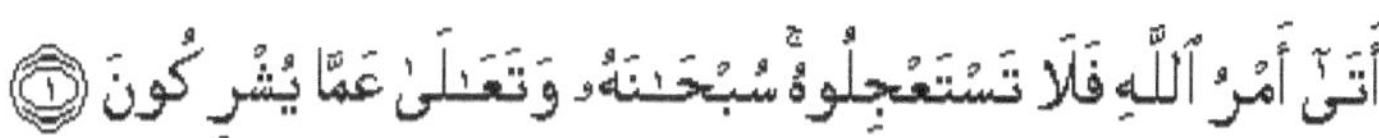

1. Ata amru Allahi fala tastaAAjiloohu subhanahu wataAAala AAamma yushrikoona

---

16:1. Allah's command is already issued! So, hasten it not.[1] Glorified and highly exalted is He above what they worship besides Him.

---

1. Relating this Verse to our present-day circumstances, we do often apparently see that an oppressor gets away with his oppression. He does not get immediate punishment. Allah tells us here, in this circumstance, that He is very much aware of the oppression done. And, in His scheme of things, He knows that appropriate action in respect of the oppression is already taken at a fixed point of time in the future. Man viz-a-viz the Creator, time is a relative term. A future event for man Is an accomplished thing for the Creator. Allah gives enough opportunities to man for reform before He strikes.

---

2. Yunazzilu almala-ikata bialrroohi min amrihi AAala man yashao min AAibadihi an anthiroo annahu la ilaha illa ana faittaqooni

---

16:2. He sends down the angels, on whom He pleases of His subjects, with the inspiration of His command: "Give the warning that there is no god but Me, and so fear Me."

خَلَقَ ٱلسَّمَـٰوَٰتِ وَٱلْأَرْضَ بِٱلْحَقِّ تَعَـٰلَىٰ عَمَّا يُشْرِكُونَ ۝

3. Khalaqa alssam*a*w*a*ti waal-ar*d*a bial*h*aqqi taAA*a*la AAamm*a* yushrikoona

16:3. He has created the heavens and the earth with the Truth and due Authority. He is far too high and exalted above what they worship besides Him.

خَلَقَ ٱلْإِنسَـٰنَ مِن نُّطْفَةٍ فَإِذَا هُوَ خَصِيمٌ مُّبِينٌ ۝

4. Khalaqa al-ins*a*na min nu*t*fatin fa-i*tha* huwa kha*s*eemun mubeen**un**

16:4. He (Allah) created man from tiny fertilized ovum. And, lo, he has become an open adversary!

وَٱلْأَنْعَـٰمَ خَلَقَهَا لَكُمْ فِيهَا دِفْءٌ وَمَنَـٰفِعُ وَمِنْهَا تَأْكُلُونَ ۝

5. Waal-anAA*a*ma khalaqah*a* lakum feeha dif-on wamanafiAAu waminh*a* ta-kuloona

16:5. And He created the cattle. You get from them warm clothing and other benefits. And from them you get meat to eat.

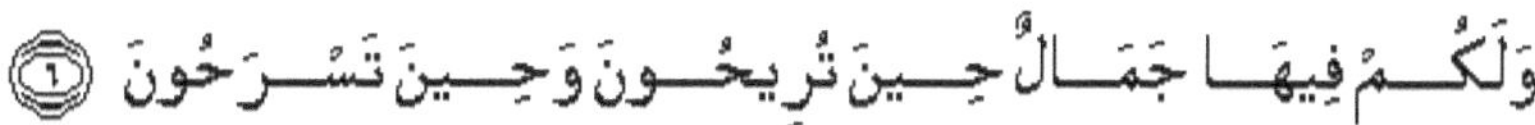

6. Walakum feeh*a* jam*a*lun *h*eena turee*h*oona wa*h*eena tasra*h*oon**a**

16:6. And you feel good when you drive them back home, and when you send them out to pasture.

وَتَحْمِلُ أَثْقَالَكُمْ إِلَىٰ بَلَدٍ لَّمْ تَكُونُواْ بَٰلِغِيهِ إِلَّا بِشِقِّ ٱلْأَنفُسِ إِنَّ رَبَّكُمْ لَرَءُوفٌ رَّحِيمٌ ۞

7. Wata*h*milu athq*a*lakum il*a* baladin lam takoonoo b*a*lighee*h*i ill*a* bishiqqi al-anfusi inna rabbakum laraoofun ra*h*eem**un**

16:7. And they carry your heavy loads to lands you could not reach but with much difficulty. Your Lord is indeed Kind, Merciful.

وَٱلْخَيْلَ وَٱلْبِغَالَ وَٱلْحَمِيرَ لِتَرْكَبُوهَا وَزِينَةً وَيَخْلُقُ مَا لَا تَعْلَمُونَ

8. Waalkhayla waalbigh*a*la waal*h*ameera litarkaboo*ha* wazeenatan wayakhluqu m*a* l*a* taAAlamoona

16:8. And horses, mules and asses for you to ride upon and as assets, and He creates what you do not know.

وَعَلَى ٱللَّهِ قَصْدُ ٱلسَّبِيلِ وَمِنْهَا جَآئِرٌ وَلَوْ شَآءَ لَهَدَىٰكُمْ أَجْمَعِينَ ۝

9. WaAAal*a* All*a*hi qa*s*du alssabeeli waminh*a* ja-irun walaw sh*a*a lahad*a*kum ajmaAAeena

16:9. And upon Allah is the determination of the Path and the deviations from it. And if He had so willed He would have certainly guided you all.[2]

2. Allah has given man the freedom to choose. It is in exercise of this freedom, that he chooses the right or the wrong path, despite His warning him plainly the consequences of following the wrong path.

هُوَ ٱلَّذِىٓ أَنزَلَ مِنَ ٱلسَّمَآءِ مَآءً لَّكُم مِّنْهُ شَرَابٌ وَمِنْهُ شَجَرٌ فِيهِ تُسِيمُونَ ۝

10. Huwa alla*thee* anzala mina alssam*a*-i m*a*an lakum minhu shar*a*bun waminhu shajarun feehi tuseemoona

16:10. He it is Who sends down water from the sky. You drink thereof, and there from you get the shrubbery upon which you let your cattle graze.

يُنۢبِتُ لَكُم بِهِ ٱلزَّرْعَ وَٱلزَّيْتُونَ وَٱلنَّخِيلَ وَٱلْأَعْنَٰبَ وَمِن كُلِّ ٱلثَّمَرَٰتِ إِنَّ فِى ذَٰلِكَ لَءَايَةً لِّقَوْمٍ يَتَفَكَّرُونَ ۝

11. Yunbitu lakum bihi alzzarAAa wa**a**lzzaytoona wa**a**lnnakheela waal-aAAn*a*ba wamin kulli alththamar*a*ti inna fee *tha*lika la*a*yatan liqawmin yatafakkaroon**a**

16:11. He causes the green cultivated fields, the olives, the palm trees, the grapes and all kinds of fruits to grow for you thereby. There is indeed a sign in that for a people who think.

وَسَخَّرَ لَكُمُ ٱلَّيْلَ وَٱلنَّهَارَ وَٱلشَّمْسَ وَٱلْقَمَرَ وَٱلنُّجُومُ مُسَخَّرَٰتٌ بِأَمْرِهِ إِنَّ فِى ذَٰلِكَ لَءَايَٰتٍ لِّقَوْمٍ يَعْقِلُونَ ۝

12. Wasakhkhara lakumu allayla wa**a**lnnah*a*ra wa**a**lshshamsa waalqamara wa**a**lnnujoomu musakhkhar*a*tun bi-amrihi inna fee *tha*lika la*a*yatin liqawmin yaAAqiloon**a**

16:12. And He has made the night, the day, the sun and the moon to work for you. And the stars are made subservient by His command. There are indeed signs in that for a people who ponder.

وَمَا ذَرَأَ لَكُمْ فِى ٱلْأَرْضِ مُخْتَلِفًا أَلْوَٰنُهُ إِنَّ فِى ذَٰلِكَ لَءَايَةً لِّقَوْمٍ يَذَّكَّرُونَ

13. Wam*a* *th*araa lakum fee al-ar*di* mukhtalifan alw*a*nuhu inna fee *tha*lika la*a*yatan liqawmin ya*ththa*kkaroon**a**

16:13. And what He has created on the earth for you are of different hues and colours. There is a sign in that for a people who reflect.[3]

3. Allah Almighty did thus inculcate the urge to think deeply over His creations mentioned in Verses 11 to 13 here. Those Muslim thinkers laid the foundation for the scientific renaissance that brought about the proliferation of modern-day knowledge. But now the Muslims have long since ceased to be the torch-bearers. They have relegated the Qur'aan to just ritual reading and have thus become the back-benchers in modern-day societies.

وَهُوَ ٱلَّذِى سَخَّرَ ٱلْبَحْرَ لِتَأْكُلُواْ مِنْهُ لَحْمًا طَرِيًّا وَتَسْتَخْرِجُواْ مِنْهُ حِلْيَةً تَلْبَسُونَهَا وَتَرَى ٱلْفُلْكَ مَوَاخِرَ فِيهِ وَلِتَبْتَغُواْ مِن فَضْلِهِۦ وَلَعَلَّكُمْ تَشْكُرُونَ ﴿١٤﴾

14. Wahuwa alla*thee* sakhkhara alba*h*ra lita/kuloo minhu la*h*man *t*ariyyan watastakhrijoo minhu *h*ilyatan talbasoona*ha* watara alfulka mawa*kh*ira feehi walitabtaghoo min fa*d*lihi walaAAallakum tashkuroo**na**

16:14. And He it is Who has made the sea subservient so that you may eat fresh flesh from it and bring out of it jewels you wear. And you see the ships cut through it so that you might seek His bounty and be thankful.

وَأَلْقَىٰ فِى ٱلْأَرْضِ رَوَاسِىَ أَن تَمِيدَ بِكُمْ وَأَنْهَٰرًا وَسُبُلًا لَّعَلَّكُمْ تَهْتَدُونَ

15. Waalq*a* fee al-ar*d*i rawasiya an tameeda bikum waanh*a*ran wasubulan laAAallakum tahtadoona

16:15. And He has cast firm anchors [mountains] in the earth lest it should shake with you.[4] And rivers and roads, that you may find your way.

---

4. The use of the word *alqa* (has cast/thrown) here is significant. It is as if the mountains were thrown into the earth from outside. Maybe, in the distant past during the formation of the earth, large meteoroids generated from a destroyed star hit the earth. The mountains have their bases dug deep down into the earth.

وَعَلَـٰمَـٰتٍ وَبِالنَّجْمِ هُـمْ يَهْتَـدُونَ ﴿١٦﴾

16. WaAAal*ama*tin wabi**al**nnajmi hum yahtadoon**a**

16:16. And they find their way by landmarks and the stars.

أَفَمَن يَخْلُقُ كَمَن لَّا يَخْلُقُ أَفَلَا تَذَكَّرُونَ ﴿١٧﴾

17. Afaman yakhluqu kaman l*a* yakhluqu afal*a* ta*th*akkaroon**a**

16:17. Is He then Who creates like the one who does not? Do you not then reflect?

وَإِن تَعُدُّوا۟ نِعْمَةَ ٱللَّـهِ لَا تُحْصُوهَآ إِنَّ ٱللَّـهَ لَغَفُورٌ رَّحِـيمٌ ﴿١٨﴾

18. Wa-in taAAuddoo niAAmata Allahi l*a* tu*h*sooh*a* inna Allaha laghafoorun ra*h*eemun

16:18. And if you would count Allah's favours, you won't be able to do it. Allah is certainly indeed Forgiving, Merciful.

وَٱللَّـهُ يَعْلَـمُ مَـا تُسِـرُّونَ وَمَـا تُعْلِنُـونَ ﴿١٩﴾

19. WaAll*a*hu yaAAlamu m*a* tusirroona wam*a* tuAAlinoon*a*

16:19. And Allah knows what you conceal and what you do openly.

وَٱلَّذِينَ يَدْعُونَ مِن دُونِ ٱللَّهِ لَا يَخْلُقُونَ شَيْئًا وَهُم يُخْلَقُونَ ﴿٢٠﴾

20. Waalla*th*eena yadAAoona min dooni All*a*hi l*a* yakhluqoona shay-an wahum yukhlaqoona

16:20. And those, whom they pray to besides Allah, have not created anything; they are themselves created!

أَمْوَٰتٌ غَـيْرُ أَحْيَـاءٍ وَمَا يَشْعُرُونَ أَيَّانَ يُبْعَثُونَ ﴿٢١﴾

21. Amw*a*tun ghayru a*h*ya-in wam*a* yashAAuroona ayy*a*na yubAAathoona

16:21. They are dead – not living – and they know not when they shall be raised.

$$\text{إِلَـٰهُكُمْ إِلَـٰهٌ وَٰحِدٌ ۚ فَٱلَّذِينَ لَا يُؤْمِنُونَ بِٱلْءَاخِرَةِ قُلُوبُهُم مُّنكِرَةٌ}$$

$$\text{وَهُم مُّسْتَكْبِرُونَ ﴿٢٢﴾}$$

22. Il*a*hukum il*a*hun w*a*hidun faalla*th*eena l*a* yu/minoona bial-*a*khirati quloobuhum munkiratun wahum mustakbiroona

16:22. The object of your worship is Allah, the One and Only! And those, who do not believe in the Hereafter, are defiant in their hearts, and arrogant.

$$\text{لَا جَرَمَ أَنَّ ٱللَّهَ يَعْلَمُ مَا يُسِرُّونَ وَمَا يُعْلِنُونَ ۚ إِنَّهُۥ لَا}$$

$$\text{يُحِبُّ ٱلْمُسْتَكْبِرِينَ ﴿٢٣﴾}$$

23. L*a* jarama anna All*a*ha yaAAlamu m*a* yusirroona wam*a* yuAAlinoona innahu l*a* yu*h*ibbu almustakbireena

16:23. Allah does indeed, without doubt, know what they hide and what they declare. He does not, indeed, love those who are arrogant.

$$\text{وَإِذَا قِيلَ لَهُم مَّاذَآ أَنزَلَ رَبُّكُمْ ۙ قَالُوٓا۟ أَسَـٰطِيرُ ٱلْأَوَّلِينَ ﴿٢٤﴾}$$

24. Wa-i*tha* qeela lahum m*a*tha anzala rabbukum q*a*loo as*a*teeru al-awwaleena

16:24. And when they are asked, “What is it that your Lord has sent down?” They say, “Stories of the ancients.”

لِيَحْمِلُوٓا۟ أَوْزَارَهُمْ كَامِلَةً يَوْمَ ٱلْقِيَـٰمَةِ ۙ وَمِنْ أَوْزَارِ ٱلَّذِينَ
يُضِلُّونَهُم بِغَيْرِ عِلْمٍ ۗ أَلَا سَآءَ مَا يَزِرُونَ ﴿٢٥﴾

25. Liya*h*miloo awz*a*rahum k*a*milatan yawma alqiy*a*mati wamin awz*a*ri alla*th*eena yu*d*illoonahum bighayri AAilmin al*a* s*a*a m*a* yaziroon**a**

16:25. By saying so they are going to bear not only their own entire burdens on the day of Resurrection, but also of the burdens of those whom they led astray with misinformation. Is it not too bad what they bear?

قَدْ مَكَرَ ٱلَّذِينَ مِن قَبْلِهِمْ فَأَتَى ٱللَّهُ بُنْيَـٰنَهُم مِّنَ ٱلْقَوَاعِدِ فَخَرَّ
عَلَيْهِمُ ٱلسَّقْفُ مِن فَوْقِهِمْ وَأَتَىٰهُمُ ٱلْعَذَابُ مِنْ حَيْثُ لَا يَشْعُرُونَ ﴿٢٦﴾

26. Qad makara alla*th*eena min qablihim faat*a* All*a*hu buny*a*nahum mina alqaw*a*AAidi fakharra AAalayhimu alssaqfu min fawqihim waat*a*humu alAAa*tha*bu min *h*aythu l*a* yashAAuroon**a**

16:26. Those before them plotted. But Allah struck their edifice at its foundations, so that the roof fell on them from above them. And the punishment came to them from whence they knew not.

ثُمَّ يَوْمَ ٱلْقِيَـٰمَةِ يُخْزِيهِمْ وَيَقُولُ أَيْنَ شُرَكَآءِىَ ٱلَّذِينَ كُنتُمْ تُشَـٰقُّونَ فِيهِمْ قَالَ ٱلَّذِينَ أُوتُوا۟ ٱلْعِلْمَ إِنَّ ٱلْخِزْىَ ٱلْيَوْمَ وَٱلسُّوٓءَ عَلَى ٱلْكَـٰفِرِينَ

27. Thumma yawma alqiy*a*mati yukhzeehim wayaqoolu ayna shurak*a*-iya alla*thee*na kuntum tush*a*qqoona feehim q*a*la alla*thee*na ootoo alAAilma inna alkhizya alyawma wa**a**lssoo-a AAal*a* alk*a*fireen**a**

16:27. Then on the Resurrection Day He will disgrace them and ask, "Where are they whom you worshipped besides Me, and for whose sake you caused discord?" Those who are endowed with knowledge will say, "Indeed, the disgrace and the evil, this day, shall be upon those who had suppressed the Truth."

ٱلَّذِينَ تَتَوَفَّىٰهُمُ ٱلْمَلَـٰٓئِكَةُ ظَالِمِىٓ أَنفُسِهِمْ فَأَلْقَوُا۟ ٱلسَّلَمَ مَا كُنَّا نَعْمَلُ مِن سُوٓءٍ بَلَىٰٓ إِنَّ ٱللَّهَ عَلِيمٌۢ بِمَا كُنتُمْ تَعْمَلُونَ

28. Alla*thee*na tatawaff*a*humu almal*a*-ikatu *tha*limee anfusihim faalqawoo alssalama m*a* kunn*a* naAAmalu min soo-in bal*a* inna All*a*ha AAaleemun bim*a* kuntum taAAmaloon**a**

16:28. Those that the angels caused to die while they indulged in deeds, which were ultimately injurious to their own selves. Then they would submit, "We didn't do anything bad." Aye! Allah does indeed know what you did.

فَٱدْخُلُوٓا۟ أَبْوَٰبَ جَهَنَّمَ خَـٰلِدِينَ فِيهَا فَلَبِئْسَ مَثْوَى ٱلْمُتَكَبِّرِينَ

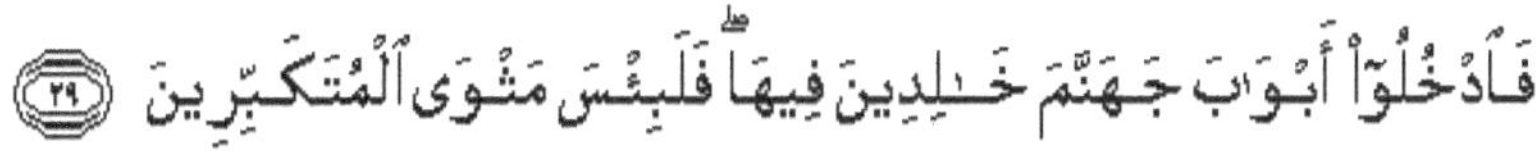

29. Faodkhuloo abw*a*ba jahannama kh*a*lideena feeh*a* falabi/sa ma*th*w*a* almutakabbireen**a**

16:29. Enter then the gates of Hell, to be there forever! And the dwelling place of the arrogant people is certainly bad.

۞ وَقِيلَ لِلَّذِينَ ٱتَّقَوْاْ مَاذَآ أَنزَلَ رَبُّكُمْ قَالُواْ خَيْرًا لِّلَّذِينَ أَحْسَنُواْ فِى هَـٰذِهِ ٱلدُّنْيَا حَسَنَةٌ وَلَدَارُ ٱلْأَخِرَةِ خَيْرٌ وَلَنِعْمَ دَارُ ٱلْمُتَّقِينَ ﴿٣٠﴾

30. Waqeela lillatheena ittaqaw matha anzala rabbukum qaloo khayran lillatheena ahsanoo fee hathihi alddunya hasanatun waladaru al-akhirati khayrun walaniAAma daru almuttaqeena

16:30. And those who fear Allah are asked, "What is it that your Lord has sent down?" They say, "That which is good." There is goodness for those who do good deeds in this world. And certainly, the abode of the Hereafter is better. And excellent certainly is the abode of those who fear Allah.

جَنَّـٰتُ عَدْنٍ يَدْخُلُونَهَا تَجْرِى مِن تَحْتِهَا ٱلْأَنْهَـٰرُ لَهُمْ فِيهَا مَا يَشَآءُونَ كَذَٰلِكَ يَجْزِى ٱللَّـهُ ٱلْمُتَّقِينَ ﴿٣١﴾

31. Jannatu AAadnin yadkhuloonaha tajree min tahtiha al-anharu lahum feeha ma yashaoona kathalika yajzee Allahu almuttaqeena

16:31. They shall enter gardens of perpetuity, having rivers flowing beneath them. They shall have, in them, what they please. Thus, does Allah reward those who fear Him.

ٱلَّذِينَ تَتَوَفَّىٰهُمُ ٱلْمَلَـٰٓئِكَةُ طَيِّبِينَ يَقُولُونَ سَلَـٰمٌ عَلَيْكُمُ ٱدْخُلُوا۟ ٱلْجَنَّةَ بِمَا كُنتُمْ تَعْمَلُونَ ﴿٣٢﴾

32. Alla*th*eena tatawaff*a*humu almal*a*-ikatu *t*ayyibeena yaqooloona sal*a*mun AAalaykumu odkhuloo aljannata bim*a* kuntum taAAmaloon*a*

16:32. Those that the angels caused to die while they did good deeds, the angels saying to them, "Peace upon you! Enter the garden as a reward for what you did."

هَـلْ يَنظُـرُونَ إِلَّآ أَن تَـأْتِيَهُمُ ٱلْمَلَـٰٓئِكَـةُ أَوْ يَـأْتِيَ أَمْـرُ رَبِّكَ كَذَٰلِكَ فَعَلَ ٱلَّذِينَ مِن قَبْلِهِمْ وَمَا ظَلَمَهُمُ ٱللَّهُ وَلَـٰكِن كَانُوٓا۟ أَنفُسَهُمْ يَظْلِمُونَ ﴿٣٣﴾

33. Hal yan*th*uroona ill*a* an ta/tiyahumu almal*a*-ikatu aw ya/tiya amru rabbika ka*th*alika faAAala alla*th*eena min qablihim wam*a* *th*alamahumu All*a*hu wal*a*kin k*a*noo anfusahum ya*th*limoon*a*

16:33. They do not wait for anything but that the angels should come to them or that the Commandment of your Lord should come to pass. That is what those before them did. And Allah oppressed them not, but they oppressed themselves.

فَأَصَـابَهُمْ سَـيِّـَٔاتُ مَـا عَمِلُـوا۟ وَحَـاقَ بِهِـم مَّـا كَـانُوا۟ بِهِۦ يَسْتَهْزِءُونَ ﴿٣٤﴾

34. Faa*s*abahum sayyi-*a*tu m*a* AAamiloo wa*h*aqa bihim m*a* k*a*noo bihi yastahzi-oon*a*

16:34. So the bad things they did shall afflict them and the things they mocked at shall besiege them.

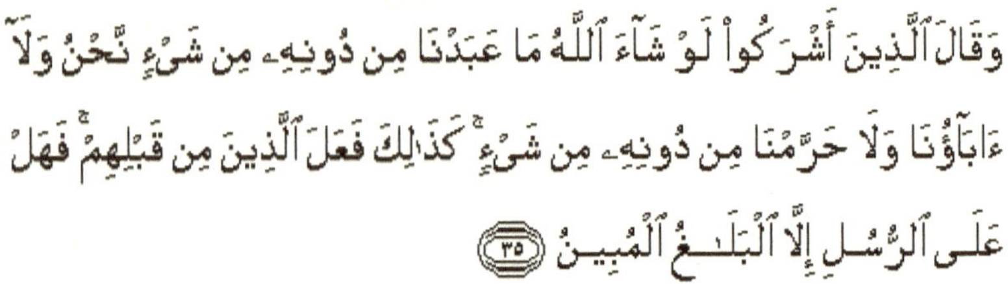

35. Waqala alla*thee*na ashrakoo law sh*a*a Allahu m*a* AAabadn*a* min doonihi min shay-in na*h*nu wala *abaona* wala *h*arramn*a* min doonihi min shay-in ka*th*alika faAAala alla*thee*na min qablihim fahal AAal*a* alrrusuli illa albala*gh*u almubeen**u**

16:35. And they who worship others besides Allah say, "Had Allah so willed, we would not have worshipped anything besides Him. Nor would our fathers do it. And we would not have prohibited anything without His Command." That is what those before them did. Are the Messengers then responsible for anything but the plain and clear conveyance of the divine Message? [5]

5. It is the responsibility of the Messengers to convey the divine Message honestly and faithfully to the people. The Messengers were not given the responsibility of punishing those who do not then come to believe in Allah, His Messenger and the Message. It is for Allah to punish them for their intransigence in this regard. HE has made it clear that there is no compulsion in religion [Verse 2:256]. Some people may then wonder as to why Prophet Muhammad (peace on him) did have all those armed conflicts with non-believers. It should be clearly borne in mind that the conflicts were not just because some people did not believe. The conflicts had occurred because the *kuffar* would not allow the believers to practice Islam in peace.

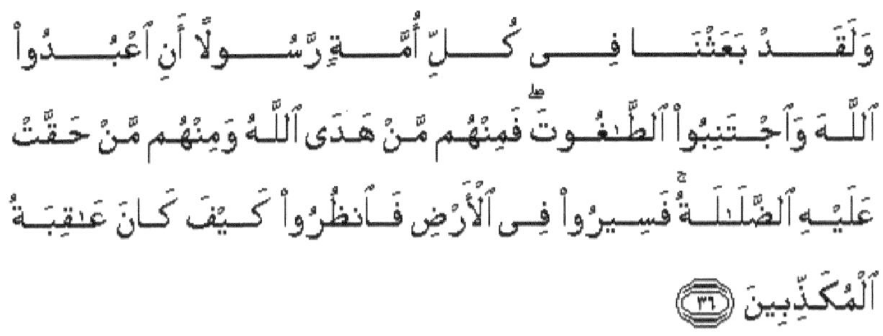

36. Walaqad baAAathna fee kulli ommatin rasoolan ani oAAbudoo Allaha waijtaniboo alttaghoota faminhum man hada Allahu waminhum man haqqat AAalayhi alddalalatu faseeroo fee al-ardi faonthuroo kayfa kana AAaqibatu almukaththibeena

16:36. And certainly We raised in every community a Messenger saying, "Worship Allah and shun whatever is worshipped other than Allah." So, there were some, among them, whom Allah guided and there were others who were destined to be misguided. Travel in the land then and see what the end of those who rejected the divine Message was.

37. In tahris AAala hudahum fa-inna Allaha la yahdee man yudillu wama lahum min nasireena

16:37. Even if you are anxious for their guidance, Allah does not indeed guide him who willfully goes astray. And there shall be none to help them.

وَأَقْسَمُواْ بِٱللَّهِ جَهْدَ أَيْمَـٰنِهِمْ لَا يَبْعَثُ ٱللَّهُ مَن يَمُوتُ بَلَىٰ وَعْدًا عَلَيْهِ حَقًّا وَلَـٰكِنَّ أَكْثَرَ ٱلنَّاسِ لَا يَعْلَمُونَ ﴿٣٨﴾

38. Waaqsamoo biAll*a*hi jahda aym*a*nihim l*a* yabAAathu All*a*hu man yamootu bal*a* waAAdan AAalayhi *h*aqqan wal*a*kinna akthara alnn*a*si l*a* yaAAlamoona

---

16:38. And they swear by Allah most solemnly that Allah will not raise anyone who dies. Yea! It is a promise binding on Him, but most people know it not.

لِيُبَيِّنَ لَهُمُ ٱلَّذِى يَخْتَلِفُونَ فِيهِ وَلِيَعْلَمَ ٱلَّذِينَ كَفَرُوٓاْ أَنَّهُمْ كَانُوا۟ كَـٰذِبِينَ ﴿٣٩﴾

39. Liyubayyina lahumu alla*thee* yakhtalifoona feehi waliyaAAlama alla*th*eena kafaroo annahum k*a*noo k*ath*ibee**n**a

---

16:39. Allah will raise the dead so that He might make matters, in which they differ, clear to them, and that those who suppress the Truth might know that they were liars.

إِنَّمَا قَوْلُنَا لِشَىْءٍ إِذَآ أَرَدْنَـٰهُ أَن نَّقُولَ لَهُۥ كُن فَيَكُونُ ﴿٤٠﴾

40. Innam*a* qawlun*a* lishay-in i*th*a aradn*a*hu an naqoola lahu kun fayakoon**u**

16:40. When We intend a thing, We just say "Be" and it is.

وَٱلَّذِينَ هَاجَرُواْ فِى ٱللَّهِ مِنۢ بَعْدِ مَا ظُلِمُواْ لَنُبَوِّئَنَّهُمْ فِى ٱلدُّنْيَا حَسَنَةً وَلَأَجْرُ ٱلْأَخِرَةِ أَكْبَرُ لَوْ كَانُواْ يَعْلَمُونَ ٤١

41. Waalla*th*eena *h*ajaroo fee All*a*hi min baAAdi m*a th*ulimoo lanubawwi-annahum fee aldduny*a h*asanatan walaajru al-*a*khirati akbaru law k*a*noo yaAAlamoona

16:41. And those who migrate for Allah's sake after they are oppressed, We will certainly resettle them in a good position in this world. And the reward of the Hereafter is certainly much greater, if they but know.

ٱلَّذِينَ صَبَرُواْ وَعَلَىٰ رَبِّهِمْ يَتَوَكَّلُونَ ٤٢

42. Alla*th*eena *s*abaroo waAAal*a* rabbihim yatawakkaloona

16:42. Those that are patient and have trust in their Lord.

وَمَآ أَرْسَلْنَا مِن قَبْلِكَ إِلَّا رِجَالًا نُّوحِىٓ إِلَيْهِمْ فَسْـَٔلُوٓاْ أَهْلَ ٱلذِّكْرِ إِن كُنتُمْ لَا تَعْلَمُونَ ٤٣

43. Wam*a* arsaln*a* min qablika ill*a* rij*a*lan noo*h*ee ilayhim fais-aloo ahla al*thth*ikri in kuntum l*a* taAAlamoona

16:43. And We did not send before you any but men to whom We revealed our Verses/signs. Ask the people of the divine Reminder/Book if you do not know.[6]

---

6. This was the divine response to the *kuffar* wondering why a man – and not an angel – had been sent as Allah's Messenger. They were asked to get confirmation from people – like the Jews – on whom the earlier divine Books had been revealed, that Allah had sent men only as His Messengers also to them.

بِالْبَيِّنَـٰتِ وَالزُّبُرِ ۗ وَأَنزَلْنَآ إِلَيْكَ الذِّكْرَ لِتُبَيِّنَ لِلنَّاسِ مَا نُزِّلَ إِلَيْهِمْ وَلَعَلَّهُمْ يَتَفَكَّرُونَ ﴿٤٤﴾

44. Bialbayyin*a*ti wa**a**lzzuburi waanzaln*a* ilayka al*thth*ikra litubayyina lilnn*a*si m*a* nuzzila ilayhim walaAAallahum yatafakkaroona

---

16:44. We had sent only men, to the earlier people, with clear signs/evidences and scriptures. And We have sent down to you the Reminder (the Qur'aan) that you may make clear to mankind what has been sent down for them, and that they may think about it.

أَفَأَمِنَ الَّذِينَ مَكَرُوا السَّيِّئَاتِ أَن يَخْسِفَ اللَّهُ بِهِمُ الْأَرْضَ أَوْ يَأْتِيَهُمُ الْعَذَابُ مِنْ حَيْثُ لَا يَشْعُرُونَ ﴿٤٥﴾

45. Afaamina alla*th*eena makaroo alssayyi-*a*ti an yakhsifa All*a*hu bihimu al-ar*d*a aw ya/tiyahumu alAAa*th*abu min *h*aythu l*a* yashAAuroona

---

16:45 Do they then who plan evil deeds feel confident that Allah will not cause the earth to swallow them, or that punishment may not overtake them from whence they know not?

أَوْ يَأْخُذَهُمْ فِى تَقَلُّبِهِمْ فَمَا هُم بِمُعْجِزِينَ ﴿٤٦﴾

46. Aw ya/khu*t*hahum fee taqallubihim fam*a* hum bimuAAjizeen*a*

16:46. Or that He may not seize them while they are on the move, and so they cannot escape?

أَوْ يَأْخُذَهُمْ عَلَىٰ تَخَوُّفٍ فَإِنَّ رَبَّكُمْ لَرَءُوفٌ رَّحِيمٌ ﴿٤٧﴾

47. Aw ya/khu*t*hahum AAal*a* takhawwufin fa-inna rabbakum laraoofun ra*h*eem**un**

16:47. Or that He may not seize them with fear and/or slow destruction? And your Lord is indeed Kind, Merciful.

أَوَلَمْ يَرَوْاْ إِلَىٰ مَا خَلَقَ ٱللَّهُ مِن شَىْءٍ يَتَفَيَّؤُاْ ظِلَٰلُهُ عَنِ ٱلْيَمِينِ وَٱلشَّمَآئِلِ سُجَّدًا لِّلَّهِ وَهُمْ دَٰخِرُونَ ﴿٤٨﴾

48. Awa lam yaraw il*a* m*a* khalaqa All*a*hu min shay-in yatafayyao *th*il*a*luhu AAani alyameeni waa**lsh**sham*a*-ili sujjadan lill*a*hi wahum d*a*khiroon*a*

16:48. Do they not see that anything, which Allah has created, casts its shadow right and left in humble prostration to Allah?

وَلِلَّهِ يَسْجُدُ مَا فِى ٱلسَّمَٰوَٰتِ وَمَا فِى ٱلْأَرْضِ مِن دَآبَّةٍ وَٱلْمَلَٰٓئِكَةُ وَهُمْ لَا يَسْتَكْبِرُونَ ۩

49. Walill*a*hi yasjudu m*a* fee alssam*a*w*a*ti wam*a* fee al-ar*d*i min d*a*bbatin waalmal*a*-ikatu wahum l*a* yastakbiroon*a*

16:49. And to Allah does prostrate any creature that is in the heavens and that is in the earth, and the angels too do protrate. And they do not show pride.

يَخَافُونَ رَبَّهُم مِّن فَوْقِهِمْ وَيَفْعَلُونَ مَا يُؤْمَرُونَ ۩

50. Yakh*a*foona rabbahum min fawqihim wayafAAaloona m*a* yu/maroon*a*

16:50. They fear their Lord over them. And they do what they are commanded.

وَقَالَ ٱللَّهُ لَا تَتَّخِذُوٓا۟ إِلَٰهَيْنِ ٱثْنَيْنِ إِنَّمَا هُوَ إِلَٰهٌ وَٰحِدٌ فَإِيَّٰىَ فَٱرْهَبُونِ

51. Waq*a*la All*a*hu l*a* tattakhi*th*oo il*a*hayni ithnayni innam*a* huwa il*a*hun w*a*hidun fa-iyy*a*ya fairhabooni

16:51. And Allah tells human beings not to take two gods. He is Allah, the One and Only. "So, Me alone should you hold in awe."[7]

7. In <u>study note 2:184</u> **we have seen why there is a sudden change from the singular to the plural form in some of the Qur'aanic Verses. The change here from the third to the first person is on the same grounds.**

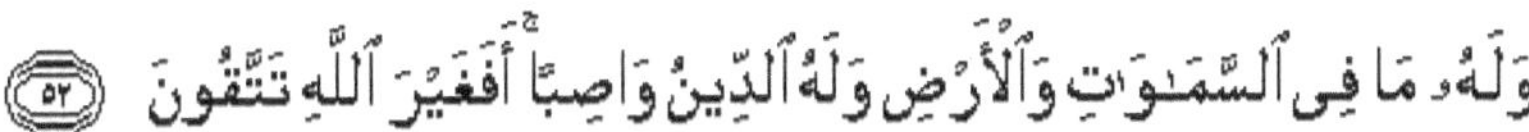

52. Walahu ma fee alssamawati waal-ardi walahu alddeenu wasiban afaghayra Allahi tattaqoona

16:52. And whatever is in the heavens and the earth is His, and the way of life ought to be for Him ever.[8] Will you then fear any being other than Allah?

8. Human beings are Allah's representatives on earth. Their way of life here should therefore be such as to please Him, and not antagonise Him.

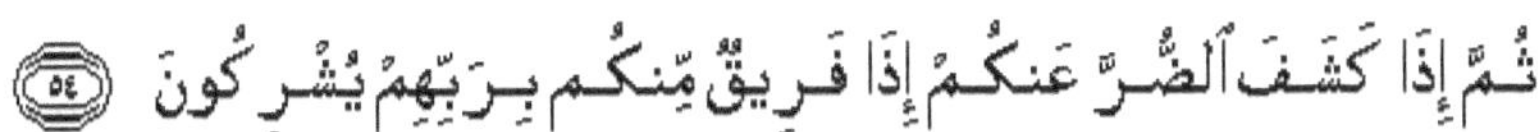

53. Wama bikum min niAAmatin famina Allahi thumma itha massakumu alddurru fa-ilayhi taj-aroona

16:53. And the good things, you have, are all from Allah. Then when anything bad afflicts you, to Him do you complain loudly!

54. Thumma itha kashafa alddurra AAankum itha fareequn minkum birabbihim yushrikoona

16:54. And yet when He removes the hardship from you, lo, some of you worship others besides their Lord!

$$لِيَكْفُرُواْ بِمَآ ءَاتَيْنَـٰهُمْ فَتَمَتَّعُواْ فَسَوْفَ تَعْلَمُونَ ۝$$

55. Liyakfuroo bima ataynahum fatamattaAAoo fasawfa taAAlamoona

16:55. And so they become ungrateful for what We have given them. Enjoy then for now! You shall soon come to know your real destiny.

$$وَيَجْعَلُونَ لِمَا لَا يَعْلَمُونَ نَصِيبًا مِّمَّا رَزَقْنَـٰهُمْ تَٱللَّهِ لَتُسْـَٔلُنَّ عَمَّا كُنتُمْ تَفْتَرُونَ ۝$$

56. WayajAAaloona lima la yaAAlamoona naseeban mimma razaqnahum taAllahi latus-alunna AAamma kuntum taftaroona

16:56. And they set apart a portion of what We have given them for those of whom they know nothing[9]. By Allah, you shall most certainly be questioned about that which you have been concocting!

9. It is a practice among polytheists to offer some material things for their deities, other than Allah, whom they worship. These deities are either fictitious things or statues of persons, dead or living. The worshippers have no incontrovertible evidences of any divine powers that are reportedly attributed to these deities. Their belief in them is based on just hearsays. The Muslims too have unfortunately fallen a prey to this *shirk*. They go to the graves of saints, with costly *chaddars* and hefty monetary donations, thinking that the saints exercise divine powers through their graves. Their thoughts and actions are utterly un-islamic, and yet they call themselves Muslims!

وَيَجْعَلُونَ لِلَّهِ الْبَنَاتِ سُبْحَانَهُ وَلَهُم مَّا يَشْتَهُونَ ۝

57. WayajAAaloona lillahi albanati subhanahu walahum ma yashtahoona

16:57. And they arbitrarily attribute daughters (angels) to Allah. HE is too glorious to have any such creaturely attribute. And, for themselves, they would have what they desire (sons)!

وَإِذَا بُشِّرَ أَحَدُهُم بِالْأُنثَىٰ ظَلَّ وَجْهُهُ مُسْوَدًّا وَهُوَ كَظِيمٌ ۝

58. Wa-itha bushshira ahaduhum bialontha thalla wajhuhu muswaddan wahuwa katheemun

16:58. And when news of a daughter being born is given to any of them, his face becomes darkened with suppressed anger.

يَتَوَارَىٰ مِنَ الْقَوْمِ مِن سُوءِ مَا بُشِّرَ بِهِ أَيُمْسِكُهُ عَلَىٰ هُونٍ أَمْ يَدُسُّهُ فِى التُّرَابِ أَلَا سَاءَ مَا يَحْكُمُونَ ۝

59. Yatawara mina alqawmi min soo-i ma bushshira bihi ayumsikuhu AAala hoonin am yadussuhu fee altturabi ala saa ma yahkumoona

16:59. He hides himself from the people because of the stigma of the news given to him. Shall he keep it despite the disgrace, or bury it in the dust? Verily, their judgment is vicious.[10]

---

10. It is sad that female infanticide is even now prevalent in some parts of the world.

لِلَّذِينَ لَا يُؤْمِنُونَ بِالْآخِرَةِ مَثَلُ السَّوْءِ وَلِلَّهِ ٱلْمَثَلُ ٱلْأَعْلَىٰ وَهُوَ ٱلْعَزِيزُ ٱلْحَكِيمُ ﴿١٠﴾

60. Lilla*th*eena l*a* yu/minoona bi**al**-*a*khirati mathalu alssaw-i walill*a*hi almathalu al-aAA*a* wahuwa alAAazeezu al*h*akeem**u**

16:60. An example of evil applies to those who believe not in the Hereafter. And the best/loftiest example applies to Allah. And He is the Omnipotent, the Wise.

وَلَوْ يُؤَاخِذُ ٱللَّهُ ٱلنَّاسَ بِظُلْمِهِم مَّا تَرَكَ عَلَيْهَا مِن دَآبَّةٍ وَلَٰكِن يُؤَخِّرُهُمْ إِلَىٰ أَجَلٍ مُّسَمًّى فَإِذَا جَاءَ أَجَلُهُمْ لَا يَسْتَأْخِرُونَ سَاعَةً وَلَا يَسْتَقْدِمُونَ ﴿١١﴾

61. Walaw yu-*a*khi*th*u All*a*hu a**l**nn*a*sa bi*th*ulmihim m*a* taraka AAalayh*a* min *d*abbatin wal*a*kin yu-akhkhiruhum il*a* ajalin musamman fa-i*th*a j*a*a ajaluhum l*a* yasta/khiroona s*a*AAatan wal*a* yastaqdimoona

---

16:61. And had Allah seized mankind for their unjust acts, He would not have left, on the earth, even a single creature. But He gives them a definite time limit. And when their time comes, they shall not be able to postpone it for a moment nor prepone it.

وَيَجْعَلُونَ لِلَّهِ مَا يَكْرَهُونَ وَتَصِفُ أَلْسِنَتُهُمُ ٱلْكَذِبَ أَنَّ لَهُمُ ٱلْحُسْنَىٰ لَا جَرَمَ أَنَّ لَهُمُ ٱلنَّارَ وَأَنَّهُم مُّفْرَطُونَ ﴿٦٢﴾

62. WayajAAaloona lill*a*hi m*a* yakrahoona watasifu alsinatuhumu alka*th*iba anna lahumu al*h*usn*a* la jarama anna lahumu alnn*a*ra waannahum mufra*t*oona

16:62 And they assign to Allah what they hate for themselves. And their tongues philosophically cover up the lie to say that for them there shall be nothing but the good. There is no doubt that for them there shall be the Fire and that they shall be hastened thereto.

تَٱللَّهِ لَقَدْ أَرْسَلْنَآ إِلَىٰ أُمَمٍ مِّن قَبْلِكَ فَزَيَّنَ لَهُمُ ٱلشَّيْطَٰنُ أَعْمَٰلَهُمْ فَهُوَ وَلِيُّهُمُ ٱلْيَوْمَ وَلَهُمْ عَذَابٌ أَلِيمٌ ﴿٦٣﴾

63. TaAll*a*hi laqad arsaln*a* il*a* omamin min qablika fazayyana lahumu alshshay*t*anu aAAm*a*lahum fahuwa waliyyuhumu alyawma walahum AAa*th*abun aleem**un**

16:63. By Allah, We did certainly send Messengers to peoples that existed before you. Then the Satan made their deeds seem good to them. And he became their *wali*[11] of the day (period). And they shall have a painful punishment.

11. See study note 2:154**.**

وَمَآ أَنزَلْنَا عَلَيْكَ ٱلْكِتَـٰبَ إِلَّا لِتُبَيِّنَ لَهُمُ ٱلَّذِى ٱخْتَلَفُوا۟ فِيهِ وَهُدًى

وَرَحْمَةً لِّقَوْمٍ يُؤْمِنُونَ ۝

64. Wam*a* anzaln*a* AAalayka alkit*a*ba ill*a* litubayyina lahumu alla*th*ee ikhtalafoo feehi wahudan wara*h*matan liqawmin yu/minoon*a*

16:64. And We have not sent down the Book to you but to make clear to them what they differ in, and as Guidance and Mercy for people who believe.

وَٱللَّهُ أَنزَلَ مِنَ ٱلسَّمَآءِ مَآءً فَأَحْيَا بِهِ ٱلْأَرْضَ بَعْدَ مَوْتِهَآ إِنَّ فِى ذَٰلِكَ

لَأَيَةً لِّقَوْمٍ يَسْمَعُونَ ۝

65. WaAll*a*hu anzala mina alssam*a*-i m*a*an faa*h*y*a* bihi al-ar*d*a baAAda mawtih*a* inna fee *th*alika laa*a*yatan liqawmin yasmaAAoon*a*

16:65. And Allah it is Who sends down water from the sky and therewith gives life to the earth after its death. There is indeed a sign[12] in that for people who listen.

---

12. The life-reviving rain is one of the innumerable signs of the existence of the Creator Who has made adequate provisions for continuance of life on earth. The earth's revival after rains is a sign also that the Creator can likewise resurrect mankind after it dies out entirely. Some other signs are mentioned in Verses 66 to 72 below. Such signs are mentioned elsewhere too in the Qur'aan.

وَإِنَّ لَكُمْ فِى ٱلْأَنْعَـٰمِ لَعِبْرَةً نُّسْقِيكُم مِّمَّا فِى بُطُونِهِۦ مِنْ بَيْنِ فَرْثٍ وَدَمٍ لَّبَنًا خَالِصًا سَآئِغًا لِّلشَّـٰرِبِينَ ۝

66. Wa-inna lakum fee al-anAAami laAAibratan nusqeekum mimma fee bu*t*oonihi min bayni farthin wadamin labanan kh*a*li*s*an sa-ighan lilshsh*a*ribeen**a**

16:66. And, indeed, in the cattle there is a lesson for you. We give you pure, potable drink of milk out of what they consume in their bellies and drawn from excreta and blood.[12a]

12a. The production of milk in cattle – or in any mammal for that matter – is succinctly described here. From the food they eat, milk precursors, along with other nutrients, are drawn into the blood, leaving excreta behind in the large intestine. The mammary gland in turn sucks the precursors from the blood circulating in the network of blood capillaries around it, to convert those (precursors) into milk. These process details, particularly of the role played by blood, came to man's knowledge centuries after the Qur'aan was revealed. Man was even unaware that blood circulates within animal bodies. Mankind – including most Muslims – however remains deeply skeptical of the divine origin of the Qur'aan!

وَمِن ثَمَرَٰتِ ٱلنَّخِيلِ وَٱلْأَعْنَـٰبِ تَتَّخِذُونَ مِنْهُ سَكَرًا وَرِزْقًا حَسَنًا إِنَّ فِى ذَٰلِكَ لَـَٔايَةً لِّقَوْمٍ يَعْقِلُونَ ۝

67. Wamin thamar*a*ti alnnakheeli waal-aAAn*a*bi tattakhi*th*oona minhu sakaran warizqan *h*asanan inna fee *tha*lika la*a*yatan liqawmin yaAAqiloon**a**

16:67. And from the fruits of the palm-tree and the vine, you get intoxication as well as good food. There is indeed a sign in that for a people who ponder.

وَأَوْحَىٰ رَبُّكَ إِلَى ٱلنَّحْلِ أَنِ ٱتَّخِذِى مِنَ ٱلْجِبَالِ بُيُوتًا وَمِنَ ٱلشَّجَرِ وَمِمَّا يَعْرِشُونَ ۝

68. Waaw*h*a rabbuka il*a* alnna*h*li ani ittakhi*th*ee mina aljib*a*li buyootan wamina alshshajari wamimm*a* yaAArishoon*a*

16:68. And your Lord inspired the bee to "have hives in the mountains, in the trees and in the buildings."

ثُمَّ كُلِى مِن كُلِّ ٱلثَّمَرَٰتِ فَٱسْلُكِى سُبُلَ رَبِّكِ ذُلُلًا يَخْرُجُ مِنْ بُطُونِهَا شَرَابٌ مُخْتَلِفٌ أَلْوَٰنُهُۥ فِيهِ شِفَآءٌ لِّلنَّاسِ إِنَّ فِى ذَٰلِكَ لَأَيَةً لِّقَوْمٍ يَتَفَكَّرُونَ ۝

69. Thumma kulee min kulli alththamar*a*ti faoslukee subula rabbiki *th*ululan yakhruju min bu*t*ooniha shar*a*bun mukhtalifun alw*a*nuhu feehi shif*a*on lilnn*a*si inna fee *th*alika la*a*yatan liqawmin yatafakkaroon*a*

16:69. "And then eat of all the fruits and tread the paths of your Lord submissively." A beverage of various colours comes forth from within it, wherein there is curative value[13] for mankind. There is indeed a sign in that for people who reflect.

---

13. Check up in google search.

وَٱللَّهُ خَلَقَكُمْ ثُمَّ يَتَوَفَّىٰكُمْ وَمِنكُم مَّن يُرَدُّ إِلَىٰٓ أَرْذَلِ ٱلْعُمُرِ لِكَىْ لَا يَعْلَمَ بَعْدَ عِلْمٍ شَيْئًا إِنَّ ٱللَّهَ عَلِيمٌ قَدِيرٌ ۝

70. WaAll*a*hu khalaqakum thumma yatawaff*a*kum waminkum man yuraddu il*a* ar*th*ali alAAumuri likay l*a* yaAAlama baAAda AAilmin shay-an inna All*a*ha AAaleemun qadee**run**

16:70. And Allah it is Who has created you. It is He then Who causes you to die. And among you there may be someone who, after having acquired knowledge, is reduced to such a decrepit state[14] of life that he knows nothing. Allah is indeed Knowledgeable, Powerful.

---

14. State of insanity or very old age, for example.

وَٱللَّهُ فَضَّلَ بَعْضَكُمْ عَلَىٰ بَعْضٍ فِى ٱلرِّزْقِ فَمَا ٱلَّذِينَ فُضِّلُوا۟ بِرَآدِّى رِزْقِهِمْ عَلَىٰ مَا مَلَكَتْ أَيْمَٰنُهُمْ فَهُمْ فِيهِ سَوَآءٌ أَفَبِنِعْمَةِ ٱللَّهِ يَجْحَدُونَ 

71. WaAll*a*hu fa*dd*ala baAA*d*akum AAal*a* baAA*d*in fee alrrizqi fam*a* alla*th*eena fu*dd*iloo bira*dd*ee rizqihim AAal*a* m*a* malakat aym*a*nuhum fahum feehi saw*a*on afabiniAAmati All*a*hi yaj*h*adoon**a**

16:71. And it is Allah Who has given some of you more/better provisions than to others. Would then those who are thus favoured give away their provisions to their slaves so that they become equal therein? Do they then deny this privilege[15] that Allah has given them?

---

15. The Qur'aan tells us that Allah has favoured some in rank over others so that the former can get work done from others (Verse 43:32), and so that He may try you in what He has given you (Verse 6:165).

وَٱللَّهُ جَعَلَ لَكُم مِّنْ أَنفُسِكُمْ أَزْوَٰجًا وَجَعَلَ لَكُم مِّنْ أَزْوَٰجِكُم بَنِينَ وَحَفَدَةً وَرَزَقَكُم مِّنَ ٱلطَّيِّبَٰتِ أَفَبِٱلْبَٰطِلِ يُؤْمِنُونَ وَبِنِعْمَتِ ٱللَّهِ هُمْ يَكْفُرُونَ ﴿٧٢﴾

72. WaAll*a*hu jaAAala lakum min anfusikum azw*a*jan wajaAAala lakum min azw*a*jikum baneena wa*h*afadatan warazaqakum mina al*tt*ayyib*a*ti afabi*a*lba*t*ili yu/minoona wabiniAAmati All*a*hi hum yakfuroona

---

16:72. And it is Allah Who has made spouses for you from among yourselves, and through your spouses He has given you sons, daughters and their further families. And He has provided wholesome food for you. Do they believe then in the falsehood and suppress the fact that it is Allah Who has given them the good things they enjoy?

وَيَعْبُدُونَ مِن دُونِ ٱللَّهِ مَا لَا يَمْلِكُ لَهُمْ رِزْقًا مِّنَ ٱلسَّمَٰوَٰتِ وَٱلْأَرْضِ شَيْـًٔا وَلَا يَسْتَطِيعُونَ ﴿٧٣﴾

73. WayaAAbudoona min dooni All*a*hi m*a* l*a* yamliku lahum rizqan mina alssam*a*w*a*ti waal-ar*d*i shay-an wal*a* yasta*t*eeAAoona

---

16:73. And they worship, besides Allah, those that possess nothing, in the heavens and the earth, wherewith to sustain their worshippers. Nor have those any power to possess anything.

$$فَلَا تَضْرِبُوا لِلَّهِ الْأَمْثَالَ إِنَّ اللَّهَ يَعْلَمُ وَأَنتُمْ لَا تَعْلَمُونَ ۝$$

74. Fala tadriboo lillahi al-amthala inna Allaha yaAAlamu waantum la taAAlamoona

16:74. So liken not anything to Allah! Indeed, Allah knows, and you do not.

$$ضَرَبَ اللَّهُ مَثَلًا عَبْدًا مَّمْلُوكًا لَّا يَقْدِرُ عَلَىٰ شَيْءٍ وَمَن رَّزَقْنَاهُ مِنَّا رِزْقًا حَسَنًا فَهُوَ يُنفِقُ مِنْهُ سِرًّا وَجَهْرًا هَلْ يَسْتَوُونَ الْحَمْدُ لِلَّهِ بَلْ أَكْثَرُهُمْ لَا يَعْلَمُونَ ۝$$

75. Daraba Allahu mathalan AAabdan mamlookan la yaqdiru AAala shay-in waman razaqnahu minna rizqan hasanan fahuwa yunfiqu minhu sirran wajahran hal yastawoona alhamdu lillahi bal aktharuhum la yaAAlamoona

16:75. Allah gives an example: a slave – property of another person – who has no power over anything, and, on the other hand, a free man whom We have given a good provision from Ourselves and he spends from it secretly and openly. Are the two alike? To Allah is due all praise! But, most of them know not.[16]

16. Polytheists do not understand even the simple thing that their deities, other than Allah, who are themselves creatures (slaves) of Allah, cannot at all be equal to Allah, their Master. The obvious inequality is illustrated by another example in Verse 76 below.

وَضَرَبَ ٱللَّهُ مَثَلًا رَّجُلَيْنِ أَحَدُهُمَآ أَبْكَمُ لَا يَقْدِرُ عَلَىٰ شَىْءٍ وَهُوَ كَلٌّ عَلَىٰ مَوْلَىٰهُ أَيْنَمَا يُوَجِّههُّ لَا يَأْتِ بِخَيْرٍ هَلْ يَسْتَوِى هُوَ وَمَن يَأْمُرُ بِالْعَدْلِ وَهُوَ عَلَىٰ صِرَٰطٍ مُّسْتَقِيمٍ ۝

76. Wa*d*araba All*a*hu mathalan rajulayni a*h*aduhum*a* abkamu l*a* yaqdiru AAal*a* shay-in wahuwa kallun AAal*a* mawl*a*hu aynam*a* yuwajjihhu l*a* ya/ti bikhayrin hal yastawee huwa waman ya/muru bi**a**lAAadli wahuwa AAal*a* sira*t*in mustaqeem**in**

16:76. And Allah gives another example, of two men, one of whom is dumb, unable to do anything, and a burden on his master. He is not good at whatever task the master gives him. Can he be held equal to him who enjoins what is just, and is himself on the right path?

وَلِلَّهِ غَيْبُ ٱلسَّمَٰوَٰتِ وَٱلْأَرْضِ وَمَآ أَمْرُ ٱلسَّاعَةِ إِلَّا كَلَمْحِ ٱلْبَصَرِ أَوْ هُوَ أَقْرَبُ إِنَّ ٱللَّهَ عَلَىٰ كُلِّ شَىْءٍ قَدِيرٌ ۝

77. Walill*a*hi ghaybu alssam*a*wati waal-ar*d*i wam*a* amru alssaAAati ill*a* kalam*h*i albacari aw huwa aqrabu inna All*a*ha AAal*a* kulli shay-in qadeer**un**

16:77. And with Allah is the knowledge of the unseen/secrets of the heavens and the earth. And the happening of the Hour is but as a momentary sight or consuming even less time. Allah indeed can do anything.

وَٱللَّهُ أَخْرَجَكُم مِّنۢ بُطُونِ أُمَّهَٰتِكُمْ لَا تَعْلَمُونَ شَيْئًا وَجَعَلَ لَكُمُ ٱلسَّمْعَ وَٱلْأَبْصَٰرَ وَٱلْأَفْـِٔدَةَ لَعَلَّكُمْ تَشْكُرُونَ ﴿٧٨﴾

78. WaAll*a*hu akhrajakum min bu*t*ooni ommah*a*tikum l*a* taAAlamoona shay-an wajaAAala lakumu alssamAAa waal-ab*s*ara waal-af-idata laAAallakum tashkuroona

---

16:78. And it is Allah Who brought you out from the wombs of your mothers, knowing nothing. And He gave you hearing and sight and intellect that you may be grateful.[17]

---

17. When a woman delivers a baby normally, we tend to forget about the wonderful process that Allah sets in motion, within the body of the mother, to get the baby out into the open world. The mother just bears the process, and it is Allah Who brings out the child. As a new-born infant, it knows nothing, but while the foetus of the child was still in the mother's womb, Allah had meticulously so fashioned it that it is now able to hear and see things. And by the time the child grows into a full-fledged man/woman, he/she acquires considerable knowledge through his/her mind gradually assimilating the things heard and seen during the intervening period. But is he/she grateful to Allah for giving him/her the faculties that enabled this acquisition?

أَلَمْ يَرَوْاْ إِلَى ٱلطَّيْرِ مُسَخَّرَٰتٍ فِى جَوِّ ٱلسَّمَآءِ مَا يُمْسِكُهُنَّ إِلَّا ٱللَّهُ إِنَّ فِى ذَٰلِكَ لَأَيَٰتٍ لِّقَوْمٍ يُؤْمِنُونَ ﴿٧٩﴾

79. Alam yaraw il*a* al*tt*ayri musakhkhar*a*tin fee jawwi alssam*a*-i m*a* yumsikuhunna ill*a* All*a*hu inna fee *tha*lika la*aya*tin liqawmin yu/minoona

---

16:79. See they not how the birds are enabled to be in mid-air above? None keeps them there but Allah! Indeed, there are signs in that for people who believe.[18]

---

18. It is in the construction of their wings that the secret of the birds' ability to fly lies. Man has built aeroplanes on the same lines. The ingenious design of the birds' wings is an unmistakable sign of the existence of the Creator of super intelligence.

وَٱللَّهُ جَعَلَ لَكُم مِّنْ بُيُوتِكُمْ سَكَنًا وَجَعَلَ لَكُم مِّن جُلُودِ ٱلْأَنْعَـٰمِ بُيُوتًا تَسْتَخِفُّونَهَا يَوْمَ ظَعْنِكُمْ وَيَوْمَ إِقَامَتِكُمْ وَمِنْ أَصْوَافِهَا وَأَوْبَارِهَا وَأَشْعَارِهَآ أَثَـٰثًا وَمَتَـٰعًا إِلَىٰ حِينٍ ۝

80. WaAllahu jaAAala lakum min buyootikum sakanan wajaAAala lakum min juloodi al-anAAami buyootan tastakhiffoonaha yawma *tha*AAnikum wayawma iqamatikum wamin a*s*wafiha waawbariha waashAAariha atha*th*an wamataAAan il*a* heenin

16:80. And Allah has facilitated for you rest, security and solace in your houses. And He has facilitated for you tents of the skins of cattle which you find light to carry when you travel and when you stay out. And of the animal wool, fur and hair, He has given you assets and possessions for a time.

وَٱللَّهُ جَعَلَ لَكُم مِّمَّا خَلَقَ ظِلَـٰلًا وَجَعَلَ لَكُم مِّنَ ٱلْجِبَالِ أَكْنَـٰنًا وَجَعَلَ لَكُمْ سَرَٰبِيلَ تَقِيكُمُ ٱلْحَرَّ وَسَرَٰبِيلَ تَقِيكُم بَأْسَكُمْ كَذَٰلِكَ يُتِمُّ نِعْمَتَهُۥ عَلَيْكُمْ لَعَلَّكُمْ تُسْلِمُونَ ۝

81. WaAllahu jaAAala lakum mimm*a* khalaqa *th*ilalan wajaAAala lakum mina aljibali aknanan wajaAAala lakum sarabeela taqeekumu alharra wasarabeela taqeekum ba/sakum ka*th*alika yutimmu niAAmatahu AAalaykum laAAallakum tuslimoona

16:81. And Allah has made for you shelters from what He has created, and places of retreat in the mountains. And He has provided for garments for you to protect you from the heat and for armour to protect you in your armed conflicts. Thus, does He complete His favour upon you in order that you submit to Him.

فَإِن تَوَلَّوْاْ فَإِنَّمَا عَلَيْكَ ٱلْبَلَـٰغُ ٱلْمُبِينُ ۝

82. Fa-in tawallaw fa-innama AAalayka albalaghu almubeenu

16:82. And if, even then, they turn away, the responsibility on you (Prophet Muhammad) is only to deliver Allah's Message clearly to the people.

يَعْرِفُونَ نِعْمَتَ ٱللَّهِ ثُمَّ يُنكِرُونَهَا وَأَكْثَرُهُمُ ٱلْكَـٰفِرُونَ ۝

83. YaAArifoona niAAmata Allahi thumma yunkiroonaha waaktharuhumu alkafiroona

16:83. They are aware of Allah's favour, yet they deny it! And most of them are those who suppress the Truth.

وَيَوْمَ نَبْعَثُ مِن كُلِّ أُمَّةٍ شَهِيدًا ثُمَّ لَا يُؤْذَنُ لِلَّذِينَ كَفَرُواْ وَلَا هُمْ يُسْتَعْتَبُونَ ۝

84. Wayawma nabAAathu min kulli ommatin shaheedan thumma la yu/thanu lillatheena kafaroo wala hum yustaAAtaboona

16:84. And One Day We will raise a witness out of every community. Then shall no leeway be given to those who suppress the Truth, nor shall they be allowed to solicit favours.

وَإِذَا رَءَا ٱلَّذِينَ ظَلَمُوٓاْ ٱلْعَذَابَ فَلَا يُخَفَّفُ عَنْهُمْ وَلَا هُمْ يُنظَرُونَ ﴿٨٥﴾

85. Wa-*itha* ra*a* alla*th*eena *th*alamoo alAA*ath*aba fal*a* yukhaffafu AAanhum wal*a* hum yun*th*aroon**a**

16:85. And when those who are wicked experience the punishment, its severity on them shall not be decreased, nor shall they be given any respite.

وَإِذَا رَءَا ٱلَّذِينَ أَشْرَكُواْ شُرَكَآءَهُمْ قَالُواْ رَبَّنَا هَـٰٓؤُلَآءِ شُرَكَآؤُنَا ٱلَّذِينَ كُنَّا نَدْعُواْ مِن دُونِكَ فَأَلْقَوْاْ إِلَيْهِمُ ٱلْقَوْلَ إِنَّكُمْ لَكَـٰذِبُونَ ﴿٨٦﴾

86. Wa-*itha* ra*a* alla*th*eena ashrakoo shurak*a*ahum q*a*loo rabban*a* h*a*ola-i shuraka*o*n*a* alla*th*eena kunn*a* nadAAoo min doonika faalqaw ilayhimu alqawla innakum laka*th*iboon**a**

16:86. And when those who worship others besides Allah see those others, they shall say, "Our Lord! These are our other gods whom we prayed to besides You." But they will retort, "Certainly indeed you are liars!"

وَأَلْقَوْاْ إِلَى ٱللَّهِ يَوْمَئِذٍ ٱلسَّلَمَ وَضَلَّ عَنْهُم مَّا كَانُوا۟ يَفْتَرُونَ ۝

87. Waalqaw ila Allahi yawma-ithin alssalama wadalla AAanhum ma kanoo yaftaroona

16:87. And they shall tender submission to Allah on that day. And what they used to concoct shall depart from them.

ٱلَّذِينَ كَفَرُواْ وَصَدُّواْ عَن سَبِيلِ ٱللَّهِ زِدْنَهُمْ عَذَابًا فَوْقَ ٱلْعَذَابِ بِمَا كَانُوا۟ يُفْسِدُونَ ۝

88. Allatheena kafaroo wasaddoo AAan sabeeli Allahi zidnahum AAathaban fawqa alAAathabi bima kanoo yufsidoona

16:88. For those who suppress the Truth and cause hindrance in Allah's Path, We will add punishment over punishment because they have been spreading corruption.

وَيَوْمَ نَبْعَثُ فِى كُلِّ أُمَّةٍ شَهِيدًا عَلَيْهِم مِّنْ أَنفُسِهِمْ وَجِئْنَا بِكَ شَهِيدًا عَلَىٰ هَٰؤُلَاءِ وَنَزَّلْنَا عَلَيْكَ ٱلْكِتَٰبَ تِبْيَٰنًا لِّكُلِّ شَىْءٍ وَهُدًى وَرَحْمَةً وَبُشْرَىٰ لِلْمُسْلِمِينَ ۝

89. Wayawma nabAAathu fee kulli ommatin shaheedan AAalayhim min anfusihim waji/na bika shaheedan AAala haola-i wanazzalna AAalayka alkitaba tibyanan likulli shay-in wahudan warahmatan wabushra lilmuslimeena

16:89. And One Day We will raise in every people a witness against them from among themselves and bring you as a witness against these. And We have revealed to you the Book explaining everything[19] clearly, and as a guidance, mercy and good news for those who submit. [20]

---

19. What does 'everything' mean here? It obviously does not mean, for example, any recipe for cooking a delicious food item. It means general principles for conduct of human life. About the recipe, in the example taken, Allah has obviously left it and such other things to be learnt through experiences of earlier people and personal innovations and inspirations. The divine Hand is inherent here too when a man innovates or invents a new thing. But the characteristics of discovery, innovation and invention are common to all human beings, whether one is a believer or not. Human beings are however given the choice of recognizing or denying the existence of One Supreme Creator of the entire Universe and everything therein. And the Kind Creator has provided innumerable and unending signs for mankind to make the right choice of recognizing His existence. Not only that, but He has sent Prophets and Messengers with divinely authored Books for their guidance <u>for making the right choice and conducting life accordingly.</u> 'Everything' in the Verse implies everything for this purpose of making the right choice and conducting life accordingly. On the exercise of this choice depends Man's fate in the Hereafter. And the stake is extremely high! And Allah could have left mankind to its fate by just providing the tell-tale numerous signs in the Universe, but He is Kind and extremely Merciful to His human creatures. HE has given them, in addition, the divine Book of Guidance, the Qur'aan, as a token of Mercy from Him. Therein He has moreover given the enticement of Paradise to mankind to help them make the right choice.

20. The unequivocal divine statement here that the Qur'aan gives clear explanation of everything makes the Book the sole authoritative source and basis for Islam, the Allah-chosen way of life for entire mankind. The equal (and in some quarters even greater) importance given to the man-influenced and error-prone *ahaadeeth* is the cause of the downfall of Muslims. Allah Ta'ala has obviously withdrawn His Hand of Mercy from them.

۞ إِنَّ ٱللَّهَ يَأْمُرُ بِٱلْعَدْلِ وَٱلْإِحْسَـٰنِ وَإِيتَآئِ ذِى ٱلْقُرْبَىٰ وَيَنْهَىٰ عَنِ ٱلْفَحْشَآءِ وَٱلْمُنكَرِ وَٱلْبَغْىِ يَعِظُكُمْ لَعَلَّكُمْ تَذَكَّرُونَ ﴿٩٠﴾

90. Inna Allaha ya/muru bialAAadli waal-ihsani wa-eeta-i *thee* alqurba wayanha AAani alfahsha-i waalmunkari waalbaghyi yaAAithukum laAAallakum tathakkaroona

---

16:90. Allah does indeed enjoin justice, kindness and giving things to near and dear ones. And He forbids obscenity, abomination and rebellion. He admonishes you that you may remember and take heed.

وَأَوْفُواْ بِعَهْدِ ٱللَّهِ إِذَا عَٰهَدتُّمْ وَلَا تَنقُضُواْ ٱلْأَيْمَٰنَ بَعْدَ تَوْكِيدِهَا وَقَدْ جَعَلْتُمُ ٱللَّهَ عَلَيْكُمْ كَفِيلًا إِنَّ ٱللَّهَ يَعْلَمُ مَا تَفْعَلُونَ ﴿٩١﴾

91. Waawfoo biAAahdi Allahi *itha* AAahadtum wala tanqudoo al-aymana baAAda tawkeediha waqad jaAAaltumu Allaha AAalaykum kafeelan inna Allaha yaAAlamu ma tafAAaloona

16:91. And fulfill Allah's covenant when you make one. And break not oaths after affirming them; for, then, you have indeed made Allah stand surety for you. Allah does indeed know what you do.

وَلَا تَكُونُواْ كَٱلَّتِى نَقَضَتْ غَزْلَهَا مِنۢ بَعْدِ قُوَّةٍ أَنكَٰثًا تَتَّخِذُونَ أَيْمَٰنَكُمْ دَخَلًا بَيْنَكُمْ أَن تَكُونَ أُمَّةٌ هِىَ أَرْبَىٰ مِنْ أُمَّةٍ إِنَّمَا يَبْلُوكُمُ ٱللَّهُ بِهِۦ وَلَيُبَيِّنَنَّ لَكُمْ يَوْمَ ٱلْقِيَٰمَةِ مَا كُنتُمْ فِيهِ تَخْتَلِفُونَ ﴿٩٢﴾

92. Wala takoonoo kaallatee naqadat ghazlaha min baAAdi quwwatin ankathan tattakhithoona aymanakum dakhalan baynakum an takoona ommatun hiya arba min ommatin innama yablookumu Allahu bihi walayubayyinanna lakum yawma alqiyamati ma kuntum feehi takhtalifoona

16:92. And be not like the woman who disintegrates her well-spun yarn into fibres.[21] You take your oaths as means of interference in one another's affairs so that one community gets bigger than another. Allah has not but put you on trial by this; and He will certainly make clear to you, on the Resurrection Day, that, about which you differed.[22]

21. The rationale for the directive in the preceding Verse not to break oaths made is explained here by use of a metaphor. A yarn spun out of several fibres has a greater strength and usefulness than the individual fibres. Likewise, a human being, individually, has little strength and usefulness. But the community, in which he lives with other human beings, gives him the necessary strength and security. He has written, and unwritten conventions made with the other people and the society in general. He cannot afford to break these conventions. He will not be able to live there otherwise.

22. At the micro level of individuals, as also at the macro level of nations, agreements and treaties are often misused for exercising undue influence on and/or for unduly usurping properties and territories of one another. Most international conflicts among nations are a result of such misuse.

وَلَوْ شَآءَ ٱللَّهُ لَجَعَلَكُمْ أُمَّةً وَاحِدَةً وَلَـٰكِن يُضِلُّ مَن يَشَآءُ وَيَهْدِى مَن يَشَآءُ وَلَتُسْـَٔلُنَّ عَمَّا كُنتُمْ تَعْمَلُونَ ۝

93. Walaw shaa Allahu lajaAAalakum ommatan wahidatan walakin yudillu man yashao wayahdee man yashao walatus-alunna AAamma kuntum taAAmaloona

16:93. And if Allah had so willed, He would certainly have made you a single community. But He causes whom He wills to go astray and guides whom He wills to go on the Right Path. And you will certainly be questioned as to what you did.[23]

23. Allah would like entire mankind to become one single community. That is why He sent His last Prophet with the last Message for them all. He has given mankind access to technologies that have rendered this world as one global village. But He won't force this desired unity; for, then, the freedom of choice, which He has bestowed on mankind, would be rendered meaningless. Man, exercising that freedom, may choose to go astray even when the Merciful Allah has given him all the warnings and guidelines, and thus come in the way of mankind becoming one community. Man is given the freedom of choice, but he has to account for all that he did here despite the warniongs and guidelines.

وَلَا تَتَّخِذُوٓاْ أَيْمَٰنَكُمْ دَخَلًۢا بَيْنَكُمْ فَتَزِلَّ قَدَمٌۢ بَعْدَ ثُبُوتِهَا

وَتَذُوقُواْ ٱلسُّوٓءَ بِمَا صَدَدتُّمْ عَن سَبِيلِ ٱللَّهِۖ وَلَكُمْ عَذَابٌ عَظِيمٌ

94. Wal*a* tattakhi*th*oo aym*a*nakum dakhalan baynakum fatazilla qadamun baAAda thubootih*a* wata*th*ooqoo alssoo-a bim*a* *s*adadtum AAan sabeeli All*a*hi walakum AAa*th*abun AAa*th*eem**un**

16:94. And take not your oaths as means of interference in one another's affairs, lest a footstep should stumble after it is firmly taken[24] and you should taste adversity because you hindered someone from Allah's Path. And grievous punishment should be your lot.

---

24. In other words, lest a man, on the verge of becoming a Muslim, should retrace his steps after observing other Muslims' deceitful conduct in the matter of the oaths they had taken.

وَلَا تَشْتَرُواْ بِعَهْدِ ٱللَّهِ ثَمَنًا قَلِيلًاۚ إِنَّمَا عِندَ ٱللَّهِ هُوَ خَيْرٌ

لَّكُمْ إِن كُنتُمْ تَعْلَمُونَ

95. Wal*a* tashtaroo biAAahdi All*a*hi thamanan qaleelan innam*a* AAinda All*a*hi huwa khayrun lakum in kuntum taAAlamoon**a**

16:95. And trade not covenant with Allah, for petty gains. That which is with Allah is certainly better for you, if you but knew.

مَـــا عِنــدَكُمْ يَنفَــدُ وَمَـــا عِنــدَ ٱللَّـــهِ بَـــاقٍ وَلَنَجْـــزِيَنَّ
ٱلَّـذِينَ صَبَرُوٓاْ أَجْرَهُم بِأَحْسَنِ مَا كَانُواْ يَعْمَلُونَ ۝

96. M*a* AAindakum yanfadu wam*a* AAinda All*a*hi b*a*qin walanajziyanna alla*th*eena *s*abaroo ajrahum bi-a*h*sani m*a* k*a*noo yaAAmaloon**a**

16:96. What is with you gets exhausted and what is with Allah endures. And We will certainly give to those who are patient their reward for the good things they did.

مَنْ عَمِلَ صَـٰلِحًا مِّن ذَكَرٍ أَوْ أُنثَىٰ وَهُوَ مُؤْمِنٌ فَلَنُحْيِيَنَّهُۥ حَيَوٰةً طَيِّبَةً
وَلَنَجْزِيَنَّهُمْ أَجْرَهُم بِأَحْسَنِ مَا كَانُواْ يَعْمَلُونَ ۝

97. Man AAamila *s*ali*h*an min *th*akarin aw ont*h*a wahuwa mu/minun falanu*h*yiyannahu *h*ayatan *t*ayyibatan walanajziyannahum ajrahum bi-a*h*sani m*a* k*a*noo yaAAmaloon**a**

16:97. Whoever, male or female, does good work, and he/she is a believer, We will certainly make him/her live a good and clean life, and We will certainly give them their reward for the good things they did.

فَإِذَا قَرَأْتَ ٱلْقُرْءَانَ فَٱسْتَعِذْ بِٱللَّهِ مِنَ ٱلشَّيْطَـٰنِ ٱلرَّجِيمِ ۝

98. Fa-i*th*a qara/ta alqur-*a*na faistaAAi*th* biAll*a*hi mina alshshay*t*ani alrrajeemi

---

16:98. And when you recite the Qur'aan, seek refuge with Allah from the accursed Satan.

إِنَّــهُۥ لَيْسَ لَــهُۥ سُـــلْطَـٰنٌ عَلَــى ٱلَّــذِينَ ءَامَنُــواْ وَعَلَــىٰ رَبِّهِـمْ يَتَوَكَّلُونَ ۝

99. Innahu laysa lahu sul*ta*nun AAal*a* alla*thee*na *a*manoo waAAal*a* rabbihim yatawakkaloon*a*

16:99. Indeed he (Satan) has no authority over those who believe and have trust in their Lord.

إِنَّمَا سُلْطَـٰنُهُۥ عَلَى ٱلَّذِينَ يَتَوَلَّوْنَهُۥ وَٱلَّذِينَ هُم بِهِۦ مُشْرِكُونَ ۝

100. Innam*a* sul*ta*nuhu AAal*a* alla*thee*na yatawallawnahu waalla*thee*na hum bihi mushrikoon*a*

16:100. His authority is only over those who befriend him and over those who worship him besides Allah.

وَإِذَا بَدَّلْنَآ ءَايَةً مَّكَانَ ءَايَةٍ وَٱللَّهُ أَعْلَمُ بِمَا يُنَزِّلُ قَالُوٓاْ إِنَّمَآ أَنتَ مُفْتَرٍۭ بَلْ أَكْثَرُهُمْ لَا يَعْلَمُونَ ۝

101. Wa-i*tha* baddaln*a* *a*yatan mak*a*na *a*yatin waAll*a*hu aAAlamu bim*a* yunazzilu q*a*loo innam*a* anta muftarin bal aktharuhum l*a* yaAAlamoon*a*

16:101 And when We change one Message[25] for another – and Allah knows best what He reveals – they say, "You are only a forger." Nay, most of them know not.

25. The Arabic word *aayat* has been used in the Qur'aan in the meaning of a sign, a miracle or a Verse of the Qur'aan. It has also the meaning of a divine Message. Every Verse of the Qur'aan is also indeed a divine Message, but the word could connote the entire divine Message, like that of the Qur'aan or the Torah. The divine Message of the Torah or of the Injeel (Gospel) was changed to the divine Message of the Qur'aan.

102. Qul nazzalahu roo*h*u alqudusi min rabbika bial*h*aqqi liyuthabbita alla*th*eena *a*manoo wahudan wabushr*a* lilmuslimeen**a**

16:102. Say, "The Holy Spirit has authoritatively revealed it (the Qur'aan) as from your Lord, in order that it may stabilise those who believe and give guidance and good news for those who submit."

103. Walaqad naAAlamu annahum yaqooloona innam*a* yuAAallimuhu basharun lis*a*nu alla*th*ee yul*h*idoona ilayhi aAAjamiyyun wah*atha* lis*a*nun AAarabiyyun mubeen**un**

16:103. And We are certainly aware that they say, "A certain man it is who teaches him." The person they are alluding to speaks a foreign tongue, and this is clear Arabic tongue!

إِنَّ ٱلَّذِينَ لَا يُؤْمِنُونَ بِـَايَـٰتِ ٱللَّهِ لَا يَهْدِيهِمُ ٱللَّهُ وَلَهُمْ عَذَابٌ أَلِيمٌ ﴿١٠٤﴾

104. Inna alla*thee*na l*a* yu/minoona bi-*aya*ti All*a*hi l*a* yahdeehimu All*a*hu walahum AAa*tha*bun aleem**un**

16:104. Allah does indeed not guide those who do not believe in His Messages. And they shall have a painful punishment.

إِنَّمَا يَفْتَرِى ٱلْكَذِبَ ٱلَّذِينَ لَا يُؤْمِنُونَ بِـَايَـٰتِ ٱللَّهِ وَأُوْلَـٰٓئِكَ هُمُ
ٱلْكَـٰذِبُونَ ﴿١٠٥﴾

105. Innam*a* yaftaree alka*thi*ba alla*thee*na l*a* yu/minoona bi-*aya*ti All*a*hi waol*a*-ika humu alk*a*thiboon**a**

16:105. Those that believe not in Allah's Messages, it is they who concoct the lie. And those are the liars.

مَنْ كَفَرَ بِٱللَّهِ مِنْ بَعْدِ إِيمَـٰنِهِۦٓ إِلَّا مَنْ أُكْرِهَ وَقَلْبُهُۥ مُطْمَئِنٌّ
بِٱلْإِيمَـٰنِ وَلَـٰكِن مَّن شَرَحَ بِٱلْكُفْرِ صَدْرًا فَعَلَيْهِمْ غَضَبٌ مِّنَ
ٱللَّهِ وَلَهُمْ عَذَابٌ عَظِيمٌ ﴿١٠٦﴾

106. Man kafara biAll*a*hi min baAAdi eem*a*nihi ill*a* man okriha waqalbuhu mu*t*ma-innun bial-eem*a*ni wal*a*kin man shara*h*a bialkufri *s*adran faAAalayhim gha*da*bun mina All*a*hi walahum AAa*tha*bun AAa*thee*m**un**

16:106. Allah's Wrath is on people who deny Allah after having believed in Him, not on those compelled while their hearts are at rest with faith, but on those that open their minds to suppression of the Truth. And they shall have the most severe punishment.

ذَٰلِكَ بِأَنَّهُمُ ٱسْتَحَبُّوا۟ ٱلْحَيَوٰةَ ٱلدُّنْيَا عَلَى ٱلْءَاخِرَةِ وَأَنَّ ٱللَّهَ لَا يَهْدِى ٱلْقَوْمَ ٱلْكَٰفِرِينَ ﴿١٠٧﴾

107. *Thalika bi-annahumu istahabboo alhayata alddunya AAala al-akhirati waanna Allaha la yahdee alqawma alkafireena*

16:107. That is because they love this worldly life more than the Hereafter, and because Allah does not guide people who suppress the Truth.

أُو۟لَٰٓئِكَ ٱلَّذِينَ طَبَعَ ٱللَّهُ عَلَىٰ قُلُوبِهِمْ وَسَمْعِهِمْ وَأَبْصَٰرِهِمْ وَأُو۟لَٰٓئِكَ هُمُ ٱلْغَٰفِلُونَ ﴿١٠٨﴾

108. *Ola-ika allatheena tabaAAa Allahu AAala quloobihim wasamAAihim waabsarihim waola-ika humu alghafiloona*

16:108. These are the people on whose hearts, hearing and eyes Allah has set a seal. And they take no heed!

لَا جَرَمَ أَنَّهُمْ فِى ٱلْءَاخِرَةِ هُمُ ٱلْخَٰسِرُونَ ﴿١٠٩﴾

109. L*a* jarama annahum fee al-*a*khirati humu alkh*a*siroon**a**

16:109. No doubt, in the Hereafter, they will be the doomed ones.

ثُـــمَّ إِنَّ رَبَّـــكَ لِلَّـــذِينَ هَـــاجَرُواْ مِـــنْ بَعْـــدِ مَـــا

فُتِنُواْ ثُـمَّ جَـــهَدُواْ وَصَــبَرُوۤاْ إِنَّ رَبَّـكَ مِـنْ بَعْدِهَا لَغَفُـورٌ رَّحِـيمٌ ۝

110. Thumma inna rabbaka lilla*th*eena *h*ajaroo min baAAdi m*a* futinoo thumma j*a*hadoo wa*s*abaroo inna rabbaka min baAAdih*a* laghafoorun ra*h*eem**un**

16:110. And then, on the other hand, your Lord is indeed Forgiving and Merciful on those who migrate after they are persecuted, then struggle hard and are patient.

۞ يَـوْمَ تَـأْتِـى كُلُّ نَفْسٍ تُجَـــٰدِلُ عَـن نَّفْسِهَا وَتُـوَفَّىٰ كُلُّ نَفْسٍ مَّا عَمِلَتْ

وَهُمْ لَا يُظْلَمُـونَ ۝

111. Yawma ta/tee kullu nafsin tuj*a*dilu AAan nafsih*a* watuwaff*a* kullu nafsin m*a* AAamilat wahum l*a* yu*th*lamoon**a**

16:111. On that Day everyone shall come, pleading for one's own self. And everyone shall be paid one's full dues, and they shall not be wronged.

وَضَرَبَ ٱللَّهُ مَثَلًا قَرْيَةً كَانَتْ ءَامِنَةً مُّطْمَئِنَّةً يَأْتِيهَا رِزْقُهَا رَغَدًا مِّن كُلِّ مَكَانٍ فَكَفَرَتْ بِأَنْعُمِ ٱللَّهِ فَأَذَٰقَهَا ٱللَّهُ لِبَاسَ ٱلْجُوعِ وَٱلْخَوْفِ بِمَا كَانُوا۟ يَصْنَعُونَ ۝

112. Wa*d*araba All*a*hu mathalan qaryatan k*a*nat *a*minatan mu*t*ma-innatan ya/teeh*a* rizquh*a* raghadan min kulli mak*a*nin fakafarat bi-anAAumi All*a*hi faa*th*aqah*a* All*a*hu lib*a*sa aljooAAi waalkhawfi bim*a* k*a*noo ya*s*naAAoona

---

16:112. And Allah gives an example of a village/town, safe and secure, to which its means of subsistence came in abundance from every quarter. Then it became ungrateful to Allah's favours. And Allah made it wear the garb of hunger and fear because of what they wrought.

وَلَقَدْ جَاءَهُمْ رَسُولٌ مِّنْهُمْ فَكَذَّبُوهُ فَأَخَذَهُمُ ٱلْعَذَابُ وَهُمْ ظَـٰلِمُونَ

113. Walaqad j*a*ahum rasoolun minhum faka*ththa*boohu faakha*th*ahumu alAAa*th*abu wahum *th*alimoona

---

16:113. And, of course, a Messenger from among them had come to them, but they rejected him. So, disaster struck them because of their wickedness.

فَكُلُوا۟ مِمَّا رَزَقَكُمُ ٱللَّهُ حَلَٰلًا طَيِّبًا وَٱشْكُرُوا۟ نِعْمَتَ ٱللَّهِ إِن كُنتُمْ إِيَّاهُ تَعْبُدُونَ ۝

114. Fakuloo mimm*a* razaqakumu All*a*hu *h*al*a*lan *t*ayyiban waoshkuroo niAAmata All*a*hi in kuntum iyy*a*hu taAAbudoon**a**

16:114. Eat then of what Allah has given you, lawful and wholesome. And be grateful for Allah's favours, if Him it is that you worship!

---

115. Innam*a* *h*arrama AAalaykumu almaytata wa**alddama wala*h*ma alkhinzeeri wam*a* ohilla lighayri All*a*hi bihi famani id*t*urra ghayra b*a*ghin wal*a* AA*a*din fa-inna All*a*ha ghafoorun ra*h*eem**un**

16:115. HE has forbidden you only carrion (what dies of itself), blood, flesh of swine and that over which any name, other than that of Allah, has been invoked. But if anyone is driven by necessity – and not desire – and does not exceed limits, then Allah is indeed Forgiving, Merciful.[26]

---

26. This Verse is, almost verbatim, the same as <u>Verse 2:173</u> **[Manzil I]. Please see study notes 281 to 285 under that Verse.**

---

116. Wal*a* taqooloo lim*a* ta*s*ifu alsinatukumu alka*th*iba *h*atha *h*alalun wa*h*atha *h*aramun litaftaroo AAal*a* All*a*hi alka*th*iba inna alla*th*eena yaftaroona AAal*a* All*a*hi alka*th*iba l*a* yufli*h*oon*a*

287

16:116. And describe not anything falsely, with your tongues, as being lawful or unlawful to concoct a lie and ascribe it to Allah. Indeed, those who concoct a lie and ascribe it to Allah shall not prosper.

مَتَـٰعٌ قَلِيلٌ وَلَهُمْ عَذَابٌ أَلِيمٌ ۝

117. Mat*a*AAun qaleelun walahum AAa*th*abun aleem**un**

16:117. They will enjoy a little and then have a painful punishment.

وَعَلَى ٱلَّذِينَ هَادُوا۟ حَرَّمْنَا مَا قَصَصْنَا عَلَيْكَ مِن قَبْلُ وَمَا ظَلَمْنَـٰهُمْ وَلَـٰكِن كَانُوٓا۟ أَنفُسَهُمْ يَظْلِمُونَ ۝

118. WaAAal*a* alla*th*eena hadoo *h*arramn*a* m*a* qa*s*a*s*na AAalayka min qablu wam*a* *th*alamn*a*hum walakin kanoo anfusahum ya*th*limoon*a*

16:118. And for those who were Jews, We prohibited what We have related to you already.[27] And We did them no wrong, but they wronged themselves.

27. **Refer** Verse 6:146.

ثُمَّ إِنَّ رَبَّكَ لِلَّذِينَ عَمِلُوا۟ ٱلسُّوٓءَ بِجَهَـٰلَةٍ ثُمَّ تَابُوا۟ مِنۢ بَعْدِ ذَٰلِكَ وَأَصْلَحُوٓا۟ إِنَّ رَبَّكَ مِنۢ بَعْدِهَا لَغَفُورٌ رَّحِيمٌ ۝

119. Thumma inna rabbaka lilla*th*eena AAamiloo alssoo-a bijah*a*latin thumma *t*aboo min baAAdi *th*alika waasla*h*oo inna rabbaka min baAAdih*a* laghafoorun ra*h*eem**un**

16:119. And your Lord is indeed Forgiving and Merciful to those who do an evil act in ignorance, then turn in repentance after that and make amends.

إِنَّ إِبْرَٰهِيمَ كَانَ أُمَّةً قَانِتًا لِّلَّهِ حَنِيفًا وَلَمْ يَكُ مِنَ ٱلْمُشْرِكِينَ ۝

120. Inna ibr*a*heema k*a*na ommatan q*a*nitan lill*a*hi *h*aneefan walam yaku mina almushrikee**na**

16:120. Abraham was indeed an institution by himself, firmly committed to Allah. And he was never a polytheist.

شَاكِرًا لِّأَنْعُمِهِ ٱجْتَبَٰهُ وَهَدَٰهُ إِلَىٰ صِرَٰطٍ مُّسْتَقِيمٍ ۝

121. Sh*a*kiran li-anAAumihi ijtab*a*hu wahad*a*hu il*a* sir*a*tin mustaqeem**in**

16:121. He was ever grateful for Allah's favours. HE chose him and guided him to the Straight Path.

وَءَاتَيْنَٰهُ فِى ٱلدُّنْيَا حَسَنَةً وَإِنَّهُۥ فِى ٱلْءَاخِرَةِ لَمِنَ ٱلصَّٰلِحِينَ

122. Waataynahu fee alddunya hasanatan wa-innahu fee al-akhirati lamina alssaliheena

16:122. And We gave him a good life in this world, and, in the next, he will indeed be among the good, righteous people.

ثُمَّ أَوْحَيْنَآ إِلَيْكَ أَنِ ٱتَّبِعْ مِلَّةَ إِبْرَٰهِيمَ حَنِيفًا وَمَا كَانَ مِنَ ٱلْمُشْرِكِينَ

123. Thumma awhayna ilayka ani ittabiAA millata ibraheema haneefan wama kana mina almushrikeena

16:123. We then instructed you to follow Abraham's lifestyle steadfastly. And he was not of the polytheists.

إِنَّمَا جُعِلَ ٱلسَّبْتُ عَلَى ٱلَّذِينَ ٱخْتَلَفُوا۟ فِيهِ وَإِنَّ رَبَّكَ لَيَحْكُمُ بَيْنَهُمْ يَوْمَ ٱلْقِيَٰمَةِ فِيمَا كَانُوا۟ فِيهِ يَخْتَلِفُونَ

124. Innama juAAila alssabtu AAala allatheena ikhtalafoo feehi wa-inna rabbaka layahkumu baynahum yawma alqiyamati feema kanoo feehi yakhtalifoona

16:124. The Sabbath[28] was ordained only for those who differed about it, and your Lord indeed will judge between them on the Resurrection Day concerning that about which they differed.

---

28. See study note 2:73 **(Chapter 2). The Jews and the Christians differ about the day of the week on which the rest day is to be observed.**

ٱدْعُ إِلَىٰ سَبِيلِ رَبِّكَ بِٱلْحِكْمَةِ وَٱلْمَوْعِظَةِ ٱلْحَسَنَةِ وَجَٰدِلْهُم بِٱلَّتِى هِىَ أَحْسَنُ إِنَّ رَبَّكَ هُوَ أَعْلَمُ بِمَن ضَلَّ عَن سَبِيلِهِ وَهُوَ أَعْلَمُ بِٱلْمُهْتَدِينَ

125. OdAAu il*a* sabeeli rabbika bial*h*ikmati waalmawAAi*th*ati al*h*asanati waj*a*dilhum biallatee hiya a*h*sanu inna rabbaka huwa aAAlamu biman *d*alla AAan sabeelihi wahuwa aAAlamu bialmuhtadeena

---

16:125. Call people to the Path of your Lord with wisdom and good counsel and argue with them in the best possible manner. Your Lord does indeed know who go astray from His path, and who follow it.

وَإِنْ عَاقَبْتُمْ فَعَاقِبُوا۟ بِمِثْلِ مَا عُوقِبْتُم بِهِۦ وَلَئِن صَبَرْتُمْ لَهُوَ خَيْرٌ لِّلصَّٰبِرِينَ

126. Wa-in AA*a*qabtum faAA*a*qiboo bimithli m*a* AAooqibtum bihi wala-in *s*abartum lahuwa khayrun li*ls*s*a*bireena

---

16:126. And if you retaliate, then retaliate with the like of that with which you were afflicted. But if you are patient, it will certainly be better for those who are patient.[29]

29. Some time back, there was that case about Danish cartoons. Some Danish newspaper had published derogatory cartoons about our Prophet (peace upon him). In pursuance of the divine directive in this Verse, the only thing the Muslims could do in retaliation was to publish an equally derogatory cartoon about Prophet Jesus (peace upon him) in one of the newspapers controlled by them. But could the Muslims do it? No, never! Because, for the Muslims Prophet Jesus is as honourable as Prophet Muhammad. The best response for the Muslims then would have been to be patient, in accordance with the divine directive in this Verse, and try and publish an article in the same Danish paper eulogizing Prophet Jesus. But the Muslims did not then follow divine directive. They called for death to the persons concerned in the publication of the said Danish cartoons and for boycott of all Danish goods. How would Allah help the Muslims if they won't follow His advice?

وَٱصْبِرْ وَمَا صَبْرُكَ إِلَّا بِٱللَّهِ وَلَا تَحْزَنْ عَلَيْهِمْ وَلَا تَكُ فِى ضَيْقٍ مِّمَّا يَمْكُرُونَ ﴿١٢٧﴾

127. Wai*s*bir wam*a* *s*abruka ill*a* biAll*a*hi wal*a* ta*h*zan AAalayhim wal*a* taku fee *d*ayqin mimm*a* yamkuroon**a**

16:127. And be patient and your patience is not but by Allah's Grace. And grieve not for them, and do not distress yourself at what they plot.

إِنَّ ٱللَّهَ مَعَ ٱلَّذِينَ ٱتَّقَوا۟ وَّٱلَّذِينَ هُم مُّحْسِنُونَ ﴿١٢٨﴾

128. Inna All*a*ha maAA*a* alla*th*eena ittaqaw waalla*th*eena hum mu*h*sinoon**a**

16:128. Allah is indeed with those who fear Him and those who do good deeds.